To my friend Maheshwari
Jagd
June 11, 2022

INDIA REBORN

BHARAT MAHAN
AS PERCEIVED BY WESTERNERS, GANDHI, NEHRU, TAGORE & OTHERS

Jagat K. Motwani, Ph.D.

Originals
Delhi-110052

Copyright © 2012 by Dr. Jagat K. Motwani
e-mail: jagatmotwani@yahoo.com

ISBN13: 978-81-8454-112-0
ISBN10: 81-8554-112-0

Published by
Originals
A-6, Nimri Commercial Centre,
Ashok Vihar Phase-IV, Delhi-110052
Phone: 27302453
e-mail: info@Lppindia.com
url: www.Lppindia.com

Cataloging in Publication Data—DK
Courtesy: D.K. Agencies (P) Ltd. <docinfo@dkagencies.com>

Motwani, Jagat K. India reborn : Bharat mahan : as perceived by westerners, Gandhi, Nehru, Tagore & others / Jagat K. Motwani.   p. cm.
Includes bibliographical references (p.   ) and index.

ISBN 13: 9788184541120
ISBN 10: 8185541120

1. India—Civilization. 2. Hindu civilization. 3. Civilization—Indic influences.   I. Title.

DDC 934   23
Printed at:
D K Fine Art Press P Ltd.
Delhi-110052

Cover
Idea: Jagat K. Motwani. Ph.D.
Design: Mr. Emad Asghar

Dedicated

to

Gandhi, Nehru, Tagore, Vivekananda, Dr. Abdul Kalam,
Gargi, Sister Nivedita

and

all those who awakened INDIA

and made

BHARAT MAHAN

Acknowledgements

The book – on various multifarious interrelated issues of human life, such as originality, identity, family, heritage, language, culture, religion, sacred scriptures – can not and should not be written without the help of several persons of various disciplines, such as history, archeology, linguistics, anthropology, sociology, etc., without whose silent and indirect cooperation the book would not be as it is. I am very grateful to all the scholars whose works have been of great help.

I am fortunate that I have received heartening comments on the book from Shri Amitabh Bachchan – the beloved idol of not only all Indian but also several Western hearts – for his fascinating art and lofty thoughts. It, I am sure, will give a great lift to the book. For that I am very grateful to Shri Amitabhji.

I am also very lucky to have Mr. Stephen Knapp, author of over twenty books, has written an appropriate FOREWORD, which will encourage readers to read it from its first word to the last.

Without the willing cooperation of my whole family – Neha, Emad, Shilpa, Daniel and Jyoti, and friend Ms. Rani Mothey – who have helped in various ways, the book would have not been as it is.

Loving appreciation for my '3-and-10-month-always-smiling prince', grandson Remi for his playful company in my study room whenever I needed to give recess to my computer-fatigued eyes.

Jagat K. Motwani, Ph.D.

PREFACE

Will Durant's observation in *'The Story of Civilization: Our Oriental Heritage'* (1963, p. 391) – "Nothing should more deeply shame the modern student than the recency and inadequacy of his acquaintance with India" – awakened me to the inadequacy of my knowledge about my own 'Mother INDIA'. Such eye-opening was prompted by an American classmate at the Fordham University, New York, where I was studying for my Ph.D. He jubilantly said that he was happy to meet a person from the great India whose Vedas give so much rich philosophy how to get serenity and peace of mind. He knew and practiced meditation and Yoga. He told me so much about Hinduism and Vedanta, that I felt myself so ashamed and small, being a national of India, particularly a Hindu.

Michael Wood, in his book *"The Story of India"*, suggested the title *"India Reborn"*. On the cover-back, it is written:

"Home today to more than a fifth of the world's population, India gave birth to the oldest and most influential civilization on Earth, to four world religions, and to the world's largest democracy. ... Now, as India bids to become a global economic giant, Michael sets out on an epic journey across this vibrant country to trace the roots of India's present in the incredible riches of her past."

While my serious review of a significant part of her ancient history, Bharat assured me of her unshakable belief in rebirth. It is great that Bharat does not believe in 'DEATH'. During her black life of more than one thousand years of shameful bondage, she continued struggling for freedom. On the very day, 15th August, 1947, Bharat was found shining with the stars of optimism and determination to regain the lost global throne. It was confirmed by her brave confrontation with belligerent neighbor on giving graceful shelter to Dalai Lama in 1962, very much befitting with the

v

Bharatiya Sanskruti (Indian culture). It confirms that Bharat is reborn and she is marching up fast to her lost Everest.

Aldous Huxley's – "Facts do not cease to exist because they are ignored." – encouraged me to unearth, as many as possible, the facts about Bharat which have been buried, ignored or historically misrepresented. This has been a long laborious library-based research to find out what various historians have said or not said about Bharat and her jewels – Aryan race, Vedas, Vedic religion (Hinduism), Sanskrit and Swastika.

I have found flood of relevant information. There are contradictions, vague assertions, and shocking distortions, deliberate fabrications and even false conclusions. They have been objectively examined and put in their right perspectives.

I found lot about India in several historical books I read for my earlier book *'None but Bharat: The Cradle of Aryans, Sanskrit, Vedas and Swastika'* which was published last year. Most of them are authored by Western scholars, some of whom have sung lot in praise of the Vedas, Upanishads and Bhagvad Gita. They also have praised the fineness of Sanskrit. Nehru, in his *'Discovery of India'*, has echoed the same, and so Gandhi, Tagore, Vivekananda and others. It infused in me the pride for my Bharat Mâtâ. I thought why not to share this with my Bharatvasis, particularly youngsters, the future of Bharat.

Jagat K. Motwani,
August 15, 2011

Amitabh Bachchan

July 15, 2011

My dear Jagat,

It is undeniable that today's youth are the makers and pillars of tomorrow's world. For us to tackle this source of immense potential and direct it towards the growth and progress of our nation, we have to instill in them the pride and love for their motherland.

I am no theologian and hence am not qualified to form an opinion. However, from what I have read of the copy of your book "Bharat Re-Born", you seem to have captured the glory and heart of Indian heritage, culture and civilization in an adept, concise and fascinating fashion.

This copy will help every "Indian" appreciate his/her legacy and make him/her proud to be "Sons/daughters of the soil"

I wish your publication a grand success. Jai Hind!

Warmly,

Amitabh Bachchan

FOREWORD

The fact of the matter is that it is getting increasingly difficult to find real knowledge about India's history, how it developed, what it has really contributed to the world, what the Vedic culture actually gave to humanity and its struggle to maintain its culture, the trials, tribulations and atrocities it has endured. Much of this history and information is no longer taught in schools, and is hardly available in universities, unless through special studies that are offered by a few colleges. Even some academics and so-called scholars, especially with Western views, actually demean and work to show the Vedic knowledge and traditions in a negative and most demeaning light, rather than showing what it really has provided for the upliftment of the consciousness of humanity.

Rarely you find individuals, like Dr. Jagat Motwani, who are courageous enough to take on special research, investigation and studies that can lead to uncovering the truth of how great was the early civilization of India or Bharatvarsha. If people really knew this information, especially Indians, they would have far greater respect for their own culture, history, and roots to their ancient traditions. Of course, India has many cultures within it, not just one. I have often said that with one tourist visa, you have access to so many cultures. But when I say culture, I mean the connection with the Vedic tradition, which is the main and original root of all of India.

There is much that can be said about the greatness of ancient India and its development, much of which was the inspiration of true social advancement. But is this knowledge to become a thing of the past? Will it one day be lost forever? And if so, is this merely because of neglect, or is it by design from those who would rather see Vedic philosophy and culture become merely a museum piece?

Rather, we can see that the Vedic civilization is still a strong part of India, its dynamics, its power, and its roots to the core values and principles that most people still follow. However, we also have to recognize that much of this is gathering momentum since it is increasingly accepted and followed outside India, all over the planet, especially in such places as the United States, Europe, Australia, South America, and so on. How is this apparent? Look around. We can easily see that one simple aspect of Vedic culture, namely *Yoga*, is gaining popularity among all ranks of people, whether poor or rich. With *Yoga* one can have deep peep within, know the deeper aspects of the Vedic philosophy, meditate for spiritual development, and understand the Vedic principles of *karma*, reincarnation, *ahimsa* and vegetarianism. In other areas we can see how *jyotish* (Vedic Astrology and astronomy) are also gaining popularity, along with *Vastu, Ayurveda*, Vedic gemology, Vedic art, Indian classical dances and music, and so on. Speaking of which, what is called world music often includes much Indian influence, and a growing form of music is now being called "mantra music". This is all happening in what could be called a spontaneous manner in the West, and Indians have little control over it, even though it is their culture which is the inspiration for it.

Is this surprising? I don't think so. Why? Because the West has always investigated things, cultures, products, philosophies, etc. with the inquisitive attitude of:

"What's in it for me? What am I going to get out of it? What is it going to do to help me reach my higher potential and bring my consciousness and awareness to a higher level, or help me attain understanding and more peace of mind?"

So if they do not see anything relevant for them, they don't take to it. And the Indian youth are very much like that today. If they do not understand something, then it makes little sense to follow it. And so, as opposed with the faddish participation in Eastern traditions by Westerners that we saw in the 1960s, even though that certainly sparked the interest of many, now we see people taking a more serious look into it. This has resulted in the recognition of the actual benefits that can be attained by any portion of the Vedic processes of self-realization, self-development and self-expression, but more importantly, actually experiencing those benefits. And once these are realized, then it grows and more people begin to investigate, try them, and tell others. As we see India becoming more Westernized and practically getting farther and farther away from their own culture, one day we may see a time, if it is not already happening, when the Vedic tradition is imported from America back to India. I've often been told by Indians themselves that India, especially the youth, have little respect for something unless it comes from the West (though I hope this trend can reverse itself, and I think it is starting to). But they should also see that an increasing number of people in the West are continually looking toward the East, especially India, for that which can satisfy their spiritual needs. When they look for something deeper, something that can put more meaning in their lives, they often look to India.

So my point in all of this is that there is a continual need to expose more people to the truths, the Vedic civilization and its culture and traditions have to offer to the people of today. Vedic is timeless wisdom. It provides universal spiritual truths, meaning that they are applicable for anyone of any background, at any time, and anywhere. It only has to be presented properly.

I have often said that many times we see remnants of ancient society, not knowing their true roots or cultural connections, and they are often simply labeled as part of a pagan or a heathen civilization. But with proper education and knowledge, we can recognize the Vedic influence in it. Then we can also begin to understand how so many areas of the planet and the various civilizations that have expanded across the globe were influenced by the oldest indigenous culture in the world, which was the Vedic culture. Only by the research of those rare scholars and historians, the true history of India and its ancient Vedic traditions is becoming more apparent and more easily understood. Only by this process is the true history of the survival of India being kept alive, even after the past 1000 years of invasions and the sacrifices made by so many millions of heroic people to defend their culture. Only by this process can the youth of today understand the struggle that was performed by their ancestors so they could enjoy the freedom they have today to participate in their great traditions. It is an example of rare *karma* to be born into Vedic society, or even learn about it in this life. Therefore, this should not be taken for granted or looked upon lightly.

This is also why I am so happy that Prof. Jagat K. Motwani, who has so nicely presented so many aspects of the points I have mentioned above in his book, "Bharat Reborn: Bharat Mahan, as Perceived by Westerners, Gandhi, Nehru, Tagore & Others." Lot of research has gone into this book to help explain and show the real and glorious nature of India's history and culture, its past accomplishments, contributions, and more importantly, what it is still capable of achieving, and, obviously, will achieve if given the chance. By this I mean that if the people in charge, such as the government and politicians, have the proper outlook and consciousness and respect for what real India has been and will be, and if they steer it in the right direction, India can reach its true potential. You cannot expect to accomplish this great destiny if you allow the wrong people remain in high places or positions.

Therefore, I encourage everyone who is interested in this topic to take a deep look into the information, given in this book, to see in a true light what India has been and can still be. I for one feel that this book should move all over the world to help people get the dust out of their eyes and get a more accurate view and understanding of India, its ancient writings, its high philosophy, its glorious character, and the potential that remains deep in the roots of its culture and its people. Dr. Motwani speaks from not only an angle of research, but also uses quotes from many other scholars and historians, and also from personal experiences, as well as of India's ancient past but also current events, all of which make for some very fascinating, uplifting and enlightening reading. Jai Hind,

Stephen Knapp
July 22, 2011

CONTENTS

Acknowledgements   iv

Preface   v

Amitabh Bachchan's comments   vii

Foreword   ix

Chapter

1. Introduction: Bharat Reborn   1
2. Vedas: The Most Ancient Scriptures of the World   9
3. Sanskrit: The Most Ancient Language   25
4. Ancient Hindu Astronauts: Unbelievable but true   41
5. Swastika: Being stolen by Europeans   53
6. Scholars on India, her Vedas and Sanskrit   61
7. India's Spiritual and Scientific Gifts to the World   71
8. India: Unity in Complexity & Beauty in Diversity   83
9. Gandhi: Hinduism, A Leaven to Wholesome Life   95
10. Tagore: Hindu Concept of Education   127
11. Inter-civilization trade: Indus, Euphrates and Nile 137
12. Colonies India Established   153
13. Ahimsa: Loss of worldwide colonies   157
14. India in Central Asia   163
15. Afghanistan: A Part of Ancient India   173
16. Iran: A Part of Ancient India   185
17. India in the Mediterranean   199
18. India in Ancient Europe   219
19. India in Ancient Americas   231
20. Far South-East Asia under Vedic Influence   241
21. India in China and Turkistan   255
22. India in Africa   263
Index   271
References and Bibliography   281

ONE

Introduction

"At one time India had a place on top of the world; there was no limit to her spiritual daring in the fields of religion, philosophy and science and her forces spread far, annexing new domains. The preceptor's seat India had thus won is now lost; now she must stand as a disciple. The reason is that fear has entered into her soul. Panic made us forbid voyaging on the high seas – whether of water or of knowledge. We belonged to the universe but relegated to the parish."

Rabindranath Tagore[*]

I wish Tagore were back to feel happy to see India (Bharat[1]) being reborn. Both 'India' and 'Bharat' have been interchageably used. India has started voyaging on the high seas of not only philosophy of life, but also of various fields of science and technology. India could not be killed, enemies wanted to. She has self-sustaining and surviving energy and unshakable conviction in rebirth. She was forced to lie down quiet and inactive. But, she was not. Life within her was active. The moment, her shackles were taken off, Bharat

---

[*]Tagore in his book 'Towards Universal Man' (1961, p. 63). The book was published on the occasion of the Centenary of the birth of Tagore on May 7, 1961. But, it must have been written before Tagore's death on 7th August, 1941.
[1] Bharat is original name of India. In the constitution of India, Bharat is given as the name of the nation. In this book Bharat is used quite often and Bharatvasi for Indian.

1

arose soaring towards the sky. Because of limitations, inflicted on by over a millennium-long cruel bondage, she will take some time – not long – to regain her lost global throne.

US Assistant Secretary of State for South and Central Asia Robert Blake said:

> "India is a rising giant whose influence is being felt not only in the Indian Ocean, but in the Americas, in Africa, the Middle East, and in Central Asia."

Will Durant, in *'Our Oriental Heritage'* (1935, p. 394), writes that the history of the beginnings of the Indian civilization, which was buried deep in the earth, is being brought out by the recent archeological researches:

> "In the days when historians supposed that history had begun with Greece, Europe gladly believed that India had been a hotbed of barbarism until the "Aryan" cousins of the European peoples had migrated from the shores of the Caspian to bring the arts and science to a savage and benighted peninsula. Recent researches have marred this comforting picture – as future researches will change the perspective of these pages. In India, as elsewhere, the beginnings of civilization are buried in the earth, and not all the spades of archeology will ever quite exhume them."

I am optimistic that the spades of archeology and the objective pen of the historians – supported by the INDEPENDENT BHARAT's might and her aroused self-image – will exhume almost all the treasures which were buried by the unprofessional colonial historians.

It is right that their "Aryan cousins" came to Europe from the Caspian shores of the Central Asia. It would be wrong to understand that the Central Asia was the native abode of the Aryans. They had gone there originally from Aryavarta (India). In ancient times, India was known as "Aryavarta", "Arya Desh", or

Introduction

"Arya Bhoomi."[2] Aryans had gone out of India – their cradle – for trade and colonization to Central Asia. It was their first stop. From there, they marched to all over the planet, including the Mediterranean, Asia Minor, Europe, and the SE Asia. It is hard to understand how Aryans became cousins of Europeans when they differ in culture, heritage, language and history, and moreover they are geographically too distant to make a family. The theory of 'Aryan invasion of India' was mischievously engineered in London, guided by Britain's world-known policy **'Divide and Rule'**.

Will Durant {William James Durant (1885-1981)}, an American historian, knew lot about Hinduism and its literature – Rāmāyana, Mahābhāratā, Shakuntalā and their poets, such as Tulsidas, Tukāram, Kabir, etc. He appreciated Hindu literature as most primitive, rich, spiritual, intellectual and philosophical. He (p.391) urges the people to know more about India, her early civilization and culture:

"Nothing should more deeply shame the modern student than the recency and inadequacy of his acquaintance with India. ... an impressive continuity of development and civilization from Mohenjo-daro, 2900 B.C. or earlier, to Gandhi, Raman and Tagore; ... this is the India that patient scholarship is now opening up, like a new intellectual continent, to that Western mind which only yesterday thought civilization an exclusively European thing."

Independent Bharat has got her crippled wings restored and energized. It has started flying high and high to kiss the sky. The day is a little far away, but very much in sight. Credit goes to her aggressive media – vocal, print, television, internet and cinema – which has been awakening the grassroots, urban as well as remote rural. It has been scaring the tax cheats, officers as well as politicians. There is an interesting TV program, known as "Office

---

[2] Max Müller, 'The Science of Language' (1890, p.291).

3

Office" which shows how open trifle bribery has been slowing down the movement of files – from table to table – in offices.

I, as an NRI, remember, long back almost every suitcase of the air passenger who resisted giving bribe was opened. The hidden overseas bank accounts of the income tax cheats are being threatened. Hope funds will soon reach home and cheats are duly punished. The proper use of the funds – roughly estimated to be over forty trillion dollars – will finance the projects to completely wipe out the poverty, but certainly reduce it to its bones. All such evils have been gradually decreasing. Cheats are numbering their days. Completely clean bribery-less India is impossible. Almost all countries are plagued with bribery in various ways. From the birth of the humanity, the man, irrespective of his religious and ethnic affiliations, has been evil. Unfortunately, God seems to have accepted His incompetence to root out this man-made cancer. Globalization of India is in its active process. It has been slowly improving the quality of the Indian manpower, industry and infrastructure.

We consider our country Bharat as female. We Bharatvasi worship her as mother – 'Bharat Mātā', 'Mother India'. I see silver-lining in uplift of women, and their fattening political muscle. In Vedas, woman has been considered strong, more honest and less greedy than man. It seems this was the reason why in the Vedic mythology, the three important portfolios were assigned to goddesses – 'education' to Sarasvati, finance to Lakshmi, and defense to Durga. Women are coming up in Indian politics. The Communist Party, which made West Bengal poor to its bones during its rule of about thirty four years, has been swept out of power by the firebrand Mamata Banerjee, seeming an incarnation of Durga. Jayalalitha Jayaraman, the leader of the opposition in Tamil Nadu has become its chief minister. There are several other women in politics such as Mayavati, the chief minister of the largest state Uttar Pradesh, Sheila Dixit, the Chief Minister of Delhi, Sushma Swaraj, the leader of the Bharatiya Janta Party, the main Opposition Party in the Indian Parliament, Sonia Gandhi, the President of the All India Ruling Congress Party, Uma Bharti, former Chief Minister of MP, etc. There are several other great women in Indian political arena. Hope they will think and behave like goddesses and raise Bharat up close to sky.

India terminated her Britain-type socialism in 1991 which has slowed down her economy for over four decades.

We come to know our Bharat much better when we see her through Western eyes. We have her clearer picture when we leave her and live somewhere overseas. Our eyes and ears become inquisitive to know our Bharat Mata more and more. Perhaps, we miss her. We hear and read what Western scholars and our great Indians – like Gandhi, Nehru, Tagore, Vivekananda, Dr. A. P. J. Abdul Kalam, Dr. K.M. Munshi and others – have said about Bharat and about her culture, Sanskrit and Vedic scriptures. It gives a thrilling feeling when we read the ancient history of Bharat's global trade and her worldwide cultural overtures, particularly her colonizing fruits all over the planet.

We identify holes in our knowledge and recognize the clouds darkening our perceptions. We see our misperceptions, perhaps caused by our self-induced ethnic inferiority complex which has been induced by wrong history. Why do we believe Western scholars, not our own Bharatiya scholars and scriptures for the same story and for the same event? We should examine why we resist seeing the truths about Bharat. Perhaps we choose not to see the positive aspects of Bharat in order to justify why we left her. Many overseas Bharatvasi criticize and belittle Bharat, we unconsciously love and adore. When any non-Indian criticizes India, we hit him/her back very hard. I, as a Fulbright student in 1966-67, felt shy telling that I was from India. The situation has changed. Now, I proudly say I am from India.

I remember at Smith College graduate school of social work, Northampton (MASS), in 1966, a Sociology professor remarked: "We got small pox from England." Grace, a British student, rose up and said: "We got smallpox from India." I got up and said: "Thank God, we have been able to control it since British left India." I was happily amazed to watch the professor and the classmates clapping hard reflecting American lofty broad-minded bias-free attitude. While getting out from the class room, Grace shouted at me, "Jagat, you didn't know I was from London." I, assertively responded, "Grace, did you not know I was from India?

You should be ashamed of your barbaric colonialism. It is dead now. India is independent."

In such situations, suppressed love for Bharat Mātā bursts out. I was surprised at my courage. America is a country of immigrants. American liberal and broadminded ethos encourages and allows one to muster the courage to be able to protect motherland, from being smeared upon with insults.

Discovery of great things about Bharat evokes a sense of pride and strength. The things, other people say about our Bharat, evoke a feeling of victory, as produced by a win of a billion-dollar lottery. Each day, since I landed at the JFK airport in June, 1970 as a Green Card immigrant, I have been learning more and more about the grandeur of Bharat. While in India, I never felt need to read what Westerners and great Indians have said about Bharat and about her treasures – Sanskrit, Vedas, Bhagvad Gita, love for knowledge, secularism, beauty in her diversity, philosophy of life, Yoga, respect for elders and Guru (teacher), etc. I have been thrilled to know what westerners have seen in our ancient scriptures, particularly Upanishads and Gita.

What Durant has written in *"The Story of Civilization: Our Oriental Heritage"* (1963), would inflate ethnic ego of every Bharatvasi. In its chapter *'The Foundations of India'*, Durant observes:

"From the time of Megasthenes, who described India to Greece ca. 302 B.C., down to the eighteenth century, India was all a marvel and a mystery to Europe. Marco Polo (1254-1323 A.D.) pictured its western fringe vaguely, Columbus blundered upon America in trying to reach it, Vasco de Gama sailed around Africa to rediscover it, and merchants spoke rapaciously of 'the wealth of Indies'. But scholars left the mine almost un-tapped."

I hope to dig deep into the mine of historical facts, the scholars have tapped or mistapped, and also those they have left untapped or ignored. I hope this book will unearth some diamonds which would shine the ancient Bharat. I know I would not be able to tell you everything you should know about the ancient Bharat and in the manner you would like to read. Indian literature is too vast an ocean for all the global army of historians. I know I will not be able to dive deep to find all the *moti* (pearls), the ancient Bharat was adorned with. I also want to tell you about my possible subjective perceptions, unconsciously evoked by my affection for my Bharat Mātā, humanly impossible to control. I would like to record what some western scholars, our great leaders and philosophers have said about the grandeur of the ancient Bharat and about her original natives (Aryans), language (Sanskrit), literature (Vedas), Swastika, culture, and also about courageous overseas adventures of Hindus and Buddhists for trade and colonization in pre-history ancient times.

I will try my best to tell as much as possible what historians have said and what they have not said. I also would try to objectively address their misrepresentations and ignorance of Indian history and culture, of course supported by documented irrefutable evidences.

The book is a library-based research to ascertain what historians, philosophers, and scholars – Western as well as Indian – have said "quote and un-quote" about the following, as based on undisputable historical documented facts:

1. Originality, antiquity and authorship of the Vedas.
2. Originality and antiquity of Sanskrit.
3. Originality and identity of the Aryans.
4. Aryan race, envied by Europeans who call it "the Jewel of the White Race".
5. Unity in Bharat's complexity, and beauty in her amazing diversity.
6. Democratic values and secularism from ancient times.
7. Love for knowledge (education).
8. Respect for guru (teacher)
9. Learned women in the remote ancient times.
10. Respect for women.
11. Bharat's windows always open to other cultures
12. Bharat's absorbing capacity to help immigrants to mainstream.

13. Bharat's inter-civilization trade in remote ancient times.
14. Colonization by ancient Aryans.

As said earlier that this book is a library-based research. Hence, request your patience with the enormous number of quotations, the book is crowded with.

TWO

Vedas: The Most Ancient Scriptures of the World

"Whatever the Vedas may be called, they are to us unique and priceless guides in opening before our eyes tombs of thought richer in relics than the royal tombs of Egypt, and more ancient and primitive in thought than the oldest hymns of Babylonian or Acadian poets. If we grant that they belonged to the second millennium before our era, we are probably on safe ground, though we should not forget that this is a constructive date only, and that such a date does not become positive by mere repetition. It may be very brave to postulate late 2000 B.C. or even 5000 B.C. as a minimum date for the Vedic hymns, but what is gained by such bravery? Such assertions are safe so far as they can not be refuted, but neither can they be proved, considering that we have no contemporaneous dates to attach them to."

Max Müller

The above is said in *"Six Systems of Indian Philosophy: Samkhya & Yoga; Nyaya & Vaiseshika"* (1899, p. 33). Max Müller (p. 24) praises India, as endowed with all the paradise-beauty, the nature can bestow:

"If I were to look over the whole world to find out the country most richly endowed with all the wealth, power,

9

and beauty that nature can bestow – in some parts a very paradise on earth – I should point to India."

The book '*The Discovery of India*' (1946) would impress any reader, as a well-researched history book, authored by Pandit Jawaharlal Nehru, an unbiased objective writer and a great statesman.

Nehru (1946, p.93) talks about the influence of the *Upanishads* on self: "The study of the Upanishads has been the solace of my life, it will be the solace of my death."

Nehru (p.79) remarks:

"The Vedic hymns have been described by Rabindranath Tagore as 'a poetic testament of a people's collective reaction to the wonder and awe of existence.' The Vedas have given us a deep peep into the philosophy of mind which has been increasingly broadening its horizon along with the advancing time.

Feuerstein & et al., in *"In Search of the Cradle of Civilization"* (1995, p. 39), observe that great philosophers around the world have been very much impressed by the *Upanishads:*

"The Upanishads, which are magnificent Gnostic treatises in the broad sense, from the capstone of the Vedic edifice. They are the best known aspect of Vedic literature and have been lauded by great thinkers through out the world."

It is soul-soothing to know that western scholars read Hindu sacred scriptures with great interest. Feuerstein & et al. (p.39) write that the German philosopher Arthur Schopenhauer has said that the *Upanishads* were comfort to him in his life and his death. Schopenhauer has remarked about the *Upanishads* in German in his book, *Upanishaden, Altindische Weisheit* (1964, p.8):

"How every line is of such strong, determined, and consistent meaning! And on every page we encounter

deep, original, lofty thoughts, while the whole is suffused
with a high and holy seriousness."

R. E. Hume, in *'The Thirteen Principal Upanishads'* (1921, p.
vii), has remarked:

"In the long history of man's endeavor to grasp the
fundamental truths of being, the metaphysical treatises
known as the Upanishads hold an honored place ... they
are replete with sublime conceptions and with intuitions
of universal truth."

Feuerstein & et al (1995, p.40) write that Max Müller, who was
critical of many aspects of the Vedic heritage, confessed toward
the end of his life: "The conception of the world as deduced from
the Veda, and chiefly from the Upanishads, is indeed astounding."[3]
Nehru (pp.92-93) quotes Arthur Schopenhauer (German
scholar, 1788-1860), the pessimist, what he has said about the
Vedic influence on the whole world:

"From every sentence (of the Upanishads) deep, original
and sublime thoughts arise, and the whole world is
pervaded by a high and holy and earnest spirit. ... In the
whole world there is no study ... so beneficial and as
elevating as that of the Upanishads. ... (They) are
products of the highest wisdom. ... It is destined sooner
or later to become the faith of the people."

Romain Rolland[4] (French writer, 1866-1944) – in a note *'On
the Hellenic-Christian Mysticism of the First Centuries and its
Relationship to Hindu Mysticism'* (as an appendix to his book on
Vivekananda) – writes: "A hundred facts testify to how great an
extent the East was mingled with Hellenic thought during the
second century of our era."

---

[3]Max Müller, *The Six Systems of Indian Philosophy*, (First published in 1899,
reprinted in 1916, xlv).
[4] Nehru, *Discovery of India*, p.92, foot note.

Nehru (p.93) writes that the most eloquent tribute to the Upanishads and the Bhagavad Gita was paid by A.E. (G.W. Russell), the Irish poet:

> "Goethe, Wordsworth, Emerson, and Thoreau among moderns have something of this vitality and wisdom, but we can find all they have said and much more in the grand sacred books of the East. The Bhagavad Gita and the Upanishads contain such godlike fullness of wisdom on all things that I feel the authors must have looked with calm remembrance back through a thousand passionate lives, full of feverish strife for and with shadows, ere they could have written with such certainty of things which the soul feels to be sure."

Vedic people of ancient times had knowledge of psychology, as evidenced by the Bhagavad Gita and the Vedas, which are much older than the Gita.

What do the Vedas teach Europeans?

Max Müller, in *'India: What Can It Teach Us?'* (1999, p. 136), writes that the Vedas can teach us lessons which nothing/no one else can. He, talking to the candidates for Civil Service in India, apprises them of the importance of the Vedas for Europeans:

> "Therefore, before opening the pages of the Veda, and giving you a description of the poetry, the religion, and philosophy of the ancient inhabitants of India, I thought it right and necessary to establish, first of all, certain points without which it would be impossible to form a right appreciation of the historical value of the Vedic hymns, and of their importance even to us who live at so great a distance from those early poets."

---

* Bhagvad Gita was the live conversation between Lord Krishna and Arjuna while the Mahabharta War between the Pandwas and the Kaurvas was in progress in about 3067 B.C.

Max Müller (1999, p.137) talks about the greatness of the Vedas, and their language Sanskrit, to which, he believed, Europeans owe lot:

"Secondly, that the ancient literature of India is not to be considered simply as a curiosity and to be handed over to the good pleasure of Oriental scholars, but that, both by its language, the Sanskrit, and by its most ancient literary documents, the Vedas, it can teach us lessons which nothing else can teach, as to the origin of our own language, the first formation of our own concepts and the true natural germs of all that is comprehended under the name of civilization, at least the civilization of the Aryan race, that race to which we and all the greatest nations of the world – the Hindus, the Persians, the Greeks and Romans, the Celts, the Slaves, and last, not least, the Teutons, belong."

Max Müller (1999, p.138) writes that the ancient literature of India "deserves the careful attention, not of Oriental scholars only, but also of every educated man and woman who wishes to know how we, even we here in England, and in this nineteenth century of ours, came to be what we are." He adds that Hindus excel in the transcendental meditation, the westerners should learn and practice.

Max Müller (1999, p. 161), talking about the lessons India can teach, writes:

"Although there is hardly any department of learning which has not received new light and new life from the ancient literature of India, yet nowhere is the light that comes to us from India so important, so novel, so rich as in the study of religion and mythology."

Max Müller (1999, p.160, footnote), talking about the progress in the research on India and her Vedas observes: "It is in the general line of progress in research that more evidence may be expected to connect Vedic thought with other cultures."

Max Müller[5], captivated by the Upanishads, writes:

> "The Upanishads are the sources of the Vedanta philosophy, a system in which human speculation seems to me to have reached its acme. ... I spend my happiest hours in reading Vedanta books. They are to me like the light of the morning, like the pure air of the mountains – so simple, so true, if once understood."

Were Vedas revealed?

Max Müller (1899, p.39), talking about Gaimini's support of the eternal character of sound (*Shabda*), remarks:

> "Having thus established to his own satisfaction the eternity of sound, Gaimini proceeds to defend the sounds or words of the Veda against all possible objections. These arguments were examined by us before, when the authorship of the Veda had to be discussed, and when it was shown that the author of the Veda could not have been a personal being, but that the Veda could only have been seen by inspired Rishis as revealed to them, not as made by them."

Nehru (1946, p.79) praises the mind (thinking process) of the composers of the Vedic hymns. Nehru did not like that the Vedas be considered as "revealed" scriptures, because, then, Nehru rightly thinks that we don't value the quality of the mind of the composers of the Vedic hymns which have the depth, too difficult for the common mind to peep into.

In Nehru's opinion, the Rig Veda unfolded the human mind, in earliest stages of thought which has opened the windows on the Vedic philosophy which has been increasingly blooming along with the time all over the planet:

[5] Ibid p. 93

Vedas: The Most Ancient Scriptures of the World

"Many Hindus look upon the Vedas as revealed scripture. This seems to me to be peculiarly unfortunate, for thus we miss their real significance – the unfolding of the human mind in the earliest stages of thought. And what a wonderful mind it was."

Nehru did not like this because, he thought then we would not value the quality of the mind of the *Rishis* who composed the hymns of the Vedas which reflect the lofty thought, the humanity should feel proud of. He praised the mind (thinking process) of the composers of the Vedas. He saw that behind the *Rig Veda* lay ages of civilized existence and thought, during which various ancient civilizations – the Indus, the Euphrates and the Nile – had grown. Therefore, it is appropriate that there should be dedication to the seers, and our ancestors who were the first path-finders.

If the Vedas are considered as "revealed" to the *Rishis* of Bharat, not authored by "a personal being," the antiquity of the Vedas can not be measured. By this, I do not want readers to think that I am buying what Gaimini or Max Müller believed that the *Vedas* were revealed to *Rishis*. The authorship of the *Rig Veda* is too ancient beyond human imagination. In such situation when the names of the composers of the various hymns of the Vedas are not known, there would be no option other than saying that the Vedas were revealed. But it is not correct. The fact is that they were composed by several *Rishis*.

The *Rig Veda*, like other *Vedas*, is a collection of *Mantras* (*Hymns*). They were composed in remote prehistory ancient times by several *Rishis*. Since the *Vedas* were not written to start with, the names of the composers are not known. Several *Rishis* might have contributed their ideas in poetry-form-hymns which came down from generation to generation by Vedic oral traditions. Technology of writing came much later. We do not have the names of the authors of the *Puranas, Brahmanas, Aranyakas, Upanishads, Sutras, Shastras, Samhitas*, etc. In those ancient times, those great *Rishis* were not egocentric, crazy about their name. Moreover, there was no sense of copyright. They were happy that they contributed some thing, the humanity needed and the future generations would love to sing.

There is such a recent example, very similar to the *Vedas*. The *Guru Granth Sahib* of Sikhs was not composed by only one person. It contains what the ten *Gurus* of Sikhs – from Guru Nanak to Guru Gobind Singh – and some other similar-thinking devotees have sung. Unlike the *Rig Veda,* the names of most of the composers of Granth Sahib are known, because of its recency.

The antiquity of the Vedas and a source of history

Max Müller talks about the antiquity of the Vedas:

"The Vedas are older than any other literary document, and give us trustworthy information of a period in the history of human thought of which we know absolutely nothing before the discovery of the Vedas."

Max Müller, in *'India: What Can It Teach Us?'* (1999, p.139), remarks that the Vedas are more primitive than any other document and that they give lot of historical data:

"The Veda may be called primitive, because there is no other literary document more primitive than it; but the language, the mythology, the religion and philosophy that meet us in the Veda open vistas of the past which no one would venture to measure in years. Nay, they contain by the side of simple, natural, childish thoughts, many ideas which to us sound modern, or secondary and tertiary, as I called them, but which nevertheless are older than any other literary document, and give us trustworthy information of a period in the history of human thought of which we know absolutely nothing before the discovery of the Vedas."

Max Müller[6], in *"History of Ancient Sanskrit Literature"* (p.557), has said:

---

[6] Taken from Stephen Knapp's *Proof of Vedic Culture's Global Existence* (2000, p. vii).

"In the *Rig Veda* we shall have before us more real antiquity than in all the inscriptions of Egypt or Ninevah. ... The *Veda* is the oldest book in existence."

In the same book (p. 63), Max Müller remarks, that the *Rig Veda* be considered as the oldest source of history, not only of India, but of the world too:

"The *Veda* has a two-fold interest. It belongs to the history of the world and to the history of India. In the history of the world the Veda fills a gap which no literary work in any other language could fill. It carries us back to times of which we have no records anywhere."

Nehru, in *'Discovery of India'* (1946, p.77), writes about the age of the *Vedas:*

"The usual date accepted by most scholars today for the hymns of the Rig Veda is 1,500 B.C., but there is tendency, ever since the Mohenjo-daro excavations, to date further back these early Indian scriptures. Whatever the exact date may be, it is probable that this literature is earlier than that of either Greece or Israel, that, in fact, it represents some of the earliest documents of the human mind that we posses. Max Muller has called it: 'The first word spoken by the Aryan man.'"

Nehru further writes that in the *Rig Veda* we shall have before us more real antiquity than in all the inscriptions of Egypt or Ninevah. The *Rig Veda* is the oldest book in existence.

Nehru (1946, p.79) talks about the *Rig Veda*, as the earliest book of the humanity which gave history of those who sought to discover the significance of the world:

"The Rig Veda, the first of the Vedas, is probably the earliest book that humanity possesses. In it we can find the first outpourings of the human mind, the glow of

17

poetry, the rupture at nature's loveliness and mystery. And in these early hymns there are, as Dr. Macnicol says, the beginnings of 'the brave adventures made so long ago and recorded here, of those who seek to discover the significance of our world and man's life within it. ... India here set out on a quest which she has never ceased to follow'."

Nehru (1946, pp. 76-77), talking about the earliest records, scriptures and mythology of India, writes about the age of the Vedas:

"Before the discovery of the Indus Valley civilization, the Vedas were supposed to be the earliest records we possess of Indian culture. There was much dispute about the chronology of the Vedic period, European scholars usually giving later dates and Indian scholars much earlier ones. ... Professor Winternitz thinks that the beginnings of Vedic literature go back to 2,000 B.C., or even 2,500 B.C. This brings us very near the Mohenjo-daro period."

In fact, the Vedas were composed earlier than 8000 B.C., as it would be shown later in this chapter. Nehru (p.79) makes a very interesting observation about the antiquity of the human civilization and its civilized thought, as reflected in the *Rig Veda*, the earliest of the Vedas:

"Yet behind the Rig Veda itself lay ages of civilized existence and thought, during which the Indus Valley and Mesopotamian and other civilizations had grown. It is appropriate, therefore, that there should be this dedication in the Rig Veda: 'To the Seers, our ancestors, the first path-finders.'"

Nehru saw that behind the *Rig Veda* itself lay ages of civilized existence and thought, during which various ancient civilizations – the Indus, the Nile, the Euphrates, etc. – had grown. Therefore, it is appropriate that there should be dedication to the seers, and our ancestors who were the first path-finders.

Hindu Calendar & the Age of Rig Veda and Sanskrit

According to the Oxford Dictionary (p.541): "Hindu calendar, a lunar calendar usually dating from 3101 B.C. and used especially in India," is roughly the same (5111 Yugabda = 3101 B.C. + 2010) as Hindus, at present, have been celebrating. This tells that Hinduism (Vedic religion) is much older than 5111. Realization of the calendar must have come much later than the birth of Hinduism (original Vedic religion). So the Vedas and their language Sanskrit should be much older than 5,111 years.

David Frawley (Sharma & Ghose, 1998, p. 140) talks about the Vedic astronomical references related to the calendar:

"The Vedas contain various astronomical references relative to the calendar. ... and several Brahamanas place the vernal equinox in the Krittik (Taurus), the summer solstice in Magha (Leo), and the winter solstice in Aquarius, a date of 2500-2000 BC. Such astronomical data reflect the Harappan and post-Harappan era, which one would expect to have an adequate calendar."

Such astronomical data suggest that the Vedas and Sanskrit are at least 4,500 years old.

Pliny and Arrian: Starting point of Vedic Chronology

Such an early date – 6676 BC or 6777 BC, as suggested by Greek historians Pliny and Arrian for the starting point for Indian (Hindu/Vedic) chronology – challenges the validity of the theory of 'Aryan invasion of India'. Feuerstein and et al (p.246) write that Greek historians Pliny and Arrian based this on the reports they got from the ambassadors at the Maurya courts that the native historical tradition of India knew of 154 kings who ruled over a period of 6,450 years. Feuerstein and et al (p.246) remark: "When we reconstruct this tradition, it appears that during the Mauryan times the calendar was taken to commence in 6676 B.C."

Break up of Himalayan glaciers: Age of the Rig Veda

Graham Hancock (2002:169) quotes B.B. Radhakrishna of the Geological Society of India (1999), who writes that the *Rig Veda* talks about the break-up of Himalayan glaciers releasing water which flowed out in seven mighty rivers (*Sapta Sindhu*). The early inhabitants of the plains burst into songs praising Lord Indra for releasing the water they very much needed. This happened during Late Pleistocene glaciations, about 10,000 years ago. Radhakrishna had said:

> "Geologist record indicates that during Late Pleistocene glaciations, waters of the Himalaya were frozen and that in place of rivers there were only glaciers, masses of solid ice. ... When the climate became warmer, the glaciers began to break up and the frozen water held by them surged forth in great floods, inundating the alluvial plain in front of the mountains. ... With the hindsight we possess as geologists, we at once see that the phenomenon described in the Rig Veda was no idle fancy but a real natural event of great significance connected with the break up of Himalayan glaciers and the release of pent-up waters in great floods."

This description of the break up of the Himalayan glaciers in the *Rig Veda* suggests beyond any doubt that the *Rig Veda* was composed at least 10,000 years back.

The archeologically excavated seals at Mohenjo-Daro and Harappa, beginning in early 1920s, shed historical light to awaken historians to the truths about the prehistory ancient Bharat, her native *Aryans*, antiquity of the *Rig Veda*, and of *Sanskrit*. Unfortunately, the wrong history, written by colonial Westerners, has not yet been corrected. Encyclopedias and text books continue to carry on the same text as written by them prior to the Indus Valley civilization saw the sunshine in 1920s.

Resemblance between Vedas and Persia's Avesta

Nehru (p.77) talks about the resemblance between the Vedas and the Persia's Avesta and between their languages, Sanskrit and Avestan respectively:

> "The Vedas were the outpourings of the Aryans as they streamed into the rich land of India. The brought their ideas with them from that common stock out of which grew the Avesta in Iran, and elaborated them in the soil of India. Even the language of the Vedas bears a striking resemblance to that of the Avesta, and it has been remarked that the Avesta is nearer the Veda than the Veda is to its own epic Sanskrit."

I agree with Nehru that Persia's Avesta and its language Avestan resemble to Bharat's Vedas and Sanskrit respectively. But I do not agree that Aryans came to India from outside and that the Vedas were brought or composed by the alleged invading Aryans. It has been historically proved that in ancient times Iran was a part of Bharat (India), culturally as well as administratively. This is discussed in the 16th Chapter, 'Iran: A Part of Ancient India'.

Arya is a Sanskrit word. Aryans were the original natives of the ancient *Aryavarta* (Bharat, India). The originality of the Aryans has been confused by the ill-based theory, 'Aryan invasion of India'. Not even one historian has yet been able to identify the country outside India which had or has Aryans as its natives and Sanskrit as its native language.

Max Müller (1899, p.34) further talks about the age of the Vedas:

> "Whatever may be the date of the Vedic hymns, whether 1500 or 15,000 B.C., they have their own unique place and stand by themselves in the literature of the world."

Stephen Knapp, in his book *"Proof of Vedic Culture's Global Existence"* (2000, p.66), talks about the antiquity of the *Vedas*:

"In the same line of thought, it has been determined that the Sanskrit *Rig-Veda* is the oldest piece of literature in the world. Reverend Morris Philip, in his book *The Teaching of the Vedas* (p.213), concludes: "After the latest researches into the history and chronology of the book of Old Testament, we may safely now call the *Rigveda* as the oldest book not only of the Aryan community, but of the whole world.""

Harry H. Hicks and Robert N. Anderson[7] have given dates of the antiquity of the Rig Veda, as given by different scholars:

* David Frawley, in *"Gods, Sages and Kings"*, on the basis of astronomical references in the *Rig Veda*, corroborating the work of other earlier scholars such as Tilak and Jacobi, go back to ca.6500 B.C.
* Probably beginning shortly after the major Indo-European "Kurganian" migration of ca 4,400 to 4,300 B.C., as described by Gumbutas, the Rig Vedic age, apparently with its inspired concepts, was conceived in India.
* According to Cambridge, "The hymns of the Rig Veda were composed in the NW of India, the country of seven rivers in about 3700 B.C.
* Hicks and Anderson have given an interesting evidence of Vedic Aryan Head from the collection of the Hicks Foundation for Cultural Preservation. They remark that extensive tests and mutually corroborative and interrelated physical, stylistic and historical evidence indicate it was cast in the 4th millennium B.C., dating 3700 B.C. It was life sized, hollow, copper-based head in a human likeness. It may be the first hard evidence relating to the original Vedic Aryans in India. They tend to emphasize: "The Head's natural style and eye treatment also provide evidence of the continuity of Vedic Aryan art styles of the 4th/3rd

---

[7] Bhu Dev Sharma and Nabarun Ghose (ed.)., *"Revisiting Indus-Sarasvati Age and Ancient India"*, WAVES, (1998, 348-350).

millennium B.C., the Harappan and Mesopotamian art, and evolution into later Hellenistic and classical Indian art."

- Feuerstein & et al (1995: 29) write about the *Rig-Veda*: "The *Rig-Veda* is the oldest book in the Sanskrit language, indeed in any Indo-European language. More than that, if we are correct, it is the oldest book in the world, and for this reason alone deserves our attention."

Feuerstein & et al (1995: 29) write that the *Rig-Veda* has a total of 1,028 hymns comprising 10,589 verses which were composed in various periods. The other three younger *Vedas* are *Sama Veda, Yajur Veda,* and *Atharva Veda.* In addition to the four *Vedas,* there were various subsidiary *Vedic* scriptures – *Puranas, Brahmanas, Aranyakas, Upanishads, Sutras, Shastras, Samhitas,* etc.

The antiquity of the *Rig Veda,* as given by various scholars, ranges from 7,500 B.C. to 3,000 B.C. considering the latest date 3,000 B.C., the age of Sanskrit should be much older than the age of its literature. The Vedas were composed at least 1,500 years prior to 1,500 B.C., the year of the alleged Aryan invasion. This challenges the validity of the Aryan invasion, according to which Sanskrit was allegedly brought in and the Vedas were composed by the invading Aryans. This also refutes the IE, according to which Sanskrit came into India from outside in about 3,000 B.C.

Nehru (1946, p. 93) talks about the individualistic philosophy of wholesome life, as contained in the Upanishads:

"There is, in the Upanishads, a continual emphasis on the fitness of the body and clarity of the mind, on the discipline of both body and mind, before effective progress can be made. The acquisition of knowledge, or any achievement, requires restraint, self-suffering, self-sacrifice. This idea of some kind of penance, *tapasya,* is inherent in Indian thought, both among thinkers at the top and the unread masses below. It is present today as it was present thousands of years ago, and it is necessary to appreciate it in order to understand the psychology underlying the mass movements which have convulsed India under the Gandhiji's leadership."

THREE

Sanskrit: The Most Ancient Language

"Sanskrit is the most apt language for Indians since most Indian languages are its offshoots."

Shaheena[♦]

"The Sanskrit language, whatever be its antiquity, is of a wonderful structure, more perfect than the Greek, more copious than the Latin, and more exquisitely refined than the either, yet bearing to both of them a stronger affinity, both in the roots of verbs and the forms of grammar, than could possibly have been produced by accident; so strong indeed, that no philologer could examine them all three, without believing them to have sprung from some common source, which, perhaps, no longer exits: there is similar reason, though not quite so forcible, for supposing that both the Gothic and Celtic, though blended with a very different idiom, had the same origin with the Sanskrit, and the Old Persian might be added to the same family."

Sir William Jones

I agree with Sir William Jones that Sanskrit has some affinity with Latin and Greek. But it is not as close as, and not of the kind as required to qualify Sanskrit to be cognate sister of any European

---

[♦] Satya Vrat Shastri, 'Sanskrit Studies: New Perspectives' (2007, p. 26).

25

language. It is too hard to agree with Jones that such affinity is due to their common origin. Sanskrit has not sprung from the same source, as Latin and Greek. Speakers of Sanskrit are ethno-culturally and historically different and geographically too distant from the Europeans. Moreover, their religions are different. Language is associated with the religion of its speakers. Thus their languages – Indic and European – can / should not be considered as the members of one and the same family. Philological resemblances can not make them cognate siblings. Such philological resemblances are caused by borrowing due to cohabitation and/or by chance or by lingual accidents.

According to Wikipedia, "Sanskrit is a historical Indo-Aryan language and the primary liturgical language of Hinduism and Buddhism. Today, it is listed as one of the 22 scheduled languages of India."

Will Durant, in *Our Oriental Heritage* (p.406), remarks:

> "The Sanskrit of the Vedas and the Epics has already earmarks of a classical and literary tongue, used only by scholars and priests; the very word Sanskrit means 'prepared, pure, perfect, sacred.' The language of the people in the Vedic age was not one but many; each tribe had its own Aryan dialect. India has never had *one* language."

Durant (p.555) talks about the transformation of Sanskrit into Prakrit – from its use by scholars to its use by public in form of various vernaculars, such as Hindi, Bengali, Punjabi, Gujarati, Marathi, Sindhi, etc.:

> "JUST as the philosophy and much of the literature of medieval Europe were composed in a dead language unintelligible to the people, so the philosophy and classic literature of India were written in a Sanskrit that had long since passed out of common parlance, but had survived as the *Esperanto* of scholars having no other common tongue. Divorced from contact with the life of the nation, this literary language became a model of scholasticism

26

and refinement; new words were formed not by the spontaneous creation of the people, but by the needs of technical discourse in the schools."

Durant (pp.574-575) talks about the literary beauty of the play *'SHAKUNTALA'* of Kalidasa which was translated into English by Sir William Jones, and praised by Goethe. Kalidasa was nominated as one of the 'Nine Gems' – poets, artists, and philosophers – by Raja Vikramaditya (380-413 A.D.).

Max Müller (1999, p.40) talks about Sanskrit, its antiquity and its relationship with other languages:

"First of all, its antiquity – for we know Sanskrit at an earlier period than Greek. But what is more important than its merely chronological antiquity is the antique state of preservation in which that Aryan language has been handed down to us. ... Sanskrit was the eldest sister of them all and could of many things which the other members of the family had quite forgotten."

It is hard to understand how Sanskrit (an Aryan language) could be handed down to Europeans when it was an Aryan language, meaning the language of Aryavarta (Bharat, India). He has not explained how it was handed down to Europe. Max Müller seems to indirectly suggest that Sanskrit is a member of the IE family. In my opinion, Sanskrit can not be genetically related to any European language because it is culturally and historically different and geographically too distant from all European languages. The IE is linguistically too diverse to be one family. Particularly, Indic languages are not and can not be genetically related to European languages. Philological similarities between some – even several – Sanskrit and European words can / should not qualify them as linguistic genetic sisters. Similarities, as said earlier, are caused by borrowing due to long cohabitation of their speakers and/or by chance.

Max Müller, in *'Science of Language'* (1891: 225-6), writes that the discovery of Sanskrit struck Lord Monboddo, like a thunderbolt just after he had finished his great work *'Of the*

Origins and Progress of Languages' (2nd edition, 6 volumes, Edinburgh, 1774). In this work, he says all the dialects of the world were derived from a language originally framed by some Egyptian gods. Later in 1792, Monboddo writes:

> "There is a language (Sanskrit) still existing, and preserved among the Brahmins of India, which is richer and in every respect a finer language than even the Greek of Homer. All the other languages of India have a great resemblance to this language, which is called the Shanscrit. ... I shall be able clearly to prove that the Greek is derived from the Shanscrit, which was the ancient language of Egypt, and was carried by the Egyptians into India, with their other arts, and into Greece by the colonies which they settled there."

If Sanskrit is the language of the Brahmins of India, how then do some linguists say that it came to India from outside? I do agree that several Sanskrit words have resemblance to Greek, but disagree with Monboddo that that Greek is derived from Sanskrit or Sanskrit from Greek. I also disagree that Sanskrit was the ancient language of Egypt. As a matter of fact, history vouches that Sanskrit-speaking Aryans had established their kingdoms in Egypt, other middle-east countries and Greece in remote ancient times. Thus, due to long cohabitation of Sanskrit-speaking Aryans with Egyptians and Greeks, Sanskrit philologically influenced the languages of Egypt and Greece. It is explained later that in ancient times that the Vedic Aryans had gone out of India for trade and had established their kingdoms in various regions all over the planet. In those days, Sanskrit could be a very popular language in Egypt and Greece, but it was not their lingua franca. India, the land of Sanskrit, is historically and culturally different and geographically too distant from Greece and Egypt to make European, Egyptian and Indic languages a family.

A few years later (1795), Lord Monboddo (Max Müller, 1891, p.226) realized that Sanskrit is not a dialect of Greek, nor Greek of Sanskrit. But, still he does not seem to be clear about the origin of

28

Sanskrit: The Most Ancient Language

Sanskrit and its relation with Greek and some Egyptian language. He writes:

> "Mr. Wilkins has proved to my conviction such a resemblance betwixt the Greek and the Shanscrit, that the one must be a dialect of the other, or both of some original language. Now the Greek is certainly not a dialect of the Shanscrit, anymore than the Shanscrit is of the Greek. They must, therefore, be both dialects of the same language; and that language could be no other than the language of Egypt, brought into India by Osiris, of which, undoubtedly, the Greek was a dialect, as I think I have proved."

It seems, both Max Müller and Sir William Jones were so much emotionally and intellectually engrossed to prove the validity of their ill-founded theory of IE (Indo-European family of languages). Hence they engineered also the theory of Aryan Invasion of India (AII), according to which Aryans invaded India in about 1500 B.C. and brought with them Sanskrit and a pantheon of Hindu gods; and composed the Vedas in about 1000 BC and even later. I feel both the theories (IE and AII) were guided by their missionary agenda to prove that all the three – Aryans, Sanskrit and the Vedas – were not originally from Aryavrata (India).

Unfortunately for them, cat is out of bag. Both the theories, AII and IE, contradict each other on both counts – (1) the story the way they came to India, and (2) on the year of entry of Sanskrit in India. According to the AII, Aryans invaded India in about 1500 B.C. and brought Sanskrit; and according to IE, speakers of Sanskrit and European languages lived some where (no consensus on their abode), and after their separation in 3000 B.C (some say 600 B.C.) Sanskrit-speaking came to India and Europeans went to Greece, Italy, etc.

According to *Samvad* (December, New Delhi, 1997, p.3), the German scholar Kurt Schildmann claims that his study of ancient inscriptions, discovered in Peru and USA, show that they are similar to ancient Sanskrit, suggesting sea fares from India might have reached Americas long back.

Glory of Sanskrit

The Columbia Encyclopedia (1993:163-4) talks about the glory of ancient Sanskrit literature, as contained in its three major Oriental dramas:

"Of the three major Oriental dramas – Sanskrit, Chinese, Japanese – the oldest is Sanskrit, although the dates of its origin are uncertain. Sanskrit drama is a part of Sanskrit literature, the classical literature of India, which flourished from about 1500 B.C. to A.D.1100. The earliest extant critical work on Sanskrit drama is attributed to Bharata, the legendary formulator of the dramatic art in India. ... The earliest-known Sanskrit playwright was Bhasa (c.3d cent. A. D.) while among the most renowned were Kalidasa, Bhavabhuti (c.8th cent. A.D.), and King Harsha."

The book '*India: What Can It Teach Us*' (1999) contains the text of the seven lectures, Max Müller delivered to the European candidates for civil service in India. He addressed several issues to help them to have clear understanding of the character of Hindus, Vedas, Vedanta, Vedic deities, significance of the study of Sanskrit and its literature. He also has addressed European misconceptions of and prejudices against India, Hindus, their deities and Vedic literature.

Max Müller (1999, p.137) has emphasized that India deserves European attention and respect because:

"(India), both by its language, the Sanskrit, and by its most ancient literary documents, the Vedas, it can teach us lessons which nothing else can teach, as to the origin of our own language, the first formation of our own concepts, and the true natural germs of all that is comprehended under the name of civilization, at least civilization of the Aryan race, that the race we and all the greatest nations of the world – the Hindus, the Persians, the Greeks and Romans, the Slaves, the Celts, and last, not least, the Teutons, belong."

Max Müller, (1999, p.138), writes that the ancient literature of the Vedic period of India deserves careful attention, not only of Oriental scholars, but also of every educated man and woman, any where, even in England. He wishes to know how we (Europeans) came to be what we are. He talks about the significance of meditation and transcendentalism in which Hindus excel:

"I wished to point out that there was another sphere of intellectual activity in which the Hindus excelled – the meditative and transcendent – and that here we might learn from them some lessons of life which we ourselves are but too apt to ignore or to despise."

Max Müller (1999, p.22) makes a pleasing remark about the respect Sanskrit commands in Germany:

"A scholar who studies Sanskrit in Germany is supposed to be initiated in the deep and dark mysteries of ancient wisdom, and a man who has traveled in India, even if he has only discovered Calcutta, or Bombay, or Madras, is listened to like another Marco Polo. In England a student of Sanskrit is generally considered a bore."

Sanskrit in China

Max Müller, in 'The Science of Language' (p. 196) talking about 'Chinese accounts of India', observes that the next nation after the Greeks that became acquainted with the language and literature of India was the Chinese. Though Buddhism was not recognized as a third-religion before the year 65 A.D., under the Emperor Ming-ti, Buddhist missionaries had reached China from India as early as the third century, 217 B.C. He further writes:

31

"The very name of Buddha, changed in Chinese into Fo-t'o and Fo[8], is pure Sanskrit, and so is every word and every thought of that religion. The language – which the Chinese pilgrims went to India to study, as the key to the sacred literature of Buddhism – was Sanskrit."

Tedd St Rain, in the Preface to *'What India Can Teach Us'* (!999), writes:

"Some of the most valuable and instructive materials in the history of man are treasured up in India, and in India only. In her classic dialect, the Sanskrit, we may read with what success ancient India conquered the elements and the world as it was then known."

He further remarks about the significance of Sanskrit:

"The study of Sanskrit, and particularly a study of the Vedic Sanskrit, is able to enlighten us and illuminate the darkest passages in the history of the human mind."

Max Müller (1999, p.39), writes that no one supposes any longer that Sanskrit was the common source of European languages:

"I am not speaking as yet of the literature of India as it is, but of something far more ancient, the language of India, or Sanskrit. No one supposes any longer that Sanskrit was the common source of Greek, Latin, and Anglo-Saxon. This used to be said, but it has long been shown that Sanskrit is only a collateral branch of the same stem from which spring Geek, Latin, Anglo-Saxon; and not only these, but all the Teutonic, all the Celtic, all the Slavonic languages, nay the languages of Persia and Armenia also."

---

[8] *Methode pour dechiffrer et transcrire les noms sanscrits qui se rencontrent dans les livres chinois, inventee et demontree* par M. Stanislas Julien, Paris, 1861, p. 103.

Sanskrit: The Most Ancient Language

I am happy about the scholarly realization that Sanskrit and European languages do not share a common origin. But, I don't agree that Sanskrit is a collateral branch of the same stem from which Sanskrit and European languages have sprung. The Indic and European are two distinctly different families of languages, culturally as well as historically. They are geographically too distant to make a family, not even a tree of languages having branches of Indic and European languages. Moreover, Sanskrit is much older than all the European languages. Philological resemblances, as seen, are caused by long close cohabitation, not by alleged common parentage. It is historically known that in ancient times, Vedic people had gone out of India for trade to several countries including European. They had established Vedic kingdoms and had colonized some countries including Greece, as shown by E. Pococke in his book, *'India in Greece* or *Truth in Mythology'* (1856).

Sanskrit and Avestan

It is true that the Persian, the language of Persia (Iran), has its origin in Sanskrit. The authors of the Vedas and worshippers of Ahuro Mazdao did live together in early ancient times. India, including Persia (Iran), was the original home of the Aryans and the Persians (Iranians). As a matter of fact, in remote ancient times, Iran was a part of Greater India (Vishaal Bharat). Both the languages, Sanskrit and Zend-Avestan, were linguistically too close to consider them as two different languages. J. P. Mallory, in *'In Search of Indo-Europeans'* (1989, p.35), has shown close linguistic relationship between Sanskrit and Iran's Avestan:

Avestan: tem amavantem yazatem
Sanskrit: tam amavantam yajatam

Avestan: surem damohu sevistem
Sanskrit: suram dhamasu savistham

Avestan: mithrem yazai zaothrabyo
Sanskrit: mitram yajai hotrabhyah

33

Mallory (p. 35) remarks:

> "The concept of a common Indo-Iranian language is indicated by the close similarities between this Indic (Sanskrit) translation of an early Iranian hymn. The god Mitra / Mithra was common to both Indians and Iranians."

In fact, these are not translations. The same Sanskrit was spoken in Avestan with little difference in phonetic pronunciation of some letters. For example:

Sanskrit	Avestan
'j'	'z'
'h'	's'
'dh'	'd'
'th'	't'
'bh'	'b'

Same way, Iranians pronounced 'Sindhu' as 'Hindu', and 'soma' as' homa'.

Dr. Poonai (Origin of Civilization and Language, 1994, p. 220) writes about the relationship between Sanskrit and the Zend-Avestan:

> "It has also been shown on the basis of statements which have been made in the oldest of the Gathas of the Zend Avesta, about mantras and personalities of the Rig Veda, that the Rig Veda predates the Gathas by several millennia and that the Vedas appear to have contributed to the content of the earliest Gathas by accumulation of concepts."

It needs to be noted that word *'Gathas'* has its origin in Sanskrit. It literally means 'stories'.

Nehru, in *'Discovery of India'* (1946, p.77), writes about the relationship between Sanskrit and Avestan:

Sanskrit: The Most Ancient Language

"Even the language of the Vedas bears a striking resemblance to that of the Avesta, and it has been remarked that Avesta is nearer to the Veda than the Veda is to its own epic Sanskrit."

Max Müller, in *'Science of Language'* (1861, p.289), remarks:

"Sanskrit and Zend share certain words and grammatical forms in common which do not exist in any other Aryan languages; and there can be no doubt that the ancestors of the poets of the Vedas and the worshippers of A*huro Mazdao* lived together for some time after they had left the original home of the whole Aryan race."

Hard to understand what Max Müller meant by the "original home of the whole Aryan race." I think, Max Müller meant Greater India when Iran remained as its part, until Iran was captured and occupied by other forces. Aryans (Hindus) and Persians (Iranians) did not leave India (the original home of the whole Aryan race). Some Avestan-speaking Zoroastrians had to leave Iran for Sanskrit-speaking India, when Iran was captured by Muslims. Most of them stayed there in Iran.

It can be understood better from the event 'Partition of India in 1947' when Muslims had Pakistan. Many Muslims opted to continue to live in India, and even some migrated back from Pakistan to India. So it happened with Zoroastrian Iranians. The ancient relationship between Iran and Bharat (India) is discussed in detail later in Chapter 16, "Iran: A Part of Ancient India.".

Dr. Poonai (p.226) gives genealogic time trend of some important IE languages:

Language Group	Approximate time of origin
Rig-Vedic Sanskrit	9000 B.C.
Zend	1500 B.C.
Greek dialects	800 B.C.
Latin languages	400 B.C.
Celtic languages	500 B.C.
Germanic languages	350 A.D.
Baltic languages	1100 A.D.

Mallory (1989, p.15) also has placed Indo-Iranian (Iranian and Indic) as the oldest group of the Indo-European languages, around 1500 B.C., along with Anatolian languages, such as Luwian, Hittite and Palaic.

Hindus: First in cultivating Science of Grammar

Max Müller, in *'The Science of Language'* (1891, pp.124-5), praises the Panini grammar:

> "The Hindus are the only nation that cultivated the science of Grammar without having received any impulse, directly or indirectly, from the Greeks. ... Sanskrit grammar arose from the study of the Vedas, the most ancient poetry of the Brahmans. ... These supplied the solid basis on which successive generations of scholars erected that astounding structure which reached its perfection in the grammar of Panini. There is no form, regular or irregular, in the whole Sanskrit language, which is not provided for in the grammar of Panini and his commentators. It is the perfection of a merely empirical analysis of language, unsurpassed, nay even un-approached, by anything in the grammatical literature of other nations."

Michael Coulson, in his book *'Sanskrit: Introduction to Classical Language'* (1992, p. xv), talks about the Panini grammar:

> "The grammar of Panini, the Astadhyayi, usually attributed to the fourth century BC, is evidently the culmination of a long and sophisticated grammatical tradition, though the perfection of his own work caused that of his predecessors to vanish."

Such recognition of Sanskrit grammar by Max Müller and by Michael Coulson seems to question the reliability and validity of linguistic congenital sisterhood of Sanskrit with Greek and Latin.

Sanskrit adored by Muslims too

Dr. Satya Vrat Shastri, in his book *"Sanskrit Studies: New Perspectives"* (2007, p. 18), remarks:

"The pursuit of Sanskrit by Muslims is not limited to the medieval or the early modern period only, it is carried on even now. The number of Muslim Sanskrit scholars pursuing Sanskrit may not be very large but it is not too small either to be ignored."

Dr. Shastri has given quite a few examples of Muslim scholars in Sanskrit, such as Shri Ghulam Dastgir of Bombay, Shri Habibur Rehman Shastri, known as Pandit Habibur Rehman, Prof. Fatehullah Mojtabai, Ms. Shaheena S., etc. Three of them need mention to emphasize Muslim interest in Sanskrit.

Sanskrit scholar Shri Ghulam Dastgir was honored in 1976 by the Government of Maharashtra. He had so much deep and abiding love for Sanskrit that he sent out invitation in Sanskrit for the marriage of his younger brother.

Ms. Shaheena. A 25 year young woman topped in the Kerala University M.A. (Sanskrit) examination. She is the second of the three daughters of Shri Shahul Hamid. She opted for Sanskrit with her parents' blessings. Dr. Shasti (p.26) talks about her that when asked by some people as to why she did not choose Arabic in place of Sanskrit, Shaheena replied: "Sanskrit is the most apt language for Indians since most Indian languages are its offshoots." Dr. Shastri writes that Shaheena wants to launch a Sanskrit magazine to help Sanskrit lovers in India express their creativity. She wants one day to teach Sanskrit. She mourns: "It is shame that this beautiful language is reduced to a Cinderella in her own land."

Prof. Fatehullah Mojtabai, former Cultural Counselor of the Embassy of Iran in India, was a noted scholar of Sanskrit and a well-known exponent of Hindu philosophy. He has translated into Persian the Gita, the *Laghuyogavāsistha* and *Mahopanisad.* Translation of Gita into Persian suggests that Prof. Mojtabai was so much impressed by the philosophy of Hinduism, as contained in Gita, that he wanted his countrymen (Iranians) should also benefit

37

from the Gita philosophy. May be his ancestors were Zoroastrians whose language Zend-Avestan was very similar to Sanskrit.

Hindus love poetry

Hindus are so much lovers of poetry that almost all ancient sacred scriptures and epics – Vedas, Upanishads, Bhagvad Gita, Rāmāyanā, Mahābhāratā, etc. – are composed in poetry form. Dr. Shastri (p.51) has remarked that poetry has been with Bharat from the times of the Vedas, and that from time to time its character has been undergoing change – from religious poetry of the Vedas to narrative poetry of the Rāmāyanā, the Mahābhāratā and the Purānas to the highly sophisticated and ornate poetry of the Mahākāvyas.

Shaheena's family finds Sanskrit *shlokas* melodious when she recites them at home. She herself says that there is poetry in every syllable of them."

Surprisingly, present cinema seems to follow the tradition. Love is expressed through song and dance. Some movies are very much stuffed with songs and dances. E. Pococke, in his book *'India in Greece'*, writes that Hindus had colonized Greece in ancient times. Every thing including mathematics was expressed in a poetry form.

Language more related to culture, rather to religion

Language is more related to culture than to religion. Some times culture is confused as religion. Any culture is much wider than religion. Therefore, the members of the same culture, though followers of different religions, may speak the same language, as is happening in India. This also is true that each culture has some of its ingredients related to various religions. Some conservative and narrow-minded persons become too sensitive to the choice of words, to insure that the word is from the language related to his/her religion.

Several ethnicities can be associated with one culture. Culture, unlike religion, doesn't have any defined restricting borders. Hence, associates of the same, rather similar culture, may follow different religions. Followers of various religions – Hinduism,

Jainism, Buddhism, Christianity, Zoroastrianism, Islam, Sikhism, Sufism, etc. – are associated with Indian culture in varying ways and in varying degrees, and so are various languages of India. This can be understood better if American culture is seen in relation to various religions and various languages of its people.

Sanskrit is primarily related to Hinduism, and then to its offshoot religions – Jainism, Buddhism and Sikhism – in varying degrees.

How did Sanskrit influence most of the world languages?

Several books, authored by European scholars, would vouch that India, with her Vedic culture expressed in Sanskrit, was all over the globe. Because of cohabitation between Sanskrit-speaking Aryans and speakers of other languages, mutual borrowing of words would be inevitable. As the result, it is natural that there would be some linguistic correspondence between Sanskrit and European languages, including Greek and Latin. But it will be wrong to interpret it as cognate or genetic relationship Sanskrit has with Greek, Latin and some other European languages.

FOUR

Ancient Hindu Astronauts: Unbelievable but True
Forgotten superior civilization

"One of the world's oldest books on astronomy is the Hindu *Sut-ya Siddhanta*. It speaks of Siddhas and Vidyahatas, or philosophers and scientists, who were able to orbit the earth in a former epoch below the moon but above the clouds."

Andrew Tomas[9]

"The importance of such studies and investigations could prove to be shocking for today's man because the existence of flying devices beyond mythology can only be explained with a forgotten superior civilization on earth."

Dr. Roberto Pinotti

This chapter will take its readers to the incredible sciences of the ancient Bharat, and to the controversial and fascinating world of Pinotti's "forgotten superior civilization", which is none but Bharat's.

Will Durant[10] has said: "As we acquire knowledge, things do not become more comprehensible, but more mysterious."

---

[9] David Hatcher Childress, in 'Technology of the Gods: The Incredible Sciences of the Ancients' Kempton, US: 2000, p.158.
[10] Ibid, p. 11.

41

Tomas further says:

"Another book from India – the *Samara-nagana Sutradharna* – contains a fantastic paragraph about the distant past when men flew in the air in skyships and heavenly beings came down from the sky. Was there a sort of two-way space traffic in a forgotten era?"

Prof. H.L. Hariyappa[11] of Mysore University, in his essay on the *Rig Veda*, writes that in a distant epoch "gods came to the earth often times, and that it was the privilege of some men to visit the immortals in heaven." The tradition of India is insistent upon the reality of this communication with other worlds during the Golden Age. The book further writes that the god Garuda is thought by Brahmins to be a combination of man and bird who travels through space.

Garuda is the national airline of Indonesia. According to the Wikipedia, the Garuda is a mythical bird or a bird-like creature that appears in both Hindu and Buddhist mythology. History tells that in ancient times Indonesia was colonized by Hindus and Buddhists, and its language Bahasa is very much influenced by Sanskrit. In Hindi, 'bhasha' (very comparable to 'Bahasa) means language. The names of several cities, like Jakarta, Surbaya, etc. and of individuals, like Sukarno, Suharto, Yudhoyona, Megavati, Sukarno-putri, (putri in Hindi means daughter) etc.. seem to have their origin in Sanskrit. Its monetary unit Rupiah is very much comparable to Indian Rupaya.

Childress (p.168) writes about the Aerial warfare in Ancient India:

"The ancient Indian epics go into considerable detail about aerial warfare over 10,000 years ago. So much detail that a famous Oxford professor included a chapter on the subject in a book on ancient warfare."

---

[11] Ibid, p. 158

Childress (p.169) writes that Dikshitar, commenting on the famous Vimana text *'Vimanika Shastra'*, says:

"In the recently published 'Samarangana Sutradhara of Bhoja' a whole chapter of 230 stanzas is devoted to the principles of construction underlying the various flying machines and other engines used for military and other purposes. The various advantages of using machines, especially flying ones, are given elaborately. Special mention is made of their attacking visible as well as invisible objects, of their use at one's will and pleasure, of their uninterrupted movements, of their strength and durability, in short of their capability to do in the air all that is done on earth."

Sanskrit scholar Ramchandra Dikshitar,[12] in his book titled *'War in Ancient India'* (1944), writes:

"No question can be more interesting than in the present circumstances of the world than India's contribution to the science of aeronautics. There are numerous illustrations in our vast Puranic and epic literature to show how well and wonderfully the ancient Indians conquered the air. To glibly characterize every thing found in this literature as imaginary and summarily dismiss it as unreal has been the practice of both Western and Eastern scholars until recently. The very idea indeed was ridiculed and people went so far as to assert that it was physically impossible for man to use flying machines. But today what with balloons, aero planes and other flying machines, a great change has come over our ideas on the subjects."[13]

---

[12] Ibid, p. 168.
[13] Ramchandra Dikshitar, *'Warfare in Ancient India'*, Madras: Oxford University Press, 1944..

Col. Henry S. Olcott (1832-1907), American author, philosopher and cofounder of the Theosophical Society, in a lecture in Allahabad in 1881, said:

"The ancient Hindus could navigate the air, and not only navigate it, but fight battles in it like so many war-eagles combating for the domination of the clouds. To be so perfect in aeronautics, they must have known all the arts and of the atmosphere, the relative temperature, humidity, density and specific gravity of the various gases."

Frederick Soddy[14] (1877-1956), a Nobel Laureate (1921, Chemistry of radioactive substance), had a great regard for the Indian epics Rāmāyanā and Mahābhāratā, from which he might have got the idea of the awesome power of the atom. Therefore, it seems he did not take the records, as contained in these ancient Hindu epics, as fables. Soddy, in *'Interpretation of Radium'* (1909), wrote:

"Can we not read into them (the texts of the epics) some justification for the belief that some forgotten race of men attained not only to the knowledge we have so recently won, but also to the power that is not yet ours?"

Dr. Vyacheslav Zaitsev[15] has said that the holy Indian (Hindu) Sages have mentioned in the Rāmāyanā that two storied celestial chariots with many windows roared off into the sky like comets. He adds that the Mahābhāratā and various Sanskrit books describe at length these chariots which were powered by winged lighting. He further remarks: "It was a ship that soared into the air, flying to both the solar and stellar regions."

Dr. Roberto Pinotti[16] – an Italian scientist who had made exhaustive study of the history of Indian astronautics – told the World Space Conference that India may have had a superior civilization with possible contacts with extraterrestrial visitors, and

---

[14] Hindu Wisdom - Vimanas
[15] ibid
[16] ibid

the flying devices 'Vimanas', as described in ancient Indian texts and that it may underline their possible connections with today's aerospace technology. He asked the delegates to examine in detail the Hindu texts instead of dismissing 'all the Vimana descriptions and traditions' as mere myths.

Dr. Pinotti asserted:

"The importance of such studies and investigations could prove to be shocking for today's man because the existence of flying devices beyond mythology can only be explained with a forgotten superior civilization on earth."

Pinotti's "forgotten superior civilization" was none but the prehistory ancient Vedic civilization.

He pointed out that Indian (Hindu) gods and heroes fought in the skies using piloted vehicles with terrible vehicles. He further said that they were similar to modern jet propelled flying machines, and that certain descriptions of the Vimanas (airplanes) seemed "too detailed and technical in nature to be labeled as myth."

Dr. Pinotti cites various texts to amazing secrets related to the operation of Vimanas, some of which could be compared to modern day use of radar, solar energy and photography. It is amazing that the ancient Indians had scientific 'Airplane manual', known as 'Vymanika Shastra'. Quoting from it, Dr. Pinotti says that the ancient flying devices of India were made from special heat-absorbing metals named 'Somaka, Soundalike and Mourthwika.' He also writes that the *Shastra* also discusses the seven kinds of mirrors and lenses installed aboard for defensive and offensive uses. He explains that the so-called 'Pinjula Mirror' offered a sort of 'visual shield' preventing the pilots from being blinded by the 'evil rays', and the weapon 'Marika' used to shoot enemy aircraft does not seem too different from what we today call laser technology.

Dr. Pinotti had made an exhaustive study of the history of Indian astronautics. He talks about another text according to which ancient Hindus knew the use of element 'fire' as could be seen from their *'Astra'* (weapons) that included *Soposamhara* (flame belching missile), *Prasvapna* (which caused sleep) and four kinds of *Agni Astras* (fire weapons) that traveled in sheets of flame and produced thunder.

It should be noted that *'Agni'* (fire) is seen as a Hindu goddess. It contributes lot to human life in various ways from life-sustaining kitchen to high technology. Its prime use in technology – manufacturing, missiles, space, astronautics, nuclear and what not – is surfacing now meeting various multifarious demands of the present complex life.

Fire is purifier too. Thus, it is used in all Hindu religious ceremonies. The seven promises, made by bride and groom, are taken while circling around fire. Even the end of the Hindu life (death) is blessed by Agni. Cremation is environment-purifying. It saves space for several beneficial uses.

Dr. Pinotti said that depictions of space travel, total destruction by incredible weapons and the fact that Vimanas (Vimans) resembled modern unidentified flying objects would suggest that India had a 'superior but forgotten civilization.' Dr. Pinotti suggests:

"In light of all this, we think it will be better to examine the Hindu texts and subject the descriptive models of Vimanas to more scientific scrutiny."

All this technical version of the construction and operation of the ancient flying machines (airplanes), as given in the ancient Hindu scriptures, can not be considered as mythological. Only the jealous technologists may say so, because they fear that their Viman (airplane) related technology may be thought, as based on the knowledge given in Hindu *Shastras* (scriptures).

The Mahābhāratā (3067 BC)[17] people did have the knowledge of not only flying machines, but also of fire missiles (Agnibans, meaning fire arrows), and TV. Sanjaya was narrating, step by step, to the blind king Dhratrashtra in his palace what was happening on

---

[17] Kosla Vepa, *'Astronomical Dating of Events & Select Vignettes from Indian History'*, Pleasanton (Ca, USA): Indic Studies Foundation, 2008.

the Kurukshetra, while the Mahābhāratā War was in progress, just like watching cricket match on TV in living room in present times. Hindus had the knowledge and technology how to create dense clouds to cover the sun and let the day look dark as seen at the sunset. Such necessity arose when Jayadratha, the powerful Raja of Sindh, was hiding himself until the sunset. Arjuna had taken an oath to kill him before the sunset, and if he failed he would kill himself in blazing fire. Arjuna wanted to kill Jayadratha, because he, with help of his army, had held Pandavas from going ahead to protect Abhimanyu, the son of Arjuna and Subhadra. He was surrounded and then killed by six great Kaurava warriors including Drona, Kripa, Karna, Ashvatthama, Kritavarman, and Brihadvalla.

To bring Jayadratha out from his hide, Lord Krishna covered the sun with his mighty potencies. It looked like sunset. Jaydratha jubilantly came out from hide to enjoy seeing Arjuna being burnt. Krishna again used his power to disburse the clouds and let the sun come out. Then Krishna told Arjuna to go and kill Jayadratha, which he did.

The question arises how the Mahābhāratā people got the ideas about the things – fire missiles, airplanes, TV, etc. Ideas don't come from nothingness. Even the idea of 'zero' came from 'numbers', because zero itself is a number. Some incidents must have prompted ideas why and how it happened. Thus, TVs, missiles, airplanes, etc. have been invented. They didn't copy the present-time inventions. The PAST can not copy the PRESENT.

It is possible the present scientists got the ideas regarding the flying machines, nuclear missiles, TV, etc. from the ancient Hindu scriptures. UFOs might have given idea of flying in the air.

The infant Hindu scientific technology did not mature into its robust adulthood, only because of historically known self-centered mentality of Hindus – secrecy – not to share knowledge with others. Every new idea was secretly confined to family only. Thus it died with the family without its ultimate development.

The Indian Emperor Ashoka[18] started a 'Secret Society of the Nine Unknown Men'. Those nine men were great scientists. Each one wrote a book on his work. One wrote on "The Secrets of

---

[18] www.hinduwisdom.inf/

Gravitation." The work of the Society was kept so secret that only the name of the book was known to historians, but it was not read nor even seen by them. The book was kept in the secret library of the Secret Society. Where? No body knows if in India, Tibet or somewhere else.

It further says that only a few years back, the Chinese discovered some Sanskrit documents in Lhasa, Tibet. The documents were sent to the University of Chandrigath to be translated. Dr. Ruth Reyna of the University said recently that the documents contain directions for building interstellar spaceships. Their method of propulsion, Reyna said, was "anti-gravitational" and was based upon a system analogous to that of "laghima," the unknown power of the ego existing in man's physiological makeup, "a centrifugal force strong enough to counteract all gravitational pull." It further says that according Hindu Yogis, it is this "Laghima' which enables a person to levitate.

Ancient Hindu Traveled in space

Dr. Reyna observes that according to the document which seems to be thousands of years old, the ancient Indians (Hindus) could use these flying machines, known by them as ''Astras'' (Weapons), for transporting some men onto any other planet.

It seems it was kept secret so that its advanced scientific inventions are not used for evil purpose of war.

Dr. A.V. Krishna[19], professor of aeronautics at the Indian Institute of Science, Bangalore says:

"It is true that the ancient Indian Vedas and other texts refer to aeronautics, space ships, flying machines, ancient astronauts. A study of the Sanskrit texts has convinced me that ancient India did know the secret of building flying machines, and those machines were patterned after space ships coming from other planets."

---

[19] Ibid.

Rāmāyanā[20] has a highly detailed story of a trip to the moon in a Vimana. It gives details about a battle with an "Asvin" (or Atlantean) airship. It further says that this is but a small bit of recent evidence of anti-gravity and aerospace technology used by Hindus. It suggests that in order to understand the technology, the 'Rama Empire' developed on the Indian sub-continent, we must go much further back in time, at least fifteen thousand years. It further says that Rama existed, apparently, parallel to the Atlantean civilization in the mid Atlantic Ocean.

I think this puzzle can be solved only when we locate the planet from where the UFOs are coming. May be, Bharatvasis (Indians) had some relationship and communication with the residents of that planet, history of which has been lost or yet to be discovered. We do not know any other planet with human life.

I would like to stress the point that Hindu traditions call heroes as gods (devas). The gods, we are referring to as flying in the space above our planet, are merely humans with great divine powers. Or since we are unable to establish their factual identity, we may take them as mythological Hindu gods. Likewise the Greek mythology talks about Atlas, Titans, Olympian gods, and Zeus, the god of heavens.

Rama and Krishna were not mythological gods. History tells that Hindus worship Sri Rama and Sri Krishna as gods. Both were great warriors with amazing vision and powers. Both, like other humans, were born and died. Both were Kshatris, not Brahmins. They respected Brahmins. Hanuman, a disciple of Sri Rama, is worshipped as a god by many Hindus.

Hinduism is being misperceived as polytheism, only because several heroes and several great sadhus (saints) are being worshipped as gods. For example Sai Baba of Shirdi, Maharashtra, is being worshipped as a god. He was born on September 28, 1838 and died on October 15, 1918. Every year over a million devotees go to Shirdi only to have darsan (sight) of his image and leave crores (billions) of rupees every year in front of his moorty as bheta (gift). Unbelievable self-made stories are being associated with him by his devotees, only to prove that he has such godly

---

[20] The Hindu Wisdom – Vimanas

powers. Hindu polytheism is the result of such misunderstanding of the difference between *devas* (gods) and God.

Concept of time: Age of the humanity

It is fascinating to see comparative concept of time between the West and the East (Hindu). Shri Aurobindo Ghosh[21] (1872-1950), a great philosopher of modern India, has said:

> "European scholarship regards human civilization as a recent progression starting yesterday with the Fiji islander, and ending today with Rockefeller, conceiving ancient culture as necessarily half savage culture. It is a superstition of modern thought that the march of knowledge has always been linear. Our vision of 'prehistory' is terribly inadequate. We have not yet rid our minds from the hold of a one-and-only God or one-and-only Book, and now a one-and-only Science."

According to 'Hinduism Today'[22]:

> "Hinduism's understanding of time is as grandiose as time itself. While most cultures base their cosmologies on familiar units such as few hundreds or thousands of years, the Hindu concept of time embraces billions and trillions of years. The *Puranas* describe time units from the infinitesimal truti, lasting 1/1,000,0000 of a second to a *mahamantavara* of 311 trillion years, Hindu sages describe time as cyclic, an endless procession of creation, preservation and dissolution. Scientists such as Carl Sagan have expressed amazement at the accuracy of space and time descriptions given by the ancient *rishis* and saints, mystically awakened senses."

---

[21] Ibid.
[22] Hinduism Today (April/May/June 2007, p. 14)

It is hard to believe all this. There are lot of commonalities and similarities in Greek and Hindu mythologies, so much that I tend to believe that there is truth in what Pococke has written in his book *'India in Greece; or Truth in Mythology'*. If we objectively examine the mythologies of the world societies, we would find in them lot of history. We can not have solid evidences of the truths in mythologies of the remote past. I get the answer in what two scholars have said – Dr. Carl Sagon: "Absence of evidence is not evidence of absence." And Aldous Huxley: "Facts do not cease to exist because they are ignored."

Lynn Thorndike (1882-1965) – American historian, author of several books including *'A History of Magic and Experimental Science'* (8 Vol.) – remarked: "Thus we see that India's marvels were not always false."

John Burrows, in 'Ancient Vimana Aircraft, remarks:

"Sanskrit texts are filled with references to gods who fought battles in the sky using Vimanas equipped with weapons."

A few of the different modes of transportation as used in pre-history ancient Bharat:

- Jalayan – a vehicle designed to operate in air as well as on water (Rig Veda 6.58. 3).
- Tritala – a vehicle consisting of three stories (RV 3.14.1).
- Trichakra Ratha – three wheeled vehicle designed to operate in air (RV 4.36.1).
- Vaayu Ratha a gas or wind-powered chariot (RV 5.41.1).
- Vidyut Ratha, a vehicle that operates on power (RV 3.14.1).

FIVE

Swastika: Being Stolen by Europeans

"One of the great enduring symbols of the whole of the Ancient World, the Swastika had wide currency as a sign of good luck and of solar beneficence. The motif occurs throughout the lands occupied by the Celts, sometimes on stonework in the company of images of the spoked wheel, another powerful sun symbol."

Sacred Symbols: The Celts[23]

It is difficult to understand why the origin of the Swastika is misrepresented. The above is right about its world-wide spread. But, it is not mentioned that India is its cradle. It is true that it is found in several European countries and among Celts and some American Indian tribes in Americas. It doesn't mean that it was born in Europe or in Americas. Swastika is a sacred symbol of the Vedic religion (Hinduism). Swastika is a Sanskrit word, meaning good luck. Swastika, in ancient times and even in present time, has been used by only Hindus in their almost all religious ceremonies. No European people have used or have been using Swastika in their religious ceremonies and no church like Hindu temples bears the sacred symbol of Swastika.

It is hard to understand why various scholars, historians and encyclopedias are biased against India and Hindus. This is evident

---

[23] The small booklet, "Sacred Symbols: The Celts" (New York: Thames and Hudson, 1995).

53

from most of the books, how European scholars – historians, linguists, anthropologists, archeologists, etc. – have misrepresented the origin of India's pride possessions, such as Swastika, Aryans, Sanskrit, Vedas, and pantheon of Hindu gods. They write that Aryans, along with a pantheon of Hindu gods and Sanskrit came to India from outside in about 1500 B.C. and later they composed the Vedas. But no historian has been able to identify the country outside India which had or has Aryans as its natives and Sanskrit as its native language. The word "Arya' is a Sanskrit word, meaning "noble".

Even a school student in India knows that India is the cradle of all the five – Swastika, Aryans, Sanskrit, Vedas and a pantheon of Hindu gods. Several historians have been allegedly writing that the alleged invading Aryans brought along with them Sanskrit, Caucasian genes and a pantheon of Hindu gods. They also write that that the Swastika has been found everywhere, but not in India. History tells that Indians also are Caucasian. No historian has been, nor will be able to identify the society, other than Hindu, which uses the Swastika in its religious ceremonies.

As a matter of fact, none, but Hindus are Aryans. The World Book Encyclopedia (1984, vol.18, p. 814a) also does not say the *Swastika* is originally associated with India and her Hindus and Hinduism:

> "Swastika is an ancient symbol often used as an ornament or a religious sign. ... The Swastika has been found on Byzantine buildings, Buddhist inscriptions, Celtic monuments, and Greek coins. Swastikas were widely used symbols among the Indians of North America and South America."

It is true that the Swastika has been found on Byzantine buildings, Buddhist inscriptions, Celtic monuments, and Greek coins. But historians don't tell how and when the Swastika travelled there from its abode India. They don't tell which society other than Hindu or Buddhist has Swastika as its religious symbol.

Swastika: Being Stolen by Europeans

Swastika is a Sanskrit word. V. S. Apte in *"The Practical Sanskrit-English Dictionary"* (1992, p.1019), has defined *Swastika:*

"A lucky object. Hindus draw the symbol of the *Swastika* in color or with raw rice on the floor alter. Hindus perform all religious rituals while sitting on the floor before starting a religious ceremony, because *Swastika* is considered a sign of a good luck."

Swastika in the Sindhu (Indus) Valley

Origin of Swastika has been historically misperceived. It has been a universal jewel, being claimed by almost all. Though historians know that it is a Sanskrit word, meaning good luck or well-being, yet they would resist saying that it originated in India, the land of the Vedas, composed in Sanskrit. Gunnar Thompson, in his book 'Nu Sun' (p.155) has given images of the Swastika as seen in Borobudur, Indus valley (Harappa), Indonesia, Copan, Honduras, and also among Buddhists, Mayans and North American Native Indians. But, he has not mentioned "among Hindus" who have been using it in their almost every religious ceremony since Hinduism was born in prehistory times – too ancient and too remote for historians. But, it is hard to understand why historians have been resisting the truth about the origin and antiquity of the Swastika and Sanskrit.

Thompson (p. 155) writes: "The Swastika is a common Old-World magic symbol attributed to Mesopotamian origins. It was present in the Yangshao culture of Neolithic China, ca. 3000 B.C." How could it originate in Mesopotamia and China? How could its age be only 5000 years when it was found among North American Natives in about ten thousand years back?

It might have been seen in Mesopotamia and China in about 3000 B.C. It does not mean it originated there. Historians know or should know that the Swastika has been found in the Indus Valley civilization. Seals of *Swastika* have been, excavated at both Indus Valley cities, Mohenjo-daro as well as Harappa. It testifies that Swastika would have been in India long before 3000 B.C.

A Seal excavated from Mohenjo-Daro.[24]

James Trager, in 'The People's Chronology' (1994, p.3), dates the Indus Valley civilization as 4000 B.C. But it is much older. It may be 7,000 B.C., as suggested by the excavations at Mehrgarh, Baluchistan, which is considered as an antecedent of the Indus Valley civilization.

Trager (p.3) tells how the people of the Indus Valley were civilized even in 4000 B.C. He writes: that the people of the Indus Valley knew irrigation system. They raised wheat, barley, peas, sesame seeds, mangoes, banana, lemon, lime, grapes for wine, and dates. Wine was also made from flowers. He further writes that

[24] Jonathan Mark Kenoyer, *Ancient Cities of The Indus Valley Civilization* (1998, pp. 85 and 108)

asses, horses, buffalos, camels, and cattle were bred. He says all this is based on the evidence, based on the excavations from Mohenjo-daro in 1922 A.D. According to Vedic (Hindu) traditions, the Vedas were composed long before 6,000 B.C.

Swastika in Americas

Appearance of the Swastika among the Native Indians in Americas has enhanced the age of Sanskrit to more than ten thousand years.

Such world-wide spread of the *Swastika* suggests that Indo-Aryans (Hindus and Buddhists) must have gone in pre-history ancient times to all the regions, as mentioned above. The Swastika found in Americas evidences that some of the Asians − who migrated to Americas via Bering Strait long back in about 8000 B.C. or even earlier − were Vedic Indo-Aryans from India. They must have used Swastika in their religious ceremonies, as Hindus have been doing in present times.

Was Swastika Nazi German?

Its use by Nazi Germans has confused the world about its origin and antiquity. There were attacks on Hindu Temple in Queens, New York, because its external wall bore the image of the Swastika. The *Swastika* was borrowed by Hitler, as explained by William L. Shirer (1959, p. 43) in his book *'The Rise and Fall of the Third Reich: A History of Nazi Germany'*. He writes that the Swastika (hakenkreus) is as old, almost, as the man on the planet.

The *Swastika* is very old, older than 10,000 years. It, in turn, reflects the age of Sanskrit, the language of the Vedas.

Europeans envy Aryans Heritage

Europeans seem to be so jealous of Hindus that they steal even their Aryan identity for themselves. They say they, not Hindus, are Aryans. Count Joseph Arthur de Gobineau, a French diplomat and a man of letters, has said:

"The jewel of the White race was the Aryan, this illustrious human family, the noblest among the White race, whose origin he traced back to Central Asia."

The Encyclopedia Americana (2003, vol. 2, p. 426) writes the same:

"Gobineau held the White race to be superior to all others and the Aryan race to be superior among whites. This theory aroused interest in Germany and was espoused by the composer Richard Wagner among others. In the 20th century it was taken up by the German dictator Adolf Hitler, who equated Aryans with Nordic race and used the theory to justify his persecution of Jews. Modern anthropologists reject the theory that there are "pure" or inherently superior human groups."

It has been shown above that Western historians, particularly European, have envied Hindus and tried to steal their treasure possessions, such as **Aryan race, Vedas, Sanskrit** and **Swastika**. They created two ill-based theories – 'Aryan invasion of India' and 'Indo-European family of languages' – according to which Aryans invaded Aryavarta (India) from outside, brought with them Sanskrit, Caucasian genes and a pantheon of Hindu gods. They write that they composed the Vedas centuries after their arrival in about 1500 B.C. They also write that Swastika is found all over, but not in India. How would historians get away free after murder of their only child 'HISTORY'? Why would **Aryans** invade their mother **Aryavarta** (later known as Bharat, India)?

History has been dominated by Europeans. During their global colonization they distorted ancient histories of Asia and Africa to suit their colonial agenda. The first print, particularly backed by the colonial might, has been too dark to erase.

Nehru (1946, p. 200) has remarked:

"The history that men and women from India made far from their homeland has still to be written. Most westerners still imagine that ancient history is largely concerned with the Mediterranean countries, and medieval and modern history is dominated by the quarrelsome little Europe. And still they make plans for the future as if Europe only counted and the rest could be fitted in anywhere."

Nehru (same page 200) cites Sir Charles Eliot[25] who has praised Hindus for their intellectual and political conquests, colonization of several territories, etc.:

'Scant justice is done to India's position in the world by those European histories which recount the exploits of her invaders and leave the impression that her own people were a feeble dreamy folk, sundered from the rest of mankind by their seas and mountain frontiers. Such a picture takes no account of the intellectual conquests of the Hindus. Even their political conquests were not contemptible, and are remarkable for the distance, if not the extent, of the territories occupied. ... But such military or commercial are insignificant compared with the spread of Indian thought."

[25] Elliot: 'Hinduism and Buddhism', vol. 1, p. xii.

SIX

Scholars on India, her Vedas and Sanskrit

"Although there is hardly any department of learning which has not received new light and new life from the ancient literature of India, yet nowhere is the light that comes to us from India so important, so novel, and so rich as in the study of (the Vedic) religion and mythology."

Max Müller,[26]

Sir Charles Eliot (1862-1931) appreciates India's gift of civilization:

"India has always given a great deal more than she has received. Civilization as we know today would not exist without India."

Francois Voltaire (1694-1778), French philosopher, known for his intelligence, wit and style, has said about the Vedic philosophy:

"Vedic metaphysics is the perennial philosophy that is at the core of all religions - a precious gift for which the West is ever indebted to the East."

---

[26] Max Müller *"India: What Can It Teach Us?"* (1999, p.161).

61

Mark Twain (1835-1910), writer, humorist, narrator, social observer, and unsurpassed in American literature, has said:

"India is the cradle of the human race, the birthplace of human speech, the mother of history, the grandmother of legend and great grandmother of tradition."

Max Müller[27] has said:

"Vedas are the oldest text of the human race. And Agni Meele Purohitam is the first verse of Rig Veda. In the most primordial time when the people of Europe were jumping like Chimpanzees, from tree to tree and branch to branch, when they did not know how to cover their bodies, but with fig leaves, did not know agriculture and lived by hunting and lived in caves, at that remote past, Indians had attained high civilization and they gave to the world universal philosophies in the form of the Vedas."

Philip Rawson, in 'The Art of Southeast Asia' (1993: 7), praises India's gift of civilization:

"The culture of India has been one of the world's most powerful civilizing forces. Countries of the Far East, including China, Korea, Japan, Tibet and Mongolia owe much of what is best in their own cultures to the inspiration of ideas imported from India. The West, too, has its own debts. ... No conquest or invasion, no forced conversion imposed."

Romain Rolland[28] (1866-1944) – French novelist, biographer, playwright and musicologist – wrote biographies of some great personalities including Mahatma Gandhi (1924). He designates India as the 'dream home' of living men:

---

[27] Prem Sabhlok, "Know thy Vedas', e-mail 3/1/2011.
[28] Jawaharlal Nehru, Discovery of India, p.89.
[28] Purnima Voria, The Economic Times, Sept. 26, 2010

"If there is one place on the face of earth where all dreams of living men have found a home from the very earliest days when man began the dream of existence, it is India."

Rolland[29], in his book on Vivekananda, writing *'On the Hellenic-Christian Mysticism of the First Centuries and its Relationship to Hindu Mysticism'*, points out:

"A hundred facts testify to how great an extent the East was mingled with Hellenic thought during the second century of our era."

Henry David Thoreau (1817-1862) displayed fascination with Indian spirituality, as reflected in the Bhagvad Gita:

"In the morning I bathe my intellect in the stupendous and cosmogonal philosophy of the Bhagavad Gita, since whose composition years of the gods have elapsed and in comparison with which our modern world and its literature seems puny and trivial."

Following is an amazing – 'Give &Take' example between America and India. Gandhi gave to Martin Luther King, Jr. what he received from Thoreau:

Thoreau → Gandhi → King:
Civil Disobedience and Nonviolence

Thoreau, a renowned indologist, was influenced by Hindu philosophy. Mahatma Gandhi received inspiration from the Thoreau's essay on *'Duty of Civil Disobedience'* (Walden, 1999, pp.265-296, originally published in 1854). He used Thoreau's weapon of *'civil disobedience'* in his bloodless nonviolent war to overpower the mighty British Empire and helped Bharat attain her independence in 1947. In turn, Dr. Martin Luther King, Jr. (1929-1968) extracted lessons of non-violence and civil disobedience

---

[29] Nehru, 'Discovery of India', p.92, footnote.

from Mahatma Gandhi, and used this knowledge to awaken his Black brethren to nonviolently fight for their political and civic rights. Un-imaginable splendid returns! America has a black president Barack Obama. Gandhi was always conscious of his debt to Thoreau, the Sage of the Walden Pond, as Martin Luther King, Jr. felt about Gandhi, the *Sant* (saint) of the *Sabarmati.* King and his wife, Loretta were invited by Prime Minister Jawaharlal Nehru to visit India. When Dr. King arrived at the Palam Airport in New Delhi, his first words in his tribute to India and Mahatma Gandhi were:

"To other countries I may go as a tourist, but to India I come as a pilgrim. This is because India means to me Mahatma Gandhi, a truly great man of the age."

Mahatma Gandhi told Indians, living in Transvaal, South Africa, about Thoreau and his tenet of civil disobedience:

"There is a deep-rooted superstition that a law cannot be disobeyed. It would be no small step forward for the community if this superstition was rooted out. When we shall have resisted the law to the last, we shall be regarded as so many Thoreaus in miniature."

Gandhi's letter in *Indian Opinion* (Oct.5, 1907)

Thoreau was imprisoned for refusing to pay his poll tax, an episode which led to writing of *On the Duty of Civil Disobedience* (Walden, p. I). Thoreau wrote in Walden, (p. 265): "I HEARTILY accept the motto: *That government is best which governs least.*" Mahatma Gandhi might have gotten the idea of *'Salt Satyagrah'* from Thoreau's defiance to pay taxes. Gandhi was fighting against the apartheid laws of South Africa. Gandhi has further written about Thoreau as a passive resister:

"David Thoreau was a great writer, philosopher, poet and with all a most practical man, that is, he taught nothing he was not prepared to practice himself. He was one of the greatest and most moral men America has produced. At the time of abolition of slavery movement, he wrote his famous essay *'On the Duty of Civil Disobedience'*. He went to gaol (jail) for the sake of his principles and suffering humanity. His essay has, therefore, been sanctified by suffering. Moreover, it is written for all time. Its incisive logic is unanswerable."

Gandhi's letter (Indian Opinion, Oct.26, 1907)

Thoreau → *Gandhi* → *Anna Hazare*
Gandhiji died, but his legacy is immortal

Gandhiji is no longer with us, but his spirit will continue to inspire and guide not only Indians, but also the whole world to fight-peacefully and nonviolently- against the government for a good cause until the humanity is alive. Gandhiji-in Anna Hazare is doing what Gandhiji would have done if he were alive. Anna will die, but Gandhi-in-him will continue to be born again and again in different Annas. India believes in reincarnation. Lord Krishna had said that whenever there would be sin, I will be born.

यदा यदा हि धर्मस्य ग्लानिर्भवति भारत। अभ्युत्थानमधर्मस्य तदात्मानं सृजाम्यहम् ॥

परित्राणाय साधूनां विनाशाय च दुष्कृताम् । धर्मसंस्थापनार्थाय सम्भवामि युगे युगे ॥

"Whenever there is decay of righteousness O! Bharatha

And a rise of unrighteousness then I manifest Myself!"

"For the protection of the good, for the destruction of the wicked
and
for the establishment of righteousness, I am born in every age."

Aurobindo Ghose[30] (1872-1950) could see positive in negative "If hatred is demoralizing, it is also stimulating," writes Ghose in one of his early essays titled *'On Nationalism'* after returning to India from England in 1893. This pithy, striking statement possibly sums

---

[30] Google, Aurobindo Ghose.

up the moral basis of violence as a stimulus among the *swadeshi* revolutionaries. In order to get rid of the torpor and inertia that one associates with the *guna* of *tamas*, political hatred must be brought into the fore as a necessary form of vitalist *rajas*. It is a deeply awe-inspiring trope in the revolutionary armory that justifies an actual, physical, political action. Aurobindo Ghose was not exempt from joyously celebrating such a moment.

On the other hand, the same man also clearly eschews such vitalistic tendencies while giving shape to his political thought.

Aurobindo[31] himself writes about his introspective moments in the prison: readings of the *Gita* and *Upanishads*, practicing yoga, hearing and feeling Vivekananda and seeing Krishna in his meditation and even levitating. It could be that going through intense physical pain and discomfort, for the middle-class revolutionary, prison also becomes a site for controlling and denying his physical, animal desires, leading to a glorification of austere practices and speculative introspection. Besides, there is also an urge to read the nation symbolically as a vast prison-house.

Will Durant, in *Our Oriental Heritage* (1935, p. 392), writes what one European scholar believes: "Indian wisdom is the profoundest that exists"; and a great novelist writes: "I have not found, in Europe or America, poets, thinkers or popular leaders equal, even comparable, to those of India today."[32]

Durant (p.392) writes: "In 1805 Colebrooke's essay *'On the Vedas'* revealed to Europe the oldest product of Indian literature; and about the same time Anquetil-Duperron's translation of a Persian translation of the *Upanishads* acquainted Schelling and Schopenhauer with what the latter called the profoundest philosophy that he had ever read."[33]

Arthur Schopenhauer (1788-1860), a German Philosopher, has said about the Upanishads:

---

[31] Ibid.

[32] Keyserling, Count H., Travel Diary of a Philosopher, 265.

[33] Winternitz, M., *A History of Indian Literature*, (pp. 18-21).

"In the whole world there is no study so beneficial and so elevating as that of Upanishads. It has been the solace of my life, it will be the solace of my death."

Nehru (pp. 92-3) says that Schopenhauer, the pessimist, is often quoted in this connection:

"From every sentence (of the Upanishads) deep, original and sublime thoughts arise, and the whole is pervaded by a high and holy and earnest spirit. ... In the whole world there is no study ... so beneficial and so elevating as that of the Upanishads. ... (They) are products of the highest wisdom. It is destined sooner or later to become the faith of the people."

All this was said long back by Western philosophers about spirituality and civilization India gave to the world, particularly to the West. Let us see what present politicians say about India and her global role.

Ahead of President Barack Obama's historic state visit to India in November, 2010, a top US diplomat has said India's rise would be consequential for the international order and deeply in the interests of America. Under Secretary of State for Political Affairs Bill Burns said:

"India's rise may be as consequential for international order, the future of the global economy and the promotion of human values as any other development in the new century unfolding before us. Without any doubt, India's rise is deeply in the interests of the United States, and our stake in India's success grows more apparent as each day passes."

This can be said about India, only because during all her life, she says what she means, even if her interests are at stake. Her vote at the UN is guided by her conscience. She supported China for her seat at the UN Security Council. I doubt very much if China will reciprocate when India is considered for the UN Security seat.

India's behavior confirms her spotless diplomatic integrity. The international community trusts her word without any doubt. It is pleasing that her diplomatic conscience has always been in tune with the dictates of the Vedas: "God is within. Do what your conscience (God) dictates."

Burns made the remarks at the awards dinner in New York where Prime Minister Dr. Manmohan Singh was presented '*The 2010 World Statesman Award*' in absentia by the 'Appeals of Conscience Foundation', a US-based interfaith coalition. Note! The award was given by 'CONSCIENCE' Foundation.

Former President George W. Bush once remarked:

> "India has a fantastic ability to grow, because her greatest export is intelligence and brainpower. ... We are grateful that the world's most skilled workers want to come to the United States. Our technology edge rests on the contributions of immigrants from places like India or China, Russia, Iran and hundreds of other countries."

Bush is referring to the contemporary brain-drain wave of Indians, driven by India's power of technology, education, intelligence, entrepreneurship and enterprise, not by its poverty as was the case of its medieval and indentured migrants. At the eve of and early 20th century, most of the immigrants from India were professionals, students, traders, and farmers.

Talking about the triumph of the East and the Hellenistic Age, Herbert J. Muller (1958, p.15) has elaborated on how Greeks profited immeasurably from their spiritual trade with the East, particularly with India:

> "At the same time, Plato's own thought was so fertile because it was not a classically ordered system but an exploration of various possibilities, a sensitive response to various influences, including Oriental thought. Its historic influence has stemmed chiefly from his inclination to a transcendental idealism, another worldly kind of

Scholars on India, her Vedas and Sanskrit

spirituality that is more typical of India than of Greece in its heyday."

V. Gordon Childe (1926, 210-212) talks about the Aryan contribution of culture, spirituality and great language Sanskrit to their colonized people:

"The lasting gift bequeathed by the Aryans to the conquered people was neither a higher material culture nor a superior physique, but a more excellent language and the mentality it generated."

Annie Besant[34] has talked about the jewels in the Mahabharata:

"Among the priceless teachings that may be found in the great Indian epic Mahabharata, there is none so rare and priceless as the Gita. ... This is the India of which I speak – the India which, as I said, is to me the Holy Land. For those who, though born for this life in a Western land, and clad in a Western body, can yet look back to earlier incarnations in which they drank the milk of spiritual wisdom from the breast of their true mother – they must feel ever the magic of her immemorial past. Must dwell ever under the spell of her deathless fascination; for they are bound to India by all the sacred memories of their past and with her, too, are bound up all the radiant hopes of their future, a future which they know they will share with her who is their true mother in the soul-life."

Victor Cousin[35] talks about the poetical and philosophical monuments of India:

"When we read with attention the poetical and philosophical monuments of the East – above all, those of India, which are beginning to spread in Europe – we

[34] India: Essays and Lectures (vol. iv) by Annie Besant, London, The Theosophical Publishing Co.,(1895, p.11).
[35] Sir John Woodroffe, "Is India Civilized: Essays on Indian Culture' (p.132).

69

discover there may be a truth, and truths so profound, which make such a contrast with the meanness of the results at which European has sometimes stopped, that we are constrained to bend the knee before the philosophy of the East, and to see in this cradle of the human race the native land of the philosophy."

Aldous Huxley[36] (1894-1963) has said about the Bhagvad Gita:

"The Bhagvad Gita is the most systematic statement of spiritual evolution of endowing value of mankind. The Gita is one of the clearest and most comprehensive summaries of the spiritual thoughts ever to have been made."

Lynn Thorndike (1882-1965) – American historian, author of several books including *'A History of Magic and Experimental Science'* (8 Vol.) – remarked: "Thus we see that India's marvels were not always false."

John Burrows; in 'Ancient Vimana Aircraft, remarks:

"Sanskrit texts are filled with references to gods who fought battles in the sky using Vimanas equipped with weapons."

---

[36] T. C. Galav: 'Philosophy of Hinduism – An Introduction' (p.65).

SEVEN

India's Spiritual & Scientific Gifts to the World

"From every sentence (of the Upanishads) deep, original and sublime thoughts arise, and the whole is pervaded by a high and holy and earnest spirit. ... In the whole world there is no study ... so beneficial and so elevating as that of the Upanishads. ... (They) are products of the highest wisdom. ... It is destined sooner or later to become the faith of the people. ... The study of the Upanishads has been the solace of my life, it will be the solace of my death."

Schopenhauer[37]

Max Müller[38] has talked about Schopenhauer who, according to him, was the last man to write at random, or to allow himself to go into ecstasies over so-called mystic and inarticulate thought:

"I am neither afraid nor ashamed to say that I share his enthusiasm for the Vedanta, and feel indebted to it for much that has been helpful to me in my passage through life. ... The Upanishads are the sources of the Vedanta philosophy, a system in which human speculation seems to me to have reached its very acme. ... I spend my happiest hours in reading Vedantic books. They are to me

---

[37] Nehru, Discovery of India (p.92).
[38] Ibid, p.93.

like the light of the morning, like the pure air of the mountains – so simple, so true, if once understood."

Nehru remarks that the discovery of Indian philosophy by Europeans "has created a powerful impression on European philosophers and thinkers."

Nehru (1946, pp. 92-93) has further discussed the spread of Indian philosophy beyond the borders of India in very early times. Early Indian thought penetrated Greece, through Iran. Plotinus traveled to the East to study Indian and Iranian philosophies, which influenced Christianity of the day. It spread throughout Europe.

Romain Rolland[39] (1866-1944) has given a note on *'The Hellenic-Christian Mysticism of the First Centuries and its relationship to Hindu mysticism'* that "a hundred facts testify to how great an extent the East was mingled with Hellenic thought during the second century of the era."

Spirituality: Gift from India to the West

India's philosophy and spirituality are too abstract to understand and least financially attractive for common Westerners, who, unlike Easterners, are more materialistic and less spiritualistic. Spirituality has attracted the upper echelon of American and European philosophers of the 19th and 20th centuries – Amos Bronson Alcott (1799-1888), Ralph Waldo Emerson (1803-1882), Edward Eldbridge Salisbury (1814-1901), Henry David Thoreau (1817-1862), Herman Melville (1819-1891), Walt Whitman (1819-1892), Sir Charles Eliot (1862-1931), Romain Rolland (1866-1944), Albert Einstein (1879-1955) – among many others. It has influenced several European philosophers – Plato (427-347 B.C.), Sir William Jones (1764-1794), and Friedrich Max Müller (1823-1900).

Albert Einstein[40] (1879-1955) wrote in his letter to Nehru on Feb.18, 1950, expressing his inability to understand the spirituality and intellectuality of India:

---

[39] Ibid, (p.92) footnote.
[40] Ibid, back cover.

Dear Mr. Nehru:

I have read with extreme interest your marvelous book The Discovery of India. The first half of it is not easy reading for a Westerner. But it gives an understanding of the glorious intellectual and spiritual tradition of your great country. The analysis you have given in the second part of the book of tragic influence and forced economic, moral and intellectual decline by the British rule and the vicious exploitation of the Indian people has deeply impressed me.

My admiration for Gandhi's and your work for liberation through non-violence and non-cooperation have become even greater than it was already before. The inner struggle to conserve objective understanding despite the pressure of tyranny from the outside and the struggle against becoming inwardly a victim of resentment and hatred may well be unique in world history. I feel deeply grateful to you for having given to me your admirable work.

With my best wishes for your important and beneficent work and with kind greetings,

Yours cordially,
Albert Einstein

Albert Einstein was born in Ulm, Germany. Later he became a Swiss citizen. He received the 1921 Nobel prize in Physics. He became an American citizen in 1940.

Oriental Spirituality in the Hellenistic Greece

Max Müller, in his book *'The Science of Language'* (1891:95), has observed that it was difficult to admit that so much influence was exercised by Hindus on Greek philosophers:

"But when Alexander went to converse with Brahmans, who were even then considered by the Greeks as the guardians of a most ancient and mysterious wisdom, their answers had to be translated by so many interpreters that one of the Brahmins themselves remarked, they must

73

become like water that had passed through many impure channels."

Talking about the triumph of the East and the Hellenistic Age, Herbert J. Muller (1958, p.15) has elaborated on how Greeks profited immeasurably from spiritual trade with the East, more typical of India:

> "At the same time, Plato's own thought was so fertile because it was not a classically ordered system but an exploration of various possibilities, a sensitive response to various influences, including Oriental thought. Its historic influence has stemmed chiefly from his inclination to a transcendental idealism, another worldly kind of spirituality that is more typical of India than of Greece in its heyday."

Plato,[41] like Hindus and Buddhists, believed in the immortality of the soul and reincarnation:

> 'Plato believed that though the body dies and disintegrates, the soul continues to live forever. After the death of the body, the soul migrates to what Plato called the realm of the pure form. After a time, the soul is reincarnated in another body and returns to the world. But the reincarnated soul retains the dim recollection of the realm of forms and yearns for it. Plato argued that people fall in love because they recognize in the beauty of their beloved the ideal form of beauty they dimly remember and seek."

A popular love song from an Indian movie echoes the Hindu belief in reincarnation, *"Aisa lagta hai ki ham agle janam men kahin mile honge."* (It seems we must have met somewhere in our previous life).

---

[41] World Book Encyclopedia (1993, vol.15, p.504)

Both doctrines, immortality of the soul and reincarnation, are the ancient basic doctrines of Hinduism and of its offshoots – Jainism, Buddhism and Sikhism. Buddhism was founded by a Hindu prince Siddhartha Gautam (563 to 483 B.C.). He was known as Buddha (enlightened) at the age of 35 when he attained supreme enlightenment.

Plato and the Upanishads

M.P. Pandit, in his book, *'Traditions in Mysticism'* (1987, p.121), has highlighted a study by Dr. Vassilis Vittaxis, a former Greek ambassador to India. Dr. Vittakis brings to light the similarities and differences between Hindu philosophy and the philosophy of Plato. For example, he likens the *nous* (mind) of Plato to the *Atman* of the Upanishads. He further draws parallels between Plato's *Division of Society* and the caste system, "Plato's Guardians, Warriors, Craftsmen have a close resemblance to the Indian Brahman, Kshatriya, Vaishya."

According to the Columbia Encyclopedia (p.2171), Plotinus (205-270), a Neoplatonist philosopher, traveled in the Eastern expedition of Gordian III, the Roman emperor in c.242 to study the philosophies of India and Persia:

"The theories of Plotinus were fundamentally those of Plato, but included elements of other Greek philosophies as well, all drawn together into an original system that rapidly won followers and had considerable influence on the thinkers of the Christian church, although Plotinus himself opposed Christianity."

There is persuasive evidence that his cosmological conception, which is the chief tenet of Neo-Platonism, was influenced by the *Vedanta* philosophy.

The influence of Vedic thought on Plato and Plotinus is one example of India's philosophical contribution to America via Europe. Unlike America's material and technological contribution to India, India's contribution to America has been intangible, abstract and philosophical. History has been hostile, unkind and indifferent to Eastern civilizations, making it difficult for present generation to know and appreciate their contribution to the mankind.

The present trend seems to be focused on the soul's solace instead of bodily pleasures. The increased awareness – that their psychological pain is caused by family disintegration and their over-indulgence in bodily pleasures and material pursuits – has led many Westerners to look toward the East for answers. Meditation, Yoga, and vegetarianism are gaining popularity amongst Americans and Europeans. Indians, like Deepak Chopra, are gaining attention of the West. It is also true that increasing number of Hindus is being attracted by non-vegetarian food.

During one of his lectures at the University of Cambridge in 1882, Friedrich Max Müller (*India: What Can It Teach Us?* (1999, p. 24) observed:

"If we were to look over the whole world to find out the country most richly endowed with all the wealth, power, and beauty that nature can bestow – in some parts a very paradise on earth – I should point to India."

"If I were asked under what sky the human mind has most full developed some of its choicest gifts, has most deeply pondered on the greatest problems of life, and has found solutions of some of them which well deserve the attention even of those who have studied Plato and Kant, I should point to India."

"And if I were to ask myself from what literature we, here in Europe, have been nurtured almost exclusively on the thoughts of Greeks and Romans, and of one Semitic race, the Jewish, may draw that corrective which is most wanted in order to make our inner life more perfect, more comprehensive, more universal, in fact more truly human, a life, not for this life only, but a transfigured and eternal life – again I should point to India."

The 'Bhajan Belt': Serenity In The Catskills

"Everything you need to know about the spiritual rhythms of the Catskill Mountains (in north New York state) is spray-painted on a rock face along Route 28. It's the sign for 'OM' – the mystic syllable of Hinduism – and it's a subtle suggestion of the energy that vibrates throughout the region. Some call it the bhajan (devotional song) belt, applying a word derived from Sanskrit for devotional song to an area that stretches from the holistic enterprises of New Paltz to a yoga ranch in Woodbourne."

Mark Healy[42]

Healy further writes that the solitude and energy of the area have not escaped the many East-leaning academics, musicians and authors who call the Bhajan (Bud-gen) belt home. Robert A.F. Thurman, a Buddhist author and scholar, has had a home in Woodstock for close to 30 years. Sharon Gannon and David Life, the influential founders of the 'Jivamukti Yoga Center' in Manhattan, New York City, purchased a place in Woodstock a few years ago. There's even a wizened local who has been known to press slips of paper inscribed with a Sanskrit mantra (*"OM mani padme hum"*) into the hands of town's people.

Quoting Healey is not to suggest that one can attain serenity and peace of mind only through Hinduism. This suggests that serenity can be realized through spirituality, meditation, Yoga and singing devotional songs. The rhythm of *bhajans* in Hindi, Sanskrit or any Indian vernacular has a peculiar soothing effect.

Albert Einstein: India's contribution to science

Several great Western scholars have emphasized India's contribution to the world. Albert Einstein (1879-1955) – American theoretical physicist, known for the formulation of the general

---

[42] Mark Healy, in "The 'Bhajan Belt': Serenity in the Catskill" (NY Times, Oct.18, 2002, Escapes section).

theory of relativity – has praised India's contribution to science: "We owe a lot to the Indians, who taught us how to count, without which no worthwhile scientific discovery could have been made."

India has given to America several scientists, technologists, Nobel Laureates, doctors, nurses, engineers, academics, economists, managers, administrators, and entrepreneurs including some in key positions.

Max Müller (1999, p.22) talks about the European charm connected with India and fancy for the wisdom of Brahmans:

> "And, strange to say, this feeling exists in England more than in any other country. In France, Germany, and Italy, even in Denmark, Sweden, and Russia, there is a vague charm connected with the name of India. One of the most beautiful poems in the German is the *Wiesheit der Brahmanen*, the "wisdom of the Brahmans," by Rückert, to my mind more rich in thought and more perfect in form than even Goethe's *West-östliecher Divan.*"

Historian Will Durant (1885-1981) thought that the West should learn from India its tolerance and gentleness and love for all living things.

Eminent French philosopher Victor Cousin[43] (1792-1867) praises India as the cradle of the human race and highest philosophy:

> "When we read with attention the poetical and philosophical monuments of the East – above all those of India, which are beginning to spread in Europe – we discover there many a truth, and truths so profound, and which make such a contrast with the meanness of the results at which European genius has some times stopped, that we are constrained to bend the knee before the philosophy of the East and to see in this cradle of the human race the native land of the highest philosophy."[44]

Stephen Knapp (p.10) has cited Will Durant in praise of India and its race, Sanskrit and philosophy :

> "India was the motherland of our race, and Sanskrit the mother of Europe's languages: she was the mother of our philosophy.

---

[43] Ibid, p. 11.
[44] Sir John Woodroffe, 'Is India Civilized: Essays on Indian Culture'..

mother through the Arabs, of much of our mathematics; mother, through the Buddha, of the ideals embodied in Christianity, mother through the village community, of self-government and democracy. Mother India is in many ways the mother of us all."

Bhagvad Gita, the most valuable gift to the West

The English novelist and essayist Aldous Huxley (1894-1963) has said that the Bhagvad Gita is for the whole world. He has further said:

"The Bhagvad Gita is the most systematic statement of spiritual evolution of endowing value of mankind. The Gita is one of the clearest and most comprehensive summaries of the spiritual thoughts ever to have been made."[45]

Prof. Fatehullah Mojtabai, former Cultural Counselor of the Embassy of Iran in India, was a noted scholar of Sanskrit and a well-known exponent of Hindu philosophy. He has translated into Persian the Gita, the *Laghuyogavāsistha* and *Mahopanisad*. He was so much impressed by the philosophy of Hinduism, as contained in Gita, that he wanted his countrymen (Iranians) should also benefit from the Gita philosophy. May be his ancestors were Zoroastrians whose language Zend-Avestan was very similar to Sanskrit.

Henry David Thoreau (1817-1862) displayed fascination with Indian spirituality, as reflected in the Bhagvad Gita:

"In the morning I bathe my intellect in the stupendous and cosmogonal philosophy of the Bhagavad Gita, since whose composition years of the gods have elapsed and in comparison with which our modern world and its literature seems puny and trivial."

A German magazine: Gifts India has given to the world

Mathematics
- The number system. Aryabhata[46] invented the concept of *zero,*

---

[45] T. C. Galav: 'Philosophy of Hinduism – An Introduction' (p.65).
[46] Google-Aryabhata (476-550 A.D., approximate) mathematician, astronomer and scientist. About him, read Chapter. "Aryabhata: Mathematician, Astronomer and Scientist.

- The decimal system was developed in India in 100 BC.
- Budhayana first calculated the value of pi. He explained the concept of what is now known as the Pythagorean Theorem. In 1999, British scholars published Budhayan's work, which dates back to the 6th Century, long before the time of European mathematicians.
- Algebra, trigonometry and calculus. Sridharacharya formulated quadratic equations in the 11th century.
- According to Forbes Magazine, Sanskrit is a suitable language for computer software.

Education

- Taxila University, the ancient seat of learning, world's first university, established in 700 BC. More than 10,500 students from all over the world studied more than 60 subjects. It was in the Punjab region, northwest of India.
- Nalanda University, was built in Baragoan in 4th century BC.

Health

- Ayurveda, the most ancient school of medicine.
- Sushruta is the father of surgery. 2600 years ago, Sushruta and a team of health scientists conducted surgeries such as cesareans, cataract, fractures and urinary stones. Usage of anesthesia was well known in ancient India.

Navigation

- The art of navigation was born in the river Sindhu (Indus), over 5000 years ago. The very word "navigation" is derived from the Sanskrit word Navgatih.

Communication

- The pioneer of wireless communication was Prof. Jagdish Bose, not Marconi; Bose had announced his achievement later after Marconi.

Sports

- Chess

Will Durant[47] has talked about India's gifts to Europe:

---

[47] Taken from 'The Power of Dharma' by Stephen Knapp (2006, p. 11)

India's Spiritual and Scientific Gifts to the World

"It is true that even across the Himalayan barrier India has sent to us such questionable gifts as grammar and logic, philosophy and fables, hypnotism and chess, and above all our numerals and our decimal system."

Indo-US relationship – "half full of cold, half full of fire"

K. R. Narayanan, India's former ambassador to the U.S. (1980-84) and the President of India (1997-2002), described Indo-U.S. relationship (1984) as "half full of cold, half full of fire," words that the Spanish poet Lorca used to describe a woman in one of his lyrics. Only two mature and responsible countries can design their 'relationship-in-fire' according to their desire. Gold turns into a beautiful piece of jewelry only after it passes through fire. The Indo-US relationship, after passing through fire for several years, has become gold. Both – India and America – tolerated fire for so many years because they knew that both, America and India, need each other. Like two true lovers, who after long bitter fire from the families, eventually marry, Delhi and Washington have strong affectionate knot, after so many (not only seven) rounds around the eye-opening fire.

Most desirable democracy

I wish Washington and Delhi have an eternal tie for the peace and the prosperity on the planet. Delhi, like Washington, has conscience. Both, unlike some world powers, say what they mean. Both have a great, but difficult, joint responsibility for global harmony. Both are great democracies. I disagree with those who say that American is the oldest democracy. They will know the truth when they know *Rām Rājya* of the Rāmāyanā period. In India *Rām Rājya* means the most desirable democracy and Lord Rama-like, the most desirable ruler.

EIGHT

India: Unity in Complexity & Beauty in Diversity

"The foreign reader ... is at once struck by two features: in the first place its unity in complexity; and, in the second, its constant efforts to impress on its hearers the idea of a single centralized India, with a heroic tradition of her own as formative and uniting impulse."[48]

Sister Nivedita (Margaret Noble)

Tagore: Individuality in union with its largeness

Tagore, in the Chapter *'Hindu University'* of his book *'Towards Universal Man'* (p.142), has beautifully described the prominence of individuality. Bharat has her mind and individuality, and urge to be great. Without this feeling, man loses himself.

Tagore stresses that the strength of man's individuality lies in his close union with the largeness, he is a part of.

It looks (hope I am correct in interpreting) Tagore warns that extreme separateness would be injurious to man as well as to the nation:

"A suppressed separateness is a terrible explosive force; some time or other it would create a mighty upset by blowing up suddenly under pressure. ... The best way to union is to honour the separateness of what is really

---

[48] Nehru, Discovery of India (p.107), taken from Sir S. Radhakrishnan's book 'Indian Philosophy'.

separate. ... All development means the unfolding of diversity in unity."

Nehru, in *'Discovery of India'* (1946, p.107), cites Sister Nivedita's perception of Bharat's diversity. Sister Nivedita, although a foreigner, understood that the Bhārat's vivid phenomenon of 'unity-in-its-diversity' is too delicate, especially for a foreign eye, to understand the truth in it. On the surface, Bharat, like an ocean, is varied, uneven and emotional, as reflected by its lingual waves and tides which, in fact, protect its well-collected, calm and grave mind, so as to be able to get seriously engrossed in addressing her complex problems. Bharat, like a mature and well-balanced person, doesn't allow her equilibrium get disturbed, so as to be able to seriously meditate to address her domestic as well as international problems.

The secret has been clearly explained by her mature behavior during her problems-ridden turbulent sixty-three-year-post-independence life. Despite host of domestic problems, compounded by irritations from the two border adversaries, India has been wisely and soberly engaged in her all well-coordinated projects – economic, agricultural, industrial, educational, technological, scientific, trade, transportation, communication, space, internet, and defense.

Fortunately, Bhārat has open mind to learn from own history and other histories. Closed mind doesn't learn much. Bhārat has been growing richer and richer, stronger and stronger, because she always keeps her ears, eyes and mind open to outside world. She has always been open to incorporate desirable cultural and philosophical orientations and perspectives from others. As rightly said by Mahatma Gandhi,[49] India invites other cultures to come in, to enrich her culture:

"I don't want my house to be walled on all sides and the windows are blinded. I want all cultures of all countries to

---

[49] Jagat Motwani, & et al (ed). 'Global Indian Diaspora: Yesterday, Today and Tomorrow' (1993, p.6).

come into my house. But I refuse to be wiped away by any culture what-so-ever."

Mahatma Gandhi

India's Diversity: Beauty, not Disunity

India is rainbow beautiful. She is a garden of flowers of diverse colors and fragrances of varied ethnic philosophies and cultures. Bharat is traditionally blessed with varied music and dance, as reflected by dances by NATRAJ, and *murli* (flute) of Krishna. All Hindu scriptures – Vedas, Upanishads, Epics, Bhagvad Gita, Shakuntala, etc. – have been composed in poetry form. In cinema, love as well as sadness are expressed through musical songs. Hindu festivals *Divali, Holi, Navratri*, etc., are celebrated with music and dance. Edward Pococke, in his book *'India in Greece'*, has written that in ancient times India had colonized Greece. As the result even the Greek mathematics was in poetry form. Surprisingly, during their recent state visit, President Mr. Obama and his wife Michelle were entertained in Mumbai by small school children with music and dance. It may be a maiden or rare example to see a president of a country, and that also of America, and his wife dancing with the children of their hostess India.

Harvard University Professor Diana L. Eck, in her book *'Darsan: Seeing the Divine Image in India'* (pp. 24-25), seems to understand "unity in India's diversity'. It would be easy for the person who understands the relationship between the Unity (God) and His diversity, expressed through His varied providence. It would be hard for many, particularly Westerners, to see monotheism in apparent polytheism of Hinduism. Varied Hindu gods and goddesses are His varied images performing His varied functions, as assigned to them. Each god/goddess (with small 'g') suggests a desirable attribute humans should incorporate.

In my opinion, there is no polytheism any where. How can it happen when GOD is ONE. Polytheism is political, only to defame other's religion. Hindus, like others, worship only one God with capital 'G', through His various manifestations – gods and goddesses. In other religions they may be known as saints. Hindus don't worship stone gods and goddesses, but their attributes and teachings, worth incorporating.

A god or goddess, man worships, is a medium connecting the devotee with God. When a devotee, bows to pray in front of a stone god/goddess, his eyes automatically get closed so as to be able to peep deep within self to feel himself with God. Hindus believe that God is within self. It is right for a Hindu to say "I am God." In meditation, in front of a divine image of a god or goddess, eyes are kept closed to have or feel the *darsan* (sight) of God – within self. This is the reason why most Hindus don't feel necessary to go to their *Mandir* (temple) regularly, because they know God is omnipresent. Hindus pray individually, not in a congregation, because they believe in his/her individual relationship with God. Hindu 'gods' and 'goddesses', like Christian saints, are various images of God. Such gods or saints, unlike God, are born and are subject to death. Some of them are mythological, such as Brahma, Vishnu, Shiva, etc. Christ, like Rama and Krishna, was a god, not God. All the three – Christ, Rama and Krishna – were born and they died.

Each god and goddess has a desirable attribute for devotees to incorporate. For example, the Darsan (seeing) of the goddess Sarasvati encourages her devotees to seek knowledge (education) with the help of his/her guru (teacher). In Hinduism there is great emphasis on the respect of the teacher (guru). It creates discipline in the class room, conducive to learning. The first school, I attended, was on 'Guruvār' (Thursday). Guruvār means the day of Guru (vār means day). Because of Hindu value attached to Sarasvati (goddess of knowledge, education), Indians, particularly Hindus, because of their education, have been all over the globe.

It is refreshing to notice that all the three important portfolios – education (knowledge), finance, and defense are assigned to goddesses Sarasvati, Laxmi and Durga respectively. In Hinduism great gods – Rama and Krishna – were *Kshatri* (warriors), not Brahmin, because only warriors can disable or kill the evil. Both Ramāyanā and Mahābharatā narrate wars between the good and the evil. History tells that in ancient Bhārat the concept of *'DEV-RAJA'*, meaning 'God-Raja' was prevalent. Why do people suffer in present times? Because, most rulers – kings, presidents, prime ministers, ministers and other officials from top to bottom – are selfish, self-centered, greedy and corrupt. I see silver lining in awakened media activity to publicly catch them for the judiciary to punish them. People are not optimistic that the judiciary is completely independent. Democracy can be effective only when there is strict independence among the three chambers – executive, legislation and judiciary – in letter as well as execution, and there is honesty and integrity. It is sad that honesty has become a rare commodity.

Prof. Diana Eck: Unity in Indian Diversity

Talking about the Indian unity in diversity, the Harvard Prof. Diana L. Eck, in her book *'Darsan: Seeing the Divine Image in India'* (1981, p.24), remarks:

"The diversity of India has been so great that it has sometimes been difficult for Westerners to recognize in India any underlying unity. As the British civil servant John Strachey put it, speaking to an audience at Cambridge University in 1859, "There is no such country, and this is the first and most essential fact about India that can be learned. ....."[50] Seeking recognizable signs of unity – common language, unifying religion, shared historical tradition – he did not see them in India."

Eck (pp. 24, 25) explains why Strachey and others have been unable to visualize unity in India's diversity:

"In part, the unity of India, which Strachey and many others like him could not see, is in its cultural genius for embracing diversity, so that diversity unites, rather than divides. ... Moving from the philosophical to the social sphere, there is the well-known diversity of interlocking and interdependent caste groups."

---

[50] Francis G. Hutchins, The Illusion of Permanence (Princeton: Princeton University Press, 1967), p. 142.

Caste system was there. But its divisive attribute was not in ancient Hindu traditions. May be because they rightly understood Eck's notion of caste system as "the diversity of interlocking and interdependent caste groups." In my opinion, ancient humanity was broadminded and inclusive. They understood that all men are created by one and the same GOD. Hence, untouchability would be disbelief in GOD, hence His insult.

Social stratification is necessary for a community – Asian, African, European or American – for its optimal smooth functioning. No society would be able to function if it has only Brahmins, Kshatries or Vaishwas. Each society has to have some who do low class jobs. No work (*karma*) is mean and no body should be considered mean or untouchable because he/she does a low job. He is much better than the Brahmin who is useless and does not do any work, and so is dependent on his family or government for his livelihood. Work (*Karma*) is worship.

I believe that no person is purely a Brahmin, Kshtriya, Vaishya or Shudra. I realized this in America that I am all the four. In my job as a social work supervisor, I, like a Brahmin teach my supervisees the theory and art of helping others. At home, I am all the four – teaching children (Brahmin), protecting house and family (Kshatri), shopping and bargaining (Vaishya), and as a Shudra, I do laundry, press clothes and clean house and even toilet. Every Shudra does all these functions in his life including the job of a Brahmin, teaching his children.

The British government of India felt threatened by the national unity behind the 1857 Mutiny. It introduced 'jati' (caste) in the 1871 Census, termed it as a privileged class, and introduced some allotments for them. The society was fragmented into various 'jatis' (castes). The poisonous fire is being enflamed by chair-greedy politicians by creating various caste-based political parties. Socially, the caste walls, determined by birth, are crumbling down by education, as evidenced by several inter-marriages. On the religious plank, followers of various religions – Hindus, Jains, Buddhists, Christians, Muslims, Sikhs, Zoroastrians, and Sufis – are unconsciously tied with strong invisible threads of culture, as described by Nehru: "India is a cultural diversity, a bundle of contradictions held together by strong but invisible threads." Like America, India is beautiful and rich in culture because of her diversity in almost every science and art of living – music, dance, dramatics, poetry, language, cuisine, dress, philosophy, sociology, literature, architecture, painting, technology, etc. India has been becoming increasingly richer in every aspect, particularly in her theosophical philosophy being fed and nourished by other cultures and religions. Surprisingly, unlike most other religions, Hinduism has never been constricted by any walls. It has always remained borderless, energizing and fresh.

Michael Wood on India

Michael Wood (born in England on July 23, 1948) – historian, broadcaster and author of several articles and books – writes that the book 'The Story of India' has come out of "(my) long attachment filled with deep respect and admiration, but most of all love for India and its cultures." Michael writes "cultures", not culture, because I understand that he was fascinated by India's rainbow of various languages, cuisines, costumes and home décors, varying from state to state, but amazingly closely tied together by one unifying secular Indian culture, in midst of hundreds of castes and several religions, such as Hinduism, Jainism, Buddhism, Judaism, Christianity, Islam, Sufism, Sikhism, etc. One would wonder how the largest democracy of the world with so many political parties has survived and has maintained good political health over sixty three years of her independence without even one single ill-incident. There was once emergency rule. The Prime Minister was obliged to lose the chair. Socialism was there until 1991. Bengal's thirty four year old communist government has been forced to leave. In my opinion, India's democracy has survived because the soul of Indians is itself democratic. In Hinduism, there are no 'dos' nor 'don'ts'. Do what conscience dictates. The same, I believe, is true of Christianity.

In The Story of India, Michael weaves a spellbinding narrative out of the 10,000 year history of the oldest and most influential civilization on earth, he fell in love with. It is said: "Now, as India bids to become a global economic giant, Michael sets out an epic journey across this vibrant country to trace the roots of India's present in the incredible riches of her past." Michael depicts an unforgettable portrait of India.

Diversity: Unfortunately misperceived

Prof. Eck (p.18) did not like what Mark Twain felt about the icons of Hindu deities he saw in Varanasi in late 19th century:

"What a swarm of them there is! The town is a vast museum of idols – and all of them crude, misshapen, and ugly. They flock through one's dreams at night, a wild mob of nightmares."

I respect Mr. Mark Twain (1835-1910), a literary giant and great novelist, for his scholarship. It is hard for me to believe that he had made such uncivilized remark. If he had literary inquisitive eye and mind, and ethics, he would have tried to know the significance and history of the idols. It is expected of such great scholars to be modest and appreciative of other cultures and religions. One, who does not have respect for other religions, can not claim his love for his own religion.

India's beautiful regional rainbow diversity, unfortunately, is being perceived by some pessimistic narrow-minded people as its disunity. In fact, beneath its apparent diversity, there is a deep hidden uniformity which has been responsible for keeping Indians sentimentally together for millennia, even in face of several divisive forces – internal as well as external. Unfortunately, many Indians are not able to see the beauty and concealed unity in India's diversity.

Nehru: Absorbing & assimilative power of Hinduism

According to Nehru,[51] several other races – Iranians, Parthians, Greeks, Bactrians, Scythians, Huns, Turks – came to India before Islam and got absorbed. Nehru cites Dodwell who remarked that India was "infinitely absorbent like the ocean". Nehru was surprised to see how these races were culturally absorbed in a caste-ridden society:

> "It is odd to think of India, with her caste system and exclusiveness, having this astonishing inclusive capacity to absorb foreign races and cultures. Perhaps it was due to this that she retained her vitality and rejuvenated herself from time to time. The Moslems, when they came, were also powerfully affected by her."

Nehru (p. 74) cites Vincent Smith: "The foreigners (Muslim Turks), like their forerunners the Sakas and the Yueh-chi, universally yielded to the wonderful assimilative power of Hinduism, and rapidly became Hinduised." I think if Vincent meant that they became Hindus by religion, he was wrong. Culturally yes. Or one can say that they got assimilated or they culturally mainstreamed. Hinduism doesn't believe in conversion. Hence, Parsees, Jews, Buddhists, Muslims, and Christians have been able to preserve their religion and imbibe the Indian basic ethos. Early Iranians, Parthians, Greeks, Bactrians, Scythians, Huns, Turks might have been religiously absorbed, as explained earlier, that they might have been immigrants in insignificant numbers.

India's unity abroad: Echoes back in India

During my visits to Fiji, Mauritius, Guyana, and Trinidad, I have seen Indian culture in its various beautiful colors among the East Indians whose ancestors had migrated there over 150 years back. I have seen saris and *bindi* on foreheads, and I enjoyed Hindi

---

[51] Discovery of India (1946, pp. 73,74)

bhajans (religious songs) in Indo-Caribbean temples and movie songs and dances in Indian festivals in Queens and on Long Island. I have gone to Guyana and Trinidad few times. I have enjoyed Divali and Holi in Trinidad.

A Guyanese dancer, Malini Bose-Shah, trained in India, runs her *Nritaya Kala Kendra* (Dance Center) in Queens for Caribbean and Indian girls who are interested in Indian classical dance. Several such other Indo-Caribbean dance schools and ROTI restaurants have also come up in America. When away from home (India), Indians enjoy the panoramic beauty of various dances – Bhārat Natyam, Kathak, Kuchipudi, Manipuri, Bhangra, Garba, etc. – and various other cultural sights and sounds on the same stage, the same night. This evidences that Indians who are found divided on regional lines are culturally united. A wedding crowd glitters with a galaxy of regional saris. The appetite of the guests is pampered by Nana Prakar (variety of) dishes, sweets, āchārs (pickles), and snacks of all regions – southern, northern, eastern, and western. Such India's beautiful, charming and inviting diversity manifests its unity in cultural events. I feel that such unity abroad is echoed back in India and makes Indians feel as ONE.

Sub-continent India: Not divided like Europe

Have scholars any explanation why Bharat is not divided like Europe? India's states could be different countries, as Europe is divided into. Amidst this colossal apparent diversity, one can distinctly feel a sense of oneness through a host of philosophical orientations (spirituality, self-realization, meditation, and Yoga) and core values, especially related to family, marriage, elders, women, children, teacher, etc. Only an ocean can conceal its confident calmness of its unity beneath its turbulent waves and tides which react collectively, as if in a concert to environment and express their complex feelings and emotions. Likewise, various regional fine arts are natural expression of the common core values and aspirations of all Indians. They culturally cement them all together. Fortunately, India, as a sub-continent, is not divided into independent countries as Europe is.

These Nehru's invisible threads of common value orientations and philosophies have kept all Indians, living home as well as abroad, tied together, despite their different religions, castes and languages. Interestingly, former generations of Indian migrants, living in indentured countries (Guyana, Suriname, Trinidad, Jamaica, Fiji, Mauritius, Africa, etc.) are much better united than the recent first generation migrants. The former, unlike the latter, seem to be casteless and more secular. Their caste, language and religion barriers seem to have been weakened by the necessity to develop a different kind of family network, as the result of being uprooted and disconnected from their original one back in India. The recent migrants will feel the same way much later after losing or forgetting their roots.

Many recent immigrants from India (NRIs) seem to have brought with them all those divisive caste, communal and linguistic biases. During my visits, I have found little caste, communal and linguistic bias in Fiji, Mauritius and Caribbean countries, where illiterate indentured laborers – mostly from Bihar and Uttar Pradesh – had migrated in 30s of the 19th century. They seem to be more broad-minded and liberated than the recently educated professional migrants. During my 1997 visit to Fiji, I found that most Indians were speaking Hindi. Everybody introduced himself/herself as Indian, not as Bihari, Hindi, Gujarati, Bengali, etc; or Hindu, Muslim, Sikh, Christian, etc. Such a great feeling of oneness is a tribute to India, the country of their ancestors.

In conclusion, I would like to say that Bhārat, despite several odds (domestic as well as external), has remained unified as the Bhārat of ancient times, because of her religion, rather culture, which is bias-free, inclusive, all-embracive, and broadminded. Diversity has enhanced her beauty.

NINE

Gandhi: Hinduism, a Leaven to Wholesome Life

"Hinduism has saved us from *Bhaya* i.e. peril. If Hinduism had not come to my rescue, the only course for me would have been suicide. I remain a Hindu because Hinduism is a leaven which makes the world worth living in. ... Hinduism teaches me that my body is a limitation of the power of the soul within."

Mahatma Gandhi

In answer to the question, "What has Hinduism done for us?", Gandhiji had answered, as above.[52]

Stephen Knapp,[53] has written what the theosophist Dr. Annie Besant, a friend of Swami Vivekananda, has talked about the role of Hinduism:

"After a study of some forty years and more of the great religions of the world, I find none so perfect, none so scientific, none so philosophical and so spiritual than the great religion known by the name of Hinduism. Make no mistake, without Hinduism, India has no future. Hinduism is the soil in which India's roots are stuck and torn out of that she will inevitably whither as a tree torn out from its

---

[52] M.K. Gandhi (ed. by Anand T. Hingorani), "My Varnashram Dharma", Bombay: Bharatiya Vidya Bhavan, 1965, (pp.64, 65).
[53] Stephen Knapp, 'The Power of the Dharma' (2006, p.10).

place. And if Hindus do not maintain Hinduism who shall save it? If India's own children do not cling to her faith who shall guard it? India alone can save India, and India and Hinduism are one."

Gandhi, talking about materialism of the West and spiritualism of Bharat, remarked:

"Just as in the West they have made wonderful discoveries in material things, similarly, Hinduism has made still more marvelous discoveries in things of religion, of the spirit, of the soul. But we have no eye for these great and fine discoveries. We are dazzled by the material progress that Western science has made. ... After all, there is some thing in Hinduism that has kept it alive up till now. It has witnessed the fall of Babylonian, Syrian, Persian and Egyptian civilization. ... Yes, I see here ancient India still living. True, there are dung heaps, too, here and there, but there are rich treasures buried under them. And the reason why it has survived is that the end which Hinduism set before it was not development along material but spiritual lines."

Gandhi[54] considered religion as duty, not privileges:

"A life of religion is not a life of privileges, but of duty. Privileges may come, as they do come to all, from a due fulfillment of duty. In the book of God, the same number of marks are assigned to the *Brahmin* that has done his task as well as to the *Bhangi* who has done *likewise*."

In Sanskrit the word *'Dharma'* means duty. Thus, Hinduism is not considered as a 'religion', but a way of life. Gandhiji primes work (*karma*), it may be of any kind. He says that the work of a Brahmin earns the same number of marks as

---

[54] Ibid, inside cover.

the work of Bhangi. In other words, a working Bhangi should get more respect than a lethargic Brahmin.

Nehru (1946, p.341) has said that Gandhi, Tagore, Vivekananda, Sir S. Radhakrishnan, etc. have enhanced Hinduism by their progressive and practical perspectives on it. Annie Besant, Sister Nivedita (Margaret Noble) and several European scholars of the nineteenth and twentieth centuries – who came in contact with Vivekananda, Gandhi, Tagore, Sir S. Radhakrishnan and other Hindu philosophers and read Vedic scriptures – Mahābhāratā, Rāmāyanā and Bhagavad Gita, Vedas, etc. – got impressed, and then influenced the people of India, particularly Hindus, with their perspectives on Hinduism and its spirituality.

Hinduism: Emphasis on *gyān* (knowledge)

The word *'Veda'* means knowledge. Hindu thirst for knowledge, external as well as internal, is at least as old as the *Vedas*, difficult to gauge exact age of. Hindus have been worshiping *Sarasvati*, the goddess of learning for un-known number of millennia.

Vivekananda, like other Hindu philosophers, emphasizes the significance of the knowledge of the inner self (*ātmagyān*):

"The goal of mankind is knowledge. ... Now this knowledge is inherent in man. No knowledge comes from outside. It is all inside. What we say a man 'knows', should, in strict psychological language, be what he 'discovers' or 'unveils', what man 'learns' is really what he discovers by taking the cover off his own soul, which is a mine of infinite knowledge."

It is a thrilling philosophy that the knowledge is inside and that has to be unveiled. What a great definition of "learning", Vivekananda has given: "What man 'learns' is really what he discovers by taking the cover off his own soul".

It is easy to have knowledge of the external world, but very difficult to have ātmagyān, knowledge of the inner-self, meaning self-awareness. In order to be able to have a deep peep within, one needs *guru* (teacher). Severe meditation and *tapasyā* (penance) are needed to be able to have a deep peep within. Psychoanalyst helps his patient to be aware of his feelings and thinking about his dear one/s, he has problem with. Mostly, psychological problems arise when one has problem with self. Meditation would help to know self in relation to the inner-self and outer-self. So much is going on within inner-self, the outer-self is scared to know. Man pushes dirt down within too deep from self. He forgets and repeatedly claims "I know myself." It is very difficult to know what we do not want to know. He forgets what he has hidden from self. It is like the self-centered person who hides his money from his family and says "I do not have any thing." My friend in Baroda found three lacs of rupees, from the house he got demolished. He had bought it to build the house of his taste and need.

Psychoanalyst is trained to help one to grope within to know what he feels about the person he has problem with. Psychoanalyst does not help his patient in his relationship with self to gain complete self-realization, required for zero distance between *ātman* and *Parmātma* (God) within. Only meditation can help in becoming one with self. It is very difficult, but it has lot of life rewards. There is a thin line between psychoanalysis and meditation, but thick line between psychoanalyst and Guru. The concept of meditation is much older than psychoanalysis, therefore it can be presumed that psychoanalysis has its origin in meditation. Only Sigmund Freud could tell if he knew and practiced meditation from which he theorized psychoanalysis. Meditation and to some extent psychoanalysis can help in knowing what creates a wall between 'self' and 'self-within'. Gurus like Vivekananda can guide and give the spiritual *gyan*.

Several Hindu philosophers have talked about the significance of knowledge (education) for improvement and development of mind. Formal or school education in relation to the knowledge will be discussed later in the chapter 'Tagore: Hindu concept of education'.

Hinduism: The Scientific Religion[55]

Hinduism is the oldest of existing religions. Several Hindu beliefs and traditions are scientific. There are scientific evidences, Hindu philosophy and its tenets are based on. There is science behind discoveries made by ancient Hindus in several elements of Hinduism. For example, self-awareness (*atmagyan*), has been proved by the Freudian science of psychoanalysis, and the art of meditation by psychoanalytical therapy.

Swami Vivekananda's concept of religion

Swami Vivekananda did not believe in rituals. He believed God is within. The quotes,[56] given here, will make clear various aspects of his concept of religion and God:

"Where can we go to find God if we can not see Him in our own hearts and in every being?"

Vivekananda has clearly said that one has not to wander around to find God, when He is sitting in own soul. It will be like a *hiran* (deer), madly wandering around for *khasturi* (perfume, scent), it is carrying with self in its nābh (navel). Spiritual growth comes from one's own inner self:

"You have to grow from the inside out. None can teach you, none can make you spiritual. There is no other teacher but your own soul. You can not believe in God until you believe in yourself."

What a great philosophy! One has not to wander around, when God is not different from self. According to Vivekananda, "The first sign of your becoming religious is that you are becoming cheerful." One can be cheerful only when one sees Him within

---

[55] Google, Hinduism – The Scientific Religion – Aryabhatta – Astronomer, Mathematician.

[56] 'Google-Swami Vivekananda quotes' is the source of all the quotes given here.

self. God is sitting within self. In Vedic religion (present Hinduism), there is prime emphasis on ātmagyān – realization of self, meaning soul merging with supreme soul. It looks easy. But it is extra-difficult. Paradoxically and unfortunately, man has distanced himself from his own soul, though zero distance between the two. It needs self-discipline and serious meditation. Ironically, man, in general, takes pride in disciplining others, not self. Most of the time, man has been distant from self, hence against himself.

Vivekananda believed that loka-seva (community service) is religion:

> "To devote your life to the good of all and to the happiness of all is religion. Whatever you do for your own sake is not religion. ... The more we come out and do good to others the more our hearts will be purified, and God will be in them."

God lives in pure hearts. If you want to have God with you, you have to make your heart pure, not think about, nor desire evil gratifications. Vivekananda makes it clear what he means by religion:

> "Religion is the manifestation of the Divinity already in man."

> "The greatest religion is to be true to your own nature. Have faith in yourself."

As if, it suggests that God and human soul are twins. Both were born together. They live together. Neither dies. Neither can live alone. Amazing philosophy that the man and God are same! No distance between the two!

Vivekananda has said:

> "You can not believe in God until you believe in yourself."

Vivekananda believed in *karma* (action, work or a deed) to get desired results. *Karma* is not destiny, as has been misperceived by many who do not have trust in self. You can make yourself what you want to be, only by *Karma*. To make *karma* effective and productive, one should have positive thinking:

"If you think about disaster, you will get it. Brood about death you hasten to demise. You think positive and masterfully with confidence and faith, life becomes more secure, more fraught with action, richer in achievement and experience."

Hinduism primes optimism and positive thinking, as reflected by the Hindu concept of death – body dies, not soul – thus unending continuity of life. See in death rebirth of a sinless beautiful infant. Do good deeds (*karma*) to beget happiness in this life and also in next life, if you believe in rebirth.

Reward for selfless love of God?

Vivekananda recommends selfless prayer:

"It is good to love God for hope of reward, but it is better to love God for love's sake; and the prayer goes: O Lord, I do not want wealth, nor children, nor learning. If it be Thy will, I shall go from birth to birth. But grant me this, that I may love Thee without hope of reward – unselfishly for love's sake."

"God is to be worshipped as the one beloved, dearer than everything in this and next life."

"The moment I have realized God sitting in the temple of every human body, the moment I stand in reverence before every human and see God in him, that moment I am free from bondage, every thing that binds vanishes, and I am free."

101

Moksha / Nirvana

The freedom from bondage, Vivekananda is talking about, is *moksha / nirvana* (freedom) from the continuing cycle of birth and death. It also means freedom from the attachments (*moha*) with dear ones which may give grief after separation. One should be concerned about the welfare of his dear ones and should do whatever he can do; but he should not feel or experience the pain, his loved one has. I remember a Hindi movie in which Omprakash, out of his love for his wife, was shown having labor pains.

Nirvana is the prime desire of Hindus, Jains, Buddhists and Sikhs. It is not easy. It needs sincere meditation and severe *tapasiya* (penance).

Sister Gargi (Marie Louise Burke)

Sister Gargi[57] (1911-2004), born as Marie Louise Burke, was very much impressed by the life of Swami Vivekananda. She did a great deal of research on his works and wrote quite a few books, including *'Swami Vivekananda in the West: New Discoveries'*. Burke took her first vows in India from the Ramakrishna Order in 1974 and was given the monastic name "Gargi" in recognition of her brilliant accomplishments as researcher and writer.

Gargi: Ancient Indian female philosopher

Marie Louise Burke was decorated with the 'GARGI', after the ancient Indian female philosopher and thinker, Gargi Vachaknu, daughter of Rishi Vachaknu. She was born in the family of Garga, 800-500 BCE. I remember that one of the girls' hostels, at the M.S. University of Baroda, my alma mater, was named 'Gargi Hall'.

Women enjoyed respect and equality in ancient India

In the ancient Vedic traditions, women enjoyed respect and equality. Women of the Vedic era were epitomes of intellectual

---

[57] Wikipedia, Sister Gargi

and spiritual attainments. Vedas talk volumes about such intellectual and spiritual women philosophers, such as Ghosha, Gargi, Lopamudra, Maitreyi, and several others. On this count – gender equality and respect for women – ancient Hindus seem to be more progressive and more civilized than the present Hindus. Ancient Bharat had a broad-minded progressive democracy, with gender equality.

Dr. Annie Besant on Hinduism

Annie Besant[58], daughter of William Wood and Emily Morris was born in London in 1847 and died in India on 20th September, 1933. She left her husband Rev. Frank Besant who was a conservative religious man. She was revolutionary, heretic, social reformer and free thinker. She was very much involved in women causes. She rejected Christianity in 1874, and became like an atheist. In 1877, she was elected as an MP of the House of Commons. In 1890s, she became supporter of Theosophy, a religious movement founded by Helena Blavatsky in 1875. Theosophy was based on Hindu-Buddhist ideas of *karma*, reincarnation and *Nirvana*. She went to live in India. She got actively involved in the 'Indian Home Rule movement'.

Annie Besant has[59] also talked about the jewels in the Mahābhāratā and the Gita:

"Among the priceless teachings that may be found in the great Indian epic Mahabharata, there is none so rare and priceless as the Gita. ... This is the India of which I speak – the India which, as I said, is to me the Holy Land. For those who, though born for this life in a Western land, and clad in a Western body, can yet look back to earlier incarnations in which they drank the milk of spiritual wisdom from the breast of their true mother – they must feel ever the magic of her immemorial past, must dwell ever under the spell of her deathless fascination; for they

---

[58] Annie Besant, Biography, Google Search
[59] Stephen Knapp, 'The Power of the Dharma' (2006, p.10)..

are bound to India by all the sacred memories of their past; and with her, too, are bound up all the radiant hopes of their future, a future which they know they will share with her who is their true mother in the soul-life."[60]

Annie Besant talks about India's 'deathless fascination'. To me it means India's belief in 'deathless life' (continuous life w/o any break) which suggests Hindu belief in *"Punner-janma"* (rebirth). It is like an unending chain of 'birth → life → death →birth', the union of birth and death, like union of 'day and night', 'light and darkness'. At higher level, it means the union between *'atma'* (*atman*) and *Parmatma*. Surprising, the words – 'death' (English), and *'maot'* (Arabic) – mean end of life. The *Dehant'*, the Sanskrit word for death, means end of only body (*deh* = body + *ant* = end), not of soul. It explains the Hindu concept of death means 'unending continuous or deathless life'. According to the Bhagvad Gita, only the body dies, the soul transmigrates into another infant body. Such optimistic view of life dilutes the fear of death. Gandhi stressed that transmigration (passage of the soul after death in another body) is not a theory, but it is a fact. It is a great contribution of Hinduism to the mankind.

Nehru (1946, p. 341) praises Annie Besant for her influence on spirituality of Hindus:

"Mrs. Annie Besant was a powerful influence in adding to the confidence of the Hindu middle classes in their spiritual and national heritage. There was a spiritual and religious element about all this, and yet there was a strong political background to it."

Is Vedic religion Monotheistic or polytheistic?

If the Vedic religion (Hinduism) is monotheistic or polytheistic would depend on the way a person wants to see it. In the usual sense of literal meaning of the word 'monotheism', Hinduism is

---

[60] Annie Besant, *'India: Essays and Lectures'* (vol. iv), London: The Theosophical Publishing Co.,(1895, p.11).

polytheistic having several gods and goddesses. But, in its real sense – differentiating gods from the almighty GOD – it is monotheistic. Hindus have only one Almighty God, and several gods and goddesses. Several *Rig Vedic* hymns talk about the unity of the Supreme Divinity.

Max Müller (1999, p.164) remarks:

> "There are hymns that assert the unity of the Divine as fearlessly as any passage of the Old Testament, or the New Testament, or the Koran."

In my opinion, most religions, including Christianity, have shades of polytheism, along with their basic monotheism. Basically, almost all the people on the planet believe in one Almighty God, of course, along with some godly persons with different names varying from language to language. Even the Almighty God has several different names corresponding to several languages. Even every child – Hindu, Christian, Jew, Muslim or of any other religion – believes in one God, pointing to the sky, thinking His abode is up there. There are other gods and goddesses ('g' small) who have different functions and attributes. Some of them are mythological.

Max Müller (1999, p.165) talks about polytheism in Greece and Rome, just like in Hinduism:

> "Our ideas of polytheism being chiefly derived from Greece and Rome, we understand by it a certain more or less organized system of gods, different in power and rank, and all subordinate to a supreme God, a Zeus or Jupiter. The Vedic polytheism differs from the Greek and Roman polytheism, and I may add, likewise from the polytheism of the Ural-Altaic, the Polynesian, the American, and most of the African races, in the same manner as a confederacy of village communities differ from a monarchy."

The Vedic polytheism does not differ much from the Greek and the Roman polytheism. All humans – Asian, Indian, African,

European or any other – believe in one Almighty God, and also they believe in His subordinates who have different names and different powers, roles and ranks. For example, the Vedic gods – Brahma (the creator), Vishnu (the care taker), and Shiva (the destroyer) – have different responsibilities to take care of the three stages of human life – birth, life, and death. Shiva's role should not be pessimistically viewed as negative. Would man feel comfortable living in deathless society of too old, sick and feeble people? There are several other gods and goddesses to take care of various needs of the life, such as wind (*Pawan*), water (*Varun*), education/knowledge (*Sarasvati*), wealth (*Laxmi*), defense (*Durga*), and others, like Rama, Krishna, etc. for different roles and different philosophies. Such gods and goddesses are known in different religions by different names, for example in Hinduism they are called '*devta*', '*devi*', and in Christianity 'saint'.

It is interesting to know what Will Durant (p. 405) has said about images in ancient Hindu world:

> "In the earlier Vedic religion there were, as far as the evidence goes, no temples and no images;[61] alters were put up anew for each sacrifice as in Zoroastrian Persia, and sacred fire lifted the offering to heaven. Vestiges of human sacrifice occur here,[62] as at the outset of almost every civilization; but they are few and uncertain."

Because of limited foggy understanding of Vedic rituals and their objectives, as the result of their limited knowledge of Sanskrit, western scholars have misinterpreted the Vedic religion and its sacred rituals. At each *hawan*, religious ceremony for peace of mind of the family, the word '*suhawa*' – pronounced at each offering of 'rice, ghee, etc.' in the sacred *agni* (fire) – has been interpreted as a sacrifice of an animal. It is offering of what (ghee, rice, etc.) was thrown into the fire, not sacrifice of a life to God. Durant's line "sacred fire lifted the offering to heaven" seems to explain that ritual did not imply sacrifice of a life. How can

---

[61] Eliot, I xv; Buddhist India, 241;Radhakrishnan, I, 108.
[62] Ibid., 107; Winternitz, 215; Gour, 5.

'sacrifice of life' happen in the society of *Rishis* who were vegetarian, and lived on vegetables, fruits and milk. The Vedic principle *'Ahimsa Parmo-Dharma'* suggests that nonviolence is the prime religion) of the Vedic people, present Hindus. It rebuts the alleged practice of sacrifice of animals and humans among Hindus. How would parents, particularly mothers, allow their child be burnt alive as sacrifice to please God. It is unbelievable that God, Who gives life, will be pleased with an offering of a life. I have not heard of any God – Hindu, Buddhist, Jewish, Christian, Muslim, or any other – will be happy with offering of a life. God gives life, does not take life. Death is the end of the suffering caused by age, physical injury, or disease. Death is God's mercy. Without death, the society will be a grave yard of alive people. Would we be able to tolerate or put up with the sight of a deathless society?

Ashvamedha: Not sacrifice of horse

Ashvamedha was not sacrifice of a horse. It was a way for a powerful king to assert his lordship over nearby small kingdoms without blood-shed. In ancient times, because of several limitations – transportation, communication, resources, army, etc. – there were mostly tiny city or town-kingdoms. He would send out his horse, along with few soldiers, to move around through the small kingdoms. He would send his army to fight any king who would resist accepting his emperorship by confronting the symbolic horse.

Rebirth: Optimism in Death

Hindus, Jains, Buddhists and Sikhs believe in rebirth. The belief in rebirth offers optimism in death. Death is not the end of life, but the beginning of a new fresh life. Life and death chase each other. There is no end to the 'birth → life → death → birth' cycle. On the same token, the belief that the sun sets is erroneous. The sun never sets. Only in the 24-hour-long revolving of the planet, the sun is not visible to the half of the humanity enjoying the rest offered by the soothing cooling darkness, bestowed by the sun. Paradoxically, the sun gives both light as well as darkness – day and night – very much needed for human life.

Body gradually decays and ultimately dies. Soul is immortal. It doesn't age. Soul transmigrates into another body, as a fresh and beautiful infant. The SOUL doesn't age and doesn't die, like the sun which never sets. The sunset is a myth.

There have been a couple of examples in India who have described their houses where they lived in their previous life. One person correctly described his previous-life home and rightly talked about his fall from its first floor balcony.

Whether rebirth is believable or not, but the feeling – a young Hindu would enjoy from the thought to continue endless life with his/her beloved for several lives to come – no billionaire can buy. Dialogues and songs in Indian movies are stuffed with oaths exchanged by loving couples to live together several lives, even after death. Such optimism is good for mental hygiene. I think cremation reflects the need to burn the body to its ashes, because unlike soul, it does not have any use after death. Thus, Hindus do not believe in the Day of Judgment.

Attachment can give pain, and wear out love

Bhagvad Gita and Vedic scriptures preach not to develop *moha* (heavy emotional attachment) for any body, because later hatred and/or separation can cause severe psychological stress. One should remain concerned about the welfare of the loved one and do whatever is needed, but not overdo to make him dependent and make self too consumed and psychologically too fatigued.

Hindus pray for *moksha / nirvana* (freedom) from the 'birth-death-birth' cycle. Life, along with pleasures, can have heavy toll of suffering too. Psychotherapy and psychoanalysis have been developed to dilute the pain. Transcendental meditation, preferably to start with the guidance of a genuine guru, can give serenity and relief from psychological suffering resulting from losses, primarily of the loving relationships. Loss of money does not give that much grief, because it can be re-earned.

Interest of Westerners in Gita

Vedic people (Hindus) of ancient times had knowledge of psychology, as evidenced by the Bhagavad Gita and the Vedas, which are much older than Gita. Henry David Thoreau (1817-1862) has said about the influence of Gita on him:

"In the morning I bathe my intellect in the stupendous and cosmogonal philosophy of the Bhagavad Gita in comparison with which our modern world and its literature seems puny and trivial."

Stephen Knapp, in *'The Power of the Dharma: An Introduction to Hinduism and Vedic Culture'* (2006, p. 3), explains why Hinduism has continued for millennia and has not been destroyed. He cites C.S Lewis, the great author and theologian:

"Finally it will come to two religions, Hinduism and Christianity. The first (Hinduism) will grow absorbing ideas and concepts from everywhere and latter (Christianity) will keep away from everything that is foreign to it."

Incorporation of foreign cultural ideas has been enriching Hinduism. It is like an ever-blowing wind, snuffing fragrance from all the ethnic philosophical flowers it touches. It is like Ganga, flowing down from the Himalayas with fresh clean water. India's religio-cultural diversity has been enlightening Hinduism which has been always open to desirable new philosophies. Hinduism is not rigid. Unlike most other religions, it is flexible and stretchable.

West's interst in Bhagvad Gita

Knapp (2006, pp.49,50) talks about West's interest in the philosophy of the Bhagvad Gita. He tells that the very first

---

* Bhagvad Gita was the live conversation between Lord Krishna and Arjuna during the Mahabharta War between Pandwas and Kaurvas, in about 3067 B.C.

translation of Gita into English was done by Charles Wilkins in 1785, with an introduction by Warren Hastings, the then British Governor General of India. Knapp adds that one of the most popular translations was done by Sir Edwin Arnold, under the title of 'The Song Celestial'. Gita won the attention of and admiration of great intellectuals and thinkers, like Von Humboldt of Germany, Emerson of America, Hagel and Schopenhauer.

Amazingly, Robert Oppenheimer, the very first Chairman of Atomic Energy Commission and the father of the Atom bomb was a great admirer of the *Bhagvad Gita*. Amazingly, he learnt Sanskrit to understand the Gita. Knapp (2006, p.50) writes that after witnessing the first atomic explosion, Oppenheimer read a couplet from Gita (Chapter 11: 12):

"If hundreds of thousands of suns rose up into the sky, they might resemble the effulgence of the Supreme Person in the universal form."

Knapp writes, that later when Oppenheimer addressed the Congress, he said that the Atom bomb reminded him of Lord Krishna who had said in the *Bhagvad Gita*: "Time I am, devourer of all."

American historian Will Durant[63] thought that the West should learn from India its tolerance and gentleness and love for all living things:

"It is true that even across the Himalayan barrier India has sent to us such questionable gifts as grammar and logic, philosophy and fables, hypnotism and chess, and above all our numerals and our decimal system."
Will Durant[64]

T. C. Galav, in *'Philosophy of Hinduism, Introduction'* (p.20), praises the philosophy of the East, particularly of India:

---

[63] Ibid. , p.11
[64] Taken from 'The Power of Dharma' by Stephen Knapp (2006, p. 11)

"Perhaps in return for conquest, arrogance and spoliation, India will teach us the tolerance and gentleness of the mature mind, the quiet content of the un-acquisitive soul, the calm of the understanding spirit, and unifying, pacifying love for all living things."

Tolerance, Gentleness and Ahimsa: Not always advisable

Tolerance and gentleness are shining diamonds of humanity, but not appropriate for all occasions, particularly when being harassed by belligerent adversaries on the border. The history shows such shining diamonds have proved darkness and shame for the Hindu Bharat, champion of *Ahimsa* and gentleness. It made it easy for the sword to force Hindus lie down to be trodden over. During last over twelve hundred years, gentleness let Bharat dismembered of Iran, Afghanistan, several countries suffixed by 'istan' in Central Asia. The last took place in 1947, when Bharat had to lose lot of its territory – Pakistan, Baluchistan, Bangladesh, Sri Lanka, Myanmar, etc. Bharat has lost several countries in South-East Asia.

I hope people will understand if I say, "I hate Ahimsa against Himsa – non-violence against violence." Such gentleness is shameful cowardice and weakness, no nation should feel proud of. I hope Delhi would not adopt Ahimsa and gentleness to guard Bharat's fragile borders. Military muscle should never be compromised for honor of India's *ahimsa* and gentleness. Violence should never be used to coerce other peoples. But, it is sacred in defense. "Never trust enemy" my father always insisted, as Sardar Patel and Chanakya did.

Stephen Knapp (2006, pp. 10-11) has said that the impressive nature of the Vedic tradition did not go unnoticed by early French thinkers like Victor Cousin (1792-1862) whose knowledge of the history of European philosophy was unrivalled:

"When we read with attention the poetical and philosophical monuments of the East – above all, those of India which are beginning to spread in Europe – we discover there many a truth, and truths so profound, and which make such a contrast with the meanness of the results at which European genius has sometimes stopped, that we are constrained to bend the knee before the philosophy of the East, and to see in this cradle of the human race the native land of the highest philosophy."[65]

Stephen Knapp, in *'The Power of Dharma'* (2006, p.11), has cited Will Durant that India was the mother of European languages and philosophy and also of mathematics and the ideals embodied in Christianity:

"India was the motherland of our race, and Sanskrit the mother of Europe's languages: she was the mother of our philosophy, mother through the Arabs, of much of our mathematics; mother, through the Buddha, of the ideals embodied in Christianity, mother through the village community, of self-government and democracy. Mother India is in many ways the mother of us all."

Knapp (p.11) has written that the English novelist and essayist Aldous Huxley[66] (1894-1963) has said that the Bhagvad Gita is for the whole world. He has further said:

"The Bhagvad Gita is the most systematic statement of spiritual evolution of endowing value of mankind. The Gita is one of the clearest and most comprehensive summaries of the spiritual thoughts ever to have been made."

What is in Hinduism, that has kept it alive?

What is that something in Hinduism that has kept it alive for millennia despite terrible odds Hindustan has been confronted with? The Vedas, Bhagvad Gita and the two Epics answer all the questions which arise in various situations confronting individuals,

---

[65] *Is India Civilized: Essay on Indian Culture*, by Sir John Woodroffe, p. 132.
[66] T. C. Galav: 'Philosophy of Hinduism – An Introduction' (p.65Car).

the society and the nation. In my opinion, the problem, an individual may have with self, can cause a serious problem, not only for his family and country, but also for others. Let me be more clear what I mean by this. The history from distant pre-history times tells that only one INDIVIDUAL – Rawan (Rāmāyanā), Duryodhan (Mahābhāratā), Hitler (2nd World War), and today Hosni Mubarak (Egypt), Col. Muammar Qaddafi (Libya), and Osama bin Laden – has been the cause of wars and unrest which have caused thousands of lives. There have been several other men like these individuals, who, I believe, had trouble with self, meaning with their own conscience. They were ego-centric and egotistic, who could not see any thing beyond self. I am happy that present India doesn't have any one like this. If some one tries to become, democracy would take care of him/her. Emergency was declared in India in 80s of the 20th century, but democracy didn't let it survive long.

Dr. Kanayalal Munshi, the founder of the Bharatiya Vidya Bhavan, has appropriately explained why Hinduism has millennia-long life despite several serious attacks on its life. Hinduism has not only survived, but has made itself richer and more beautiful, because of its progressive attitude to include whatever is good in any other culture. It is flexible and stretchable, not rigid. It stretches itself to appropriately and adequately meet the increasing demands of the changing times. Hinduism has no rigid boundaries. It does not have any 'dos', nor any 'don'ts'. It has been expanding, keeping pace with the complex humanity. Paradoxically, one can see unity in its complexity and beauty in its diversity. Because of its 'unity in diversity', Hinduism has been able to preserve its monotheism, being expressed by its polytheistic appearance. This is too delicate a concept for common mind. If Hinduism was conservative and rigid, it would have been brittle like glass.

Gandhiji loved and revered Hinduism a great deal. He has said: "Cow worship is a great idea which is capable of expansion." He praises the freedom of Hinduism from the modern proselytization. He believed that the contribution of the four Ashrams of Hinduism is unique. There is nothing like it in the whole world. Gandhiji[67] has lamented that Hinduism has been misrepresented so is its *Varnashram* which is being confused as caste system:

> "Today, *Varnashram Dharma* and Hinduism are misrepresented and denied by its votaries. The remedy is not destruction, but correction. Let us reproduce the true Hindu spirit, and then ask whether it satisfies the soul or not."[68]

Gandhiji was right that Hinduism has been misrepresented. Several Western scholars, because of their ignorance and resistance to understand and respect other cultures, have misrepresented other cultures including the Vedas and Hinduism. For example, Prof. Stanley Wolpert, in his book *'A New History of India'* (p.25), has misinterpreted the word *'Dasa'* as slave, so as to say that the ancient India practiced slavery. As a matter of fact the word *'Dasa'* means *Sewak* (servant). India never had slavery. Slavery is historically associated with only Americans and Europeans – British, French, Spanish, Dutch, and Portuguese.

Gandhi[69]: Varnashram is not caste system

Gandhiji has stressed:

> "*Varna* has nothing to do with caste. Caste is an excrescence, just like untouchability, upon Hinduism. All the excrescences that are emphasized today were never part of Hinduism. *Varnashram* is not caste. I hold that there is nothing in common between caste and *Varna*. Whilst *Varna* gives life, caste kills it."

---

[67] M.K. Gandhi (ed. by Anand T. Hingorani), "My Varnashram Dharma", Bombay: Bharatiya Vidya Bhavan, 1965, (p..66)
[68] Young India, November 24, 1927.
[69] M. K. Gandhi, *'My Varnashram Dharma'*, ed.by Anand T. Hingorani, Bharatiya Vidya Bhavan, Bombay, 1965.

Will Durant, in *'Our Oriental Heritage'* (1935, p. 398), explains how and when Varna was perceived as caste: "The early Hindu word for caste is *varna*, color. This was translated by the Portuguese invaders as *caste*, from the Latin *castus*, pure."

Gandhiji explains that the *Rishis*, after incessant experiment and research, arrived at this fourfold division, the four ways of earning one's livelihood. There was flexibility in terms of changing occupation – one could move up the ladder, and some may be obliged by to step down depending upon the circumstances and self-deficits, he is confronted with. But there was no attribute of untouchability associated with any kind of work. There was sense of 'dignity of labor', respect for *karma*, meaning work. Racism, in America, was even worse than the caste system until prohibition was strictly enforced. In fifties of the twentieth century blacks had separate seats on buses and there were a couple of instances that they were lynched. Yet all White hearts don't seem to be cleansed. In India also, caste has been legally prohibited. But the desired enforcement of the caste-related laws needs lot of support of the Hindu heart, like that of Gandhiji.

This is the way present societies – developed and developing – are divided into four divisions, as ascertained by the kind of work they are doing. The work, guided by brain (knowledge) is most prized, and the work done while on sweated feet is least desired. The quality of the *Karma* (work) is graded by the knowledge and the technological skill of the worker, of course super-judged by the quality of its purpose or mission. Purpose of the *Karma* should be selfless and in the interest of the society. Brahmin, the person of knowledge (*Gyan*), like present highly educated person, occupies the highest chair. So the four *Varnas*, four categories of work (*karma*) to earn livelihood, were devised. Gita suggests that both, *Gyan* (knowledge) and *Karma* (activity), are necessary for living a satisfying life. There should be inter-occupation mobility. One can move up from a restaurant-waiter to a medical doctor who might have used waiter's job, or any other low job, to pay for his higher education. I have seen a brother of a doctor doing menial jobs. He should be respected because there is his *karma* (work, activity) in earning his livelihood. Inactivity (*karmaheenta*) is to be disliked, but not the *karmaheen* (inactive) person. He deserves opportunity and assistance to get work and rise. Hatred, in any form and for any rationale, should not be condoned. It is an uncivilized and inhuman attitude. Therefore, in Gandhi's or any one's opinion, the attitude of untouchability is not civilized. In psychotherapy, alcoholism is to be hated, not the alcoholic; theft should be condemned, not the thief. There must be some unavoidable circumstance obliging one to drink, steal, or unavailability of job. In every human being, all the three *gunas* (qualities, aptitudes) – *satto* (divine, super good), *rajas* (human, normal), and *tammo* (inhuman, evil) – are inherent, changing in response to one's circumstances and ability to balance one's ego in war between his id and super-ego.

Should any *karma* (work, activity) be considered hateful?

To supplement my family income, I worked as a bus conductor during my vacation from my school teaching job. There is nothing wrong if a son of a Brahmin does a menial job, when compelled by circumstances. A working *bhangi* is entitled to more respect than an inactive lazy Brahmin. Menial job is much better than remaining unemployed. Developed countries have people to do menial jobs, but they are not considered as *Achhoot* (untouchable). Unfortunately, in India they are. It is not a civilized attitude. Gandhiji suggested that the people doing menial jobs should be called as *"Harijans"* meaning the people of God. Changing the name doesn't help. Attitudes are to be changed.

In present times, there is no society – developed or developing – whose population is not divided into these four segments. No society can optimally function without the help of the lowest, meaning the fourth labor class. Cobblers, Barbers, Smiths are seen occupying high positions in developed as well as developing societies. In India, Dalits are occupying respectful high positions, like ministers and even chief ministers – whom Brahmins are saluting. Very recently, an upper caste official was seen dusting the slippers of a *dalit* chief minister in public. In short, position or money – *brahmin* or *dalit* – is worshipped.

Unfortunately, in Hindu society, some of the fourth class workers are considered as *"Shudra* or *achhoot"* (untouchable).

This is very wrong. Ancient Bharat did not have untouchables. From that sense, ancient Bharatvasi (Indians) can be considered more civilized than the present who, like ancient Bharatvasis, do not appreciate the dignity of labor and *karmasheelta* of the sweating labor.

Sindhi: A caste-less society, why not others?

The original residents of the Mohenjo-daro (Indus Valley Civilization, 3500–2300 B.C.), the ancestors of present Sindhi Hindus did not have any untouchable. So was true about the rest of the ancient Bharat. In ancient times, Hindus had not even heard of caste system. The present Sindhi Hindus – descendents of their Mohenjodaro ancestors – do not have any untouchable. Then, why do other Hindus have?

For Sindhi Hindus, work is worship. They are hardworking (*karmasheel*). I remember we Sindhis were getting irritated when we, as migrants from Sindh after the unfortunate partition of India in 1947, were considered as *Sharnarthi* (refugees). We were saying: "We are *Pursharthi*, not *Sharnnarthi*." We proved it. Sindhi Hindus, in general, are economically comfortable. Sindhi beggar is rare. No work is bad. Mostly Sindhi surnames are not caste-based, because they do not believe in caste. Their surnames are family-based. For example 'Karamchandanis' are children of their great-great-great-grand father 'Karamchand'. So 'Motwani' of 'Motumal', 'Advani' of 'Adumal', 'Ramchandani' of 'Ramchand', so on.

The British government, in order to fragment Indian nation into pieces, brought the idea of mention of "*Jati*" in the Census after fearing the Indian unity as was reflected by the '1857 Revolt' for independence of India. At present there is political movement to eliminate the mention of '*Jati*' in the Census of India.

Woman in ancient Vedic times

Durant (p.401) observes:

"Woman enjoyed far greater freedom in the Vedic period than in later period. She had more choice of her mate than the forms of marriage might suggest. (He seems to refer to the ancient system of *Swamber*). She appeared freely at feasts and dances, and joined in religious sacrifice. She could study, and like Gargi, engage in philosophic disputation."

In remote ancient times of the *Rāmāyanā* and the *Mahābhāratā*, women had respect and power. In family, the mother and the wife exercised her authority. I remember in forties of the twentieth century, my grand father used to discuss his political and social issues with his mother. I think, in present times, authority is tied with money. Woman, because of her triple responsibility – wife, mother, and household – gets little time to earn. This has been compounded because of disintegration of joint family.

With advance of time and because of the awakening of the modern woman due to socio-cultural globalization, the status of the Indian woman, more so of the urban, is becoming the same, comparable to the Western woman. Urban Indian are increasingly becoming two-income families. Many women have been well educated to assume outdoor employment responsibilities, well-compared to man. The present woman, oriental or occidental, is demanding, rather earning, more independence, which, unfortunately has been at the cost of marriage and care of children. The ego – male as well as female, as exhibited by gender competition and sense of individualism, rather than coexistence and cooperation – has been responsible for disintegration of family and gradual disappearance of marriage. Realistic fear of divorce and widowhood necessitates woman to work long to earn adequate retirement benefits to survive independently. This has become a painful reality because of aversion to joint family. Married children, though willing to, may not take responsibility of the care of their widowed elderly parent, particularly mother, may be because of marital conflict.

This – that woman in ancient times had respect and power in the family – may be unbelievable for present Indians. Vedas and Epics talk about several great women, like Gargi, Ghosha,

Lopamudra, Maitrey, etc. All this would appear true when we read or watch the *leelas* (dramas, plays), known as *Ram Leelas* and *Krishna Leelas* of the great epics, *Rāmāyanā* and *Mahābhāratā*, played on streets, in temples, and as televised. I remember the days when Rāmānand Sagar's *Mahābhāratā* was weekly televised, the streets were deserted by televisions. The doors of the 'television homes' were left open welcoming the neighbors who did not have TV. It was watched by all Indians, irrespective of their religious affinity. *Mahābhāratā* is thrilling with war-oriented strategically suspenseful events showing respect for and authority of the woman. *Mahābhāratā* has history. It is educational, full of ancient Indian philosophy and values – family, *guru-shikshak* (teacher-student) and also war-oriented ethics.

The *Rāmāyanā* stresses on values related to government and family relations, including marital, parent-child, sibling, and all other family relations. *Rāmāyanā* emphasis has also been on democracy – the people's *Rāj*, popularly known as *Ramrajya* (good government). *'Rāmrājya'* is being considered as a good democracy even in present times.

Satee, not known in ancient Vedic period

Will Durant (p. 402) observes that the practice of *Satee* (cremation of widow alive along with the body of her husband) "was almost unknown in Vedic times." It came much later when widows, particularly young, didn't feel safe from being abused. Circumstances had changed because of change in India's socio-cultural demography due to new non-Vedic immigrants. Widow re-marriage was not culturally approved. *Satee* was not a custom. It was a circumstance-responding practice which fortunately did not survive long. Some women volunteered impressed by their sentiments for their departed husband, some because of fear of loneliness, and some might have been forced by their in-laws because of their selfish inhuman agenda. We should be happy that legal prohibition has been effectively enforced. It is a severely punishable crime.

It is shame that some Hindus, although having such a great enviable heritage, are going backward. Europeans envied the

Aryan (Hindu) heritage. They thought it was their heritage. The title *"Our Oriental Heritage"* of Will Durant's book proves the point.

The history of assaults, domestic as well as external, on Hinduism during last over fourteen centuries would awaken Hindus to make desirable adjustments in response to the demands of the time. More important is that Hindus should objectively examine why some Hindus walk out to embrace Jainism, Buddhism and Sikhism, although their core philosophy of life is not different from Hinduism. I think caste system and some senseless religious rituals have been tarnishing Hinduism. Gandhiji has rightly asserted: "Caste is an excrescence, just like untouchability, upon Hinduism." According to him, all the excrescences that are emphasized today, were never part of Hinduism. Hindus should look back and try to be the same as they were in ancient times.

Hinduism may be understood better when it is seen in comparison to other major religions, particularly religions in the West. The culture of the West is different from the culture of the East. Religion and culture are close to each other. Religion influences the culture. I am unable to explain differences between various religions, because I have little knowledge about other religions. Even I don't know my own religion Hinduism as much as I would like to know.

I know, rather I earnestly believe that any religion of the East or of the West, is to bring peace to self, family, community and whole humanity. Basics of all religions are similar because all of them talk about one and the same Almighty God. Differences, the cause of inter-fights are created by the people who have little knowledge of religion, particularly of own. They don't know God and they don't understand what God wants. Basically, religion is supposed to show the path to Almighty God, Allah, Ishwar, etc. God wants to be reachable. Therefore, He has given several paths to Him. God may have names, as many as languages. Different names of God, as per different languages, have confused people who are confused about, rather ignorant of God and their own religion.

God is great and so kind that He has suggested several paths to reach Him. Religion should allow its every disciple to choose path of his / her choice. Why to fight on the path, God has allowed? All religions have the same sacred mission of all-pervasive peace. Unfortunately, the man, particularly self-styled religious man, has abused religion, divided God, and spread division, hatred and unrest.

Various philosophies have significant bearing on serenity within self, togetherness within own family, oneness in own community, and international coexistence. Peace stems from the feeling of union with self which has been difficult to realize because man himself is at odds with self. I had seen a book with its title, '*Man against Himself*'. Religion can help in bringing 'zero distance' between man and man, and between man and God.

According to Hinduism, God is within self. Paradoxically, because of his self-centeredness, the man has distanced himself from self, thus from God.

Unity of Divinity: Misperceived, thus Confused

The man himself has distorted the institution of religion so as to serve self, rather than the humanity. Unity of divinity has been challenged. Supremacy of God (one Almighty God) has been misrepresented, ironically by civilized hypocritical religious leaders, believing that peoples of different religions have their own God, different from others. According to misguided religious leaders, there are as many Gods as the religions.

How can evangelism be sacred when God is one?

Why conversions under the nose of the one Almighty God? How can the Christian gospel to convert be godly when His global providence is challenged and reduced by the gospel? It is not the fault of the language to have different names of God. Why Christian 'God' be different from Islamic 'Allah' and from Hindu 'Ishwar'? The lingual difference is being manipulated and misrepresented to serve a segment rather than the whole. No segment of people will be beneficially served, if they are at odds with Almighty God.

The major living religions[70]

1. Eastern – Hinduism, Jainism, Buddhism, Zoroastrianism, and Sikhism.
2. Western – Judaism, Christianity, Islam and Sufism

Hinduism is the oldest religion. Its age is not known. Other oriental religions – Jainism, Buddhism, and Zoroastrianism – may be as old as Judaism, but older than Christianity, Islam, Sufism, Sikhism and some other religions, not mentioned here. Judaism is the parent of Christianity and Islam. Sikhism is quite recent, 15th century A.D.

World's Major Religions [71]

Religion	Founder	Place	Year[72]
Hinduism	Natural	India (Bharat)	10,000+ BC
Zoroastrianism*	Zarathustra	Iran	600 BC
Jainism*	Vardaman Mahāvir	India	527 BC
Buddhism*	Siddharth Gautam	Nepal-India	544 BC
Judaism*	Abraham	Jerusalem	6th and 5th BC
Christianity	Jesus Christ	Jerusalem	0 AD
Islam, Sufism	Muhammad	Mecca, Arabia	570/571 AD
Sikhism[73]	Guru Nanak	Punjab, India	15[th]cen. A.D

---

[70] Some religions are not included.

[71] Only well-known religions are included. Source – Google Search, Dr. Peter Clarke, *World's Religions: Understanding the Living Faiths*, and R. C. Zaehner: *World's Religions*

[72] Are approximates.

[73] Later it was enhanced to 'Khalsa Pantha' by the 10th Guru Gobind Singh in 1699.

*All the four – Zoroastrianism, Jainism, Buddhism and Judaism – seem to be contemporary.

The Zoroastrianism of Iran can be understood better only in the light of the following ancient historical relationships:

- between India and Iran,
- particularly between Sanskrit and Avestan, and
- Vedas and Avesta.

The Avesta is close to the Vedas. Its language Avestan was too close to Sanskrit to distinguish one from the other as seen from the following few sentences.

Avestan:	tem amavantem yazatem
Sanskrit:	tam amavantam yajatam
Avestan:	surem damohu sevistem
Sanskrit:	suram dhamasu savistham
Avestan:	mithrem yazai zaothrabyo
Sanskrit:	mitram yajai hotrabhyah

Very close linguistic correspondence between Sanskrit and Avestan words (given by Burrow, p. 4), as shown above, will puzzle many to think if Avestan and Sanskrit are two different languages.

Will Durant, in *'Our Oriental Heritage'* (p.406), remarks that Sanskrit was a near relative of the early Persian dialect in which the Avesta was composed.

Benjamin Walker, in *'The Hindu World: An Encyclopedic Survey of Hinduism'* (vol. 2, p 353), writes about inter-mixing of old Iranian and Indian (Hindu) gods and deities.

Max Müller, in *'The Science of Language'* (1891, p.289), remarks:

"Sanskrit and Zend share certain words and grammatical forms in common which do not exist in any other Aryan languages; and there can be no doubt that the ancestors of the poets of the Vedas and the worshippers of A*huro mazdao* lived together for some time after they had left the original home of the whole Aryan race."

Max Müller (p. 293) remarks: "Now *Airya* in Zend (like in Sanskrit) means venerable, and is at the same time the name of the people."[74] He (p. 292) remarks: "In India, as we saw, the name of Arya, as a national name."

'Gathas' (hymns of the Avesta) is a Sanskritic word, meaning stories. Both Hindus and Zoroastrians worship fire, and both wear sacred thread – *Janeoo* (Hindus) and *Kusti* (Zoroastrians). Hindus wear *Janeoo* hanging from the shoulder, and Zoroastrians wear *Kusti* around the waist. Zoroastrians, like Hindus, believe in 'after life.' Both Hindus and Zoroastrians, unlike Christians, sit on the floor to pray.

Avestan "Vohu Mana" means good mind. 'Mana', in Sanskrit, means mind. The Avestan 'Asha' (the spirit of truth) means 'hope' in Sanskrit.

History tells that in ancient times, Iran, like Afghanistan, was a part of India.[75] Iran was a land of Aryans.

Hinduism, Jainism, Buddhism and Sikhism

Jainism, Buddhism and Sikhism are offshoots of the Vedic religion (present Hinduism). All the four oriental religions – Hinduism, Jainism, Buddhism and Sikhism – have similar basic tenets, such as:

1. **Concept of rebirth and reincarnation**, that only the body ages and ultimately dies. Soul is always fresh, immortal and eternal. At death, it transmigrates into the body of a newly-born baby. It means life is a continuous

---

[74] Lassen, *Ind. Alt.* b. i. s. 6.
[75] Read the Chapter, "Iran: A Part of Ancient India."

unending eternal *Chakra* (wheel) – **birth** → **life** → **death**→ **birth**. Hinduism suggests, like life and time, marriage is eternal, and so religion is eternal. Hinduism is called "Sanatan Dharma. The word 'Sanatan' means eternal. When life is eternal, then why to cry over death? What a life-enriching optimism!

2. **Moksha / Nirvana,** meaning freedom from the *Chakra* of birth and death. All the four – Hindus, Jain, Buddhists and Sikhs – believe that Moksha / Nirvana can be realized by serious meditation and tedious *tapasya* (penance or penitence).

3. All the four believe in *ahimsa* (nonviolence) in varying degrees. Jainism believes in zero violence, to the extent that they do not eat root vegetables like potato and they cover their nose so that even insects are not hurt. Hinduism believes in *ahimsa*, but not that seriously as the Jain and Buddhists do. For example, according to the Bhagvad Gita, violence against cruel and violent people is nonviolence.

4. All the religions – oriental as well as occidental – have philosophy of spirituality. But Westerners, in general, are comparatively more materialistic and Easterners more spiritualistic. This is very much reflected by the higher material achievements in the West, particularly in Europe and America achieved by inhuman uncivilized colonization and slavery.

5. Hindus believe in divine unity – unity of God and man – meaning God is within self. There are no 'dos' or 'don'ts' in Hinduism. Conscience, meaning God within, dictates what is right and what is wrong. Lie for godly result is truth. For example, if wicked persons chasing a girl at the multiple crossing ask you "Which way did the girl go" your wrong answer would be truth.

All the four – Hindus, Jains, Buddhists and Sikhs cremate the dead.

TEN

Tagore: Hindu Concept of Education

"Our present system of education, however, does not allow us to cultivate them (thought and imagination). ... And unless we cultivate them in childhood we can not have them when we are grown up."

Tagore

The Nobel Laureate Rabindranath Tagore (1861-1941), in *'Towards Universal Man'* (1961, pp. 43-45), has said that thought and imagination are indispensable to make life meaningfully active and productive. Both can be better cultivated if early education is given in native language.

He explains why so. Our children learn foreign language (English) for their several beginning years. Most of the content of the texts, they study, is also foreign. It is of little use because it talks about the culture and history which are foreign and irrelevant to Indian life. The young students rigorously cram the content. Retention is stressful because there is little feeling with the content. Own language – Bengali, Hindi, or any other vernacular – is fluid, flowing like Ganga and Jamuna, with colorful flowers of our culture. Own language facilitates thinking, conceptualization' and expression of the ideas akin to our culture which is most dear to heart and fruitful for mind.

Tagore (p. 43) has vividly explained how early education in English would arrest child's thinking, imagination and expression:

"Our present system of education, however, does not allow us to cultivate them (thought and imagination). ... To learn the English language is difficult enough, but to familiarize ourselves with English thought and feeling is even more difficult, and takes a long time during which our thinking capacity remains inactive for lack of an outlet. ... To read without thinking is like accumulating building materials without building any thing."

Life: A great school

At college for B.A. (1948-1952), as a part of my English course, I had to read Shakespeare's play Othello. What was its use to me? Othello did not tell me any thing of my interest. Othello did not tell me any thing about my culture and heritage, I would have loved to know. Shakuntala, translated into English, I believe by Sir William Jones, would have been better. Moreover, English of Shakespeare (1564-1616) was difficult to understand, because it was not the same as the present English.

Tagore has helped in understanding the difference between early education in own native language and in foreign language. Native language facilitates thinking and conceptualization to promote literary creativity. My father Khushiram (1887-1967) had matriculation in Sindhi, which used be known as 'Sindhi final'. He was not considered 'educated' because he did not know English. Now, having read what Tagore has said about education, I feel my father was much more educated than I am, even with Ph.D. I could not know what he had known about our culture, heritage and history from the several books written in Sindhi. It was easy for him to understand because they were written in Sindhi. English did not connect me with myself, nor with my culture. My father knew about our culture, philosophy and religion much more than I know even now. He knew Gurmukhi, the script of Guru Granth Sahib. He used to read Guru Granth Sahib, and Sindhi translations of Sukhamani, Nanakprakash, Gita, Rāmāyanā, Mahābhāratā, etc.

The education, thus informally acquired, made my father understand the significance of respecting the individuality of others, even of his son. In Indian society, generally father tells his son: "My son, you have to listen to me what to do in this situation. I know better than you know." After M.A. in Social Work (MSW) in 1958, I worked as a welfare officer in Ahmedabad, close to my home town Baroda, for monthly salary of Rs. 325. A few months later, I received an offer of a teaching job (lecturer) at a graduate school of Social Work in Benaras, about 1000 miles from home town Baroda for a monthly salary of only Rs. 225. My father knew that I liked teaching. I had been a teacher in schools while I was going to college for my B.A., M.A. and M.S.W. It was monthly loss of about Rs. 100, too big in those times, and I had to maintain two homes, one at Baroda for elderly parents and my college-going younger brother. My father, when asked, happily said: "My son, you have to make the decision, you are capable to. You know your interest and plans for your future. You have to assume responsibility of your life. I should not." It is hard to believe that an Indian father would allow his son to change his job for that lower salary and be far away from home. But, as I see, my father had become much more educated and mature than an M.A. graduate, through his study of the books on Indian life, family and on parent-child relationship. I took the Benaras job. Fortunately, after a year, I was back to Baroda to teach at Baroda University for salary, even better than I was getting at Ahmedabad as a welfare officer. This teaching job helped me to get Fulbright scholarship and later Green Card and citizenship of America.

I am fully convinced that informal life education, despite English illiteracy, makes one adequately educated and mature to optimally take care of self and family. Life, equipped with adequate education in native language, is a great school.

Tagore (p.44) calls initial education in a foreign language 'joyless', because it is a burden of the load of foreign words:

"In our lives that auspicious moment is wasted in joyless education. From childhood to adolescence and again from adolescence to manhood, we are coolies of the goddess of learning, carrying loads of words on our folded backs."

I will call it a dry, meaningless, wasteful and inappropriate education, if it is given in a foreign language in early years of life when foundation of personality is laid. Tagore (p.44) explains why and how education in own language right from childhood helps in early maturity of the desired personality:

"It follows, therefore, that if I want my son to grow into a man, I should see that he grows up like a man right from childhood. Otherwise he will always remain a child."

Tagore was not against foreign language. He had enough of it. I hope I am right that he felt that education in English, the world's language, should be given after the foundation in native education is adequately solid to be able to meaningfully examine and understand the foreign cultural, literary and historical content. Then, sharing and comparison between the two cultures would become intelligible, mature and mutually respectful. Education in a foreign language during adulthood would be meaningful and more productive. Each language has its own culture and history. The adequate knowledge of own language and own culture facilitates understanding of foreign languages and foreign cultures. In my opinion, early education in foreign language may arrest acceptance of own culture.

The undue emphasis on English in metropolitan cities – Mumbai, Delhi, Kolkata, Chennai, Bangalore, etc. – has been hurting knowledge of Indian culture among new generation youngsters. They are becoming foreigners, not only in own country, but also in own family, creating undue distance between generations. English-medium schools have been mushrooming. There is nothing wrong in that if the texts have content related to Indian culture and history. The selection of texts should be in the hands of those Indians who have Indian heart for Indian culture.

Tagore (pp.203-204) explains this:

"As the secret pricking goes on, we in our fretfulness ascribe the cause of irritation to some outside intrusion. We say that the only thing wrong in our education is that it is not in our absolute control; that the boat is sea-worthy, only the helm has to be in our hands to save it from wreckage. Lately, most of our attempts to establish national schools and universities were made with the idea that it was external independence which was needed. We forget that the same weakness in our character or circumstances which inevitably draws us on the slippery slope of imitation, will pursue us when our independence is merely of the outside."

It is rightly said that imitation in education is dangerously slippery.

Are education and life one?

Education in native language enriches its speakers with the stories and legends about their culture and heritage which have significant connection with their lives and their inner self. Tagore (p.45) has explained how our education in foreign language has robbed us of all that our own language would have given:

"Since our education bears no relation to our life, the books we read paint no vivid pictures of our homes, extol no ideals of our society. The daily pursuits of our lives find no place in those pages, nor do we meet there any body or any thing we happily recognize as our friends and relatives, our sky and earth, our mornings and evenings, or our cornfields and rivers. Education and life can never become one in such circumstances, and are bound to remain separated by a barrier. Our education may be compared to rainfall on a spot that is a long way from our roots. Not enough moisture seeps through the intervening barrier of earth to quench our thirst."

Tagore is trying to draw our attention to: "Our education may be compared to rainfall on a spot that is a far way from our roots." Distance between the rainfall of education from the roots of .culture is useless and dangerous for the nation. What is the use of such education?

The essay in my mother-tongue Sindhi, I read in early years of my life, has left its impress on my mind and heart, too hard to forget. It encouraged me get education and give it to others.

Therefore I became teacher. The essay goes like this. Candidates for job of a teacher were being interviewed. The selection committee left a book on the floor between the entrance and the table in front of them. Several candidates ignored the book. One lady picked it, kissed it and left it on the table, before taking her seat. She was selected. She convinced the committee that she had respect for the knowledge, she was being hired to give to her students.

We should take serious note of what Tagore has suggested that education and life should become one, not away from our roots. It is also true that we should have the education which would irrigate and nourish our literary garden with flowers of languages rich in varied ethnic colors and fragrances. Therefore, education of English, the world's language, is also very important.

Languages enrich each other. Each language has its own culture, own history and own literature. Cultures and histories have wealth of knowledge which can raise the horizon of one's mind with insights into the problems related to various situations – individual, societal, national and international. Coexistence of various languages with the 'Give & Take' spirit would make a great contribution to the wealth of human wisdom for desirable peaceful life. A language in isolation would shrink like a barren land without rain.

Tagore (p.202) suggests that our education, schools and universities should strengthen the Indian mind to address India's problems in its own Indian way:

"INDIA HAS proved that it has its own mind, which has been deeply concerned to solve according to its light the problems of existence. India's aim in education is to enable this mind to fulfill its quest in its own individual way."

What a great thoughtful suggestion, Tagore (pp. 202-203) has given about the mission of the education. He suggests that the education can be fruitful only when it is in close contact with the complete Indian life, and the schools should have Indian heart:

Tagore: Hindu Concept of Education

"Further, our education should be in constant touch with our complete life, economic, intellectual, aesthetic, social, and spiritual; and our schools should be at the very heart of our society, connected with it by the living bonds of varied co-operation. For, true education is to realize at every step how our training and knowledge have an organic connection with our surroundings."

The value of education is gauged by its relevance to life. Tagore, after a brief stay at the law school in England, returned to India to pursue the career of his liking, as a poet, writer, philosopher, playwright and educator. Continuing his education at the law school would have been the most irreparable loss of his life.

Rabindranath Tagore[76] was born in Calcutta in a wealthy Brahmin (Thokur) family. After a brief stay in England (1878) to attempt to study law, he returned to India, and instead pursued a career as a writer, playwright, songwriter, poet, philosopher and educator. During the first 51 years of his life he achieved some success in Calcutta. This all suddenly changed in 1912. He then returned to England along with his son for the first time since his failed attempt at law school as a teenager. On the way over to England he began translating his latest selections of poems, Gitanjali, into English. Almost all of his work prior to that time had been written in Bengali. Upon arrival, his son left his father's brief case with this notebook in the London subway. Fortunately, an honest person turned in the briefcase. Tagore's one friend in England, a famous artist he had met in India, Rothenstein, learned of the translation, and asked to see it. Reluctantly, with much persuasion, Tagore let him have the notebook. The painter could not believe his eyes. The poems were incredible. He called his friend, W.B. Yeats, and finally talked Yeats into looking at the hand scrawled notebook.

The rest, as they say, is history. Yeats was enthralled. He later wrote the introduction to Gitanjali when it was published in September 1912 in a limited edition by the India Society in

---

[76] Google

London. Thereafter, both the poetry and the man were an instant sensation, first in London literary circles, and soon thereafter in the entire world. His spiritual presence was awesome. His words evoked great beauty. Nobody had ever read anything like it. A glimpse of the mysticism and sentimental beauty of Indian culture were revealed to the West for the first time. Less than a year later, in 1913, Rabindranath received the Nobel Prize for literature. He was the first non-westerner to be so honored. Overnight he was famous and began world lecture tours promoting inter-cultural harmony and understanding. In 1915 he was knighted by the British King George V. When not traveling he stayed at his family home outside of Calcutta, where he remained very active as a literary, spiritual and social-political force.

In 1919, following the Amritsar massacre of 400 Indian demonstrators by British troops, Sir Tagore renounced his Knighthood. Although a good friend of Mohandas Karamchand Gandhi, most of the time Tagore stayed out of politics. He was opposed to nationalism and militarism as a matter of principle, and instead promoted spiritual values and the creation of a new world culture founded in multi-culturalism, diversity and tolerance. He served as a spiritual and creative beacon to his countrymen, and indeed, the whole world. He used the funds from his writing and lecturing to expand upon the school he had founded in 1901 now known as Vishva Bharati. The alternative to the poor system of education imposed by the British, combined the best of traditional Hindu education with Western ideals. Tagore's multi-cultural educational efforts were an inspiration to many, including his friend, Count Hermann Keyserling of Estonia. Count Keyserling founded his own school in 1920 patterned upon Tagore's school, and the ancient universities which existed in Northern India under Buddhist rule over 2,000 years ago under the name School of Wisdom. Tagore led the opening program of the School of Wisdom in 1920, and participated in several of its programs thereafter.

Vedic Knowledge: Vast and borderless

Indian literature is a vast garden of flowers, varied in ethnic colors and fragrances. It would not be so if we don't know English and also some other languages, and their literature. More languages, better for knowledge which would be deep and wide. Knowledge is too vast, varied and borderless for any individual. The person, who claims to be extra-learned with ultimate knowledge, is too ignorant, even of the concept of knowledge and its breadth and depth. He is ignorant of his ignorance, like lamp can not see darkness under itself. Amazing, the knowledge, man has acquired during his millennia-long life, is not yet complete. Man still needs to sweat several millennia to know what human mind has in its store. It is delightful to know that God has created the ever-growing mind to fruitfully chase limitless knowledge which again encourages mind to create more knowledge; thus mutual non-stop chase between mind and knowledge: mind → knowledge → mind.

Several, more Gandhis, Nehrus, Tagores, Vivekanandas, Gargis, Buddhas, Nanaks, Eliots, Shakespeares, Thoreaus, etc. would not be enough to cover all the vast landscape of varied knowledge, even if..... they all sweat for millennia to come. There are more than 4,000 languages. Each language has its own literature with its own different knowledge, at least partially different from others. The human mind will continue to conceive much more, quite different and varied knowledge to meet the varied human needs of the changing times. Mind is too deep for the man to touch the bottom of his own mind. The man is revolving like the earth he is standing on.

Pain incites adventure

Adventure is the secret of human pains and pleasures. One values and enjoys pleasures more only when he understands and enjoys his pains. Again one can find real education in pains, as Gautam Buddha and several others have found. Pain is giver. Land of pains can never be barren. This is the secret of Hinduism and of its survival to justify its name "SANATAN", meaning ETERNAL.

135

ELEVEN

Inter-civilization Trade: Indus, Euphrates and Nile

"Who could have imagined that latitudes so northerly as the line of the Oxus and the northern Indus would have sent forth the inhabitants of their frozen domains to colonise the sultry clime of Egypt and Palestine! Yet so it was. These were the Indian tribes that, under the appellation of "SURYA"[77] or "the Sun," gave its enduring name to the vast province of "SURIA," now Syria. It is in Palestine that this martial race will be found settled in the greatest force."

E. Pococke, in 'India in Greece' (p.182)

Who could have thought that the natives of the Indus Valley (Sindhu-Sarasvati Valley) would have navigated to Mesopotamia (Iraq), Egypt, Syria, Palestine, Asia Minor (Turkey) region about 5000 years back?

V. Gordon Childe, in 'New Light on the Most Ancient East' (1928, p.186), writes about direct commercial trade the Indus Valley had with the Tigris-Euphrates, Mesopotamia:

"The best-dated imports in Mesopotamia, providing a *terminus ante quem* for the Harappa period, belong to the Sargonid age. Only a couple of 'seals' and stone vases imported into both areas from an intermediate centre

---

[77] Suryavanshi, an Indian warrior clan. Surya means sun.

illustrate trade connections in Early Dynastic times, before 2350 B.C. Other Indus 'seals' from a post-Akhadian context in Mesopotamia imply a persistence of the Harappa civilization down 2000 B.C."

Childe, in *'The Aryans'* (1926, p. 34), talks about the ancient inter-civilization contacts between India and Mesopotamia:

"Here we have for the first time positive evidence of intercourse between India and Western Asia before the first millennium – and these connections were evidently very ancient, presumably anterior to the general adoption of the cylinder seal in Mesopotamia about 2800 B.C."

Chester G. Starr, in *'A History of the Ancient World'* (1991, p.113), also writes about the ancient trade connection between Indus and the Mesopotamia civilizations:

"Indian stamp seals and Mesopotamia cylinder seals turned up in sites of other area. This trade endured from about 2500 into the second millennium."

He further writes about the difference between the quality of life in the two civilizations, better in the Indus Valley. He also identifies traces of the Vedic religion in the Indus Valley:

"Yet the Indus civilization was quite distinct. Its walls and buildings were erected in baked bricks, not the sun-dried bricks of Mesopotamia; drainage systems excelled those found anywhere else at this period. .. A male god, three-faced, flanked by animals, and seated in a yoga-like posture reminds one of the later god Siva."

Geoffrey Bibby, in *'Looking for Dilmun'* (1969:177), talks about two sorts of round seals found in Ur and Mohenjo-Daro – high-bossed type with bulls and Indus script from Mohenjo-Daro and low-bossed from Bahrain. He writes: "So the Indus civilization had been tentatively dated to the last three centuries of the third millennium B.C."

Bibby (p.174) cites Gadd's article *"Seals of Ancient Indian Style Found at Ur"* to show that there were trade connections between Mohenjo-daro and Mesopotamia. He further tells that the seals bore the figure of a bull which was surmounted by an inscription in the unknown language of the Indus Valley civilization.

Bibby (p. 221) talks about identifying the Makan and Meluhha of the Ur traders, whether their trade was with Africa or India:

"But it is difficult to fit in an African location to the text of the Ur tablets or to the facts of archeology. Distance alone was a factor, and though I had never been conservative in my estimation of the distances which trading vessels could cover. I could not ignore the fact that the sailing distance from Bahrain to Africa was twice that from Bahrain to India. Ivory and gold, which were products of Meluhha, could come equally from Africa and from India, but the carnelian of Meluhha could only come from Rajputana in India."

Rajputana is on the north-eastern border of Sindh and not far away from the river Sindhu (Indus). On pages 192-3, Bibby talks about ships loaded with cargoes of timber, ivory, lapis lazuli and carnelian beads from the cities of the Indus Valley civilization to Dilmun, Bahrain. He also talks about movement of foreign merchants and use of weights and measures in the Indus Valley civilization, Mesopotamia and Dilmun. On page 184, Bibby says that those cubes of polished flint used as weights were in common use only in the Indus Valley civilization. On page 341, Bibby writes: "Oppenheim's theory was that Dilmun's prosperity had depended on the transit trade of luxury goods from the Indus Valley civilization and copper from Makan."

Bibby (p.278) talks about the pottery – delicate thin vases with black-painted patterns of criss-crossed triangles and chains of semi-circles and zigzag bands – belonged to the range of wares found in Iran and Baluchistan, and designated generally as chalcolithic, ranging from the fourth to the second millennium B.C.

Bibby (pp. 279-280) seems to suggest that the cultures of Baluchistan and Kulli were racial antecedent of the Indus people. He writes :

"It was not the Kulli people who originated the Indus civilization, on the contrary, the Indus civilization in its period of greatest expansion reached out and colonized much of the territory held by the Kulli villagers."

Baluchistan was a significant part of the Sindhu (Indus) civilization, and so was Iran governed by Bharat in ancient times. Bibby talks about one vessel bore the painted figure of the Brahmin bull. He (p.278) seems to suggest their connection with the Sindhu (Indus) Valley civilization:

"Some of the pottery could give a closer dating. There were a couple of small cracker-barrel-shaped jars in grey, covered with bands of the black designs from shoulder to flat base, which even I could recognize as typical of the Kulli culture, while a shoulder-sherd of a larger red-brown vessel bore the painted figure of a humped bull, the Brahmin bull of India, which was equally typically Kulli. This needs explanation."

Dr. Poonai, in *'Origin of Civilization and Language'* (1994, pp. 157-8), has talked about such migrations from India in ancient times. He says that several Rig-Vedic Sanskrit-speaking Aryan clans emigrated westwards beyond the Aegean area. In the early part of the third millennium B.C., the states of Caria, Miletus, Lydia, Troy and Phrygia, and neighboring lands were already occupied by peoples who spoke Sanskritic dialects.

It is amazing to see the kind and size of the trade the Indus people had with the people of the Euphrates and Nile civilizations in ancient times. The present spread of global Indian trade seems to be the mirror of India's ancient inter-civilization trade. It has been on the increasing swift move to kiss the sky. Its further global movement is being custom-tailored in Delhi by American President Mr. Barack Obama and Indian Prime Minister Dr. Manmohan Singh (November, 2010).

V. Gordon Childe, in *'The Aryans: A Study of Indo-European Origins'* (1987, p.30), writes what happened to the Aryan (Mitanni) small kingdoms in Palestine:

> "In Palestine the Aryan names have totally disappeared by 1000 B.C., and even in the Mitanni region they have scarcely a vestige behind them. Here at least Aryan speech succumbed to Semitic and Asianic dialects, and small Aryan aristocracies were absorbed by the native population."

This clearly suggests that Aryans, known as Mitanni, were there who had established their aristocracies which succumbed to Semitic and other Asianic powers. Some or most got absorbed among the native people, and the rest might have left for India, the home of their ancestors. They, being warriors, might have traveled to India in armored horse-driven chariots. They might have been mistaken as invaders and must have faced some military confrontation from the then natives of India.

Childe writes on the same page that the Mitanni documents suggest that they were written in the language very close to the Indian, as reflected by the remote hymns of the *Rig Veda*:

> "The Indians' language approximates most closely to that of the Mitanni documents and has been preserved from a remote date in the hymns of the Rig Veda. This priceless document also furnishes precious historical data."

This clearly suggests two things:

1. Mitanni were Aryans (Hindus), and
2. The Rig Veda had history.

141

Childes (pp.16-34) talks about the Aryan dynasts in Mesopotamia, Babylonia, Egypt, and its near regions, as early as fourth millennium:

"Aryan peoples first emerge from the gloom of prehistory in the northern borders of the Fertile Crescent of the Ancient East. The oldest Aryan names and words that have come down to us are inscribed upon cuneiform tablets from Babylonia, Egypt, and Cappadocia. But these first historic Aryans appear as late intruders in a region illumined by the light of written documents from the end of the 4th millennium. In Mesopotamia and the adjoining countries they have invaded the domain hitherto occupied by peoples of different antecedents."

Childe's statement, "But these first historic Aryans appear as late intruders in a region ... In Mesopotamia and the adjoining countries they have invaded the domain," clearly suggests that those Aryans were not the natives of the Mesopotamia region, they were invaders. Childe doesn't tell from where those Aryans came. Childe himself, Max Müller and several scholars have said that *Aryavarta* (India, Bharat) is the cradle of the Aryans.

Childe, in *"The Aryans"* (1926, p. 17), writes: "But by the middle of the 2nd millennium we find Aryan princes installed within the Fertile Crescent, heirs of the civilization created by Sumerian and Semite."

Childe (p. 18) further writes:

"The precursors of the Aryan invaders may be found among the Kassites, who established a dynasty at Babylon about 1760 B.C. ... Moreover, the majority of the personal names of the period collected by Clay[78] suggest rather a kinship between the Kassites and the Asianic folk to the north-west. Yet in the names of their kings occur elements recalling Indo-Iranian deities – Surias (Sun-god

---

[78] Yale Oriental Series,1.

cf. Sans. *Surya*), Indas (cf.Sans. *Indra*), Maruttas (cf. Sans. Marutah, storm-god)."

Childe (p.18) talks about horse-driven chariots introduced by Kassites and Aryan princes:

"Moreover, these Kassites introduced the use of the horse for drawing chariots into the Ancient East and its later Babylonian name *susu* seems to be derived from the Indo-Iranian form *asua* (in Sanskrit, A*sva*, means horse). It is then highly probable that the Kassite's invasion was due to the pressure of Aryan tribes on the high lands of Iran, and that its leaders were actually Aryan princes."

Horse-driven chariots were used in the Mahābhāratā war which happened in 3067 B.C.[79], long before Kassite presence in Babylon. As a matter of fact, Kassites were Vedic (Hindu) *Kshtries* (warrior tribe) from India and Iran. In that remote period, Iran was a part of India, as reflected by very close linguistic correspondence between Sanskrit and Avestan, and also similarities in religious philosophy, deities, and rituals, for example worship of fire.

Mitanni Aryan dynasty ruling in Mesopotamia

In fact, all the three – Mitanni, Kassite and Hittite – were Indo-Aryans. They were *Kshatries* (warriors) of Bharat who had gone out and had established their kingdoms in Asia Minor and Mesopotamia region. Ironically, though from India, they had fights as indicated by their peace treaty of 1350 BC at Boghazkoi or Boghas Keui, Western Asia, which was the capital of Hittites. In the treaty, Vedic (Hindu) gods were invoked as witnesses, because both the parties were Hindus. History tells about fights even between brothers. The Mahābhāratā war was between two first cousins, the *Pandawas* and the *Kaurwas*.

---

[79] Kosla Vepa, "Astronomical Dating of Events & Select Vignettes from Indian History" (2008, P. 37).

Childe (p.18) writes that the diplomatic archives, found at 'Tell el-Amarna', tell that a distinctively Mitanni Aryan dynasty had its kingdom on the Upper Euphrates. Their princes had Aryan names, Sutarna, Dusratta, and Artatama, who worshipped Indo-Iranian (better specific terms 'Vedic' or 'Hindu', instead of 'Indo-Iranian') deities, because the four gods – Indra, Varuna, Mitra, and the Nasatya, invoked as witnesses in the treaty – were Vedic gods. The treaty was also signed by two Vedic kings.

Childe (pp.18-19) talks about an other document which recently turned up among the Hittites archives from Boghas Keui, significantly dealing with horse-breeding which contains a series of Aryan (Sanskrit) numbers – a*aika* (1), *teras* (3), *panza* (5), *satta* (7), and *nav* (9). Childe (p.19) also mentions that there existed among the Mitanni, a class of warriors *'Marianna'* which compares with the Sanskrit *'marya'*, meaning young heroes.

All whatever has been said above about the Aryan dynasts – Kassites established their kingdoms in Babylon in about 1760 B.C., and Mitanni in Mesopotamia and its adjoining regions – makes clear beyond any doubt that they were Sanskrit-knowing Aryans who worshipped Vedic deities whose names appear in the *Rig Veda*. It is clear that Sanskrit knowing Vedic Aryans were there before 1760 B.C., may be even as early as the end of 4th millennium B.C. They were not the natives of those regions, they were intruders or traders,

I fully agree that in ancient times, as early as 2500-3500 B.C., when the Indus Valley civilization was flourishing, adventurous and enterprising Aryans had gone out from India to so many regions of the world for trade. They had established their Vedic/Hindu kingdoms. They didn't move out from S. Russia and Turkistan as suggested above by the Columbia Encyclopedia. Neither S. Russia nor Turkistan had Aryans as their natives any time. On the contrary, the migratory Sanskrit-speaking Aryans had gone to S. Russia and Turkistan from India.

Childe, in the Chapter VIII *'The Aryans in the South Russia'* of his book 'The Aryans' (1926, pp. 183-206), has given several evidences – correspondence between things of the South Russia and the Aryans, such as armory, wheeled vehicles, clay model of wagon, burial rites, etc – to prove that Aryans were in South

Russia. I agree that Aryans were there, but it would be wrong to say that the Aryans were the natives of South Russia. They initially went there as traders. Later they established their kingdom. It seems the Europeans, particularly the British, learned from the ancient history of the Aryans to first sneak in as traders to pave the way to their kingdom.

The Aryans were there until about 1500 B.C. when they were overpowered by some other forces. Most of them stayed there and eventually got absorbed. Some of them attempted to return to India, the country of their ancestors. They, being from warrior royal families traveled in armored horse-driven chariots. They were mistaken as invaders and thus met some violent military confrontation.

S. R. Rao tells what Sir Mortimer Wheeler has said about the Harappan civilization:

"He (Wheeler) was of the view that the unchallenged integrity of the Harappans was responsible for its isolation and consequent failure to make any permanent contribution to the History of Civilization. But it will be presently seen that as a maritime power the Harappans developed brisk overseas trade and established merchant colonies in Bahrain, Failaka and the Euphrates-Tigris Valley."

Maritime trading links with Mesopotamia

Andrew Robinson, in *'Lost Languages'* (2002, p. 266), writes:

"It (Indus Valley civilization) had regular maritime trading links with the Persian Gulf and Mesopotamia, where Indus seals have been discovered." Indus traders had reached Mesopotamia by sea too. They knew ship-building technology. They had productive sea-faring trading connections with Egypt and several middle-east countries, particularly Bahrain."

Indus Valley: Inter-civilization trade-related technologies

E. Pococke (p.44) praises Hindus for their navigation capabilities in ancient times, as early as Indus Civilization:

> "The distance of the Nile from the Indian shores forms no objection to the surmise: the sail that spread for Ceylon could waft for the Red Sea, which the fleets of Tyre, of Soloman, and of Hiram covered about this time. That the Hindoos navigated the ocean from the earliest ages, the traces of their religion in the isles of the Archipelago sufficiently attest. That the people of the country of the Indus ranked as navigators, in the most venerable antiquity, is perfectively clear, from the ancient Institutes of Menu, where "merchants who traffic beyond sea, and bring presents to the king," are expressly mentioned. ... These Institutes of Menu, running up to the vast antiquity of B.C. 1400, give an idea of the early commercial energies of India; which all my subsequent observations will fully carry out."

In footnote, Pococke writes that according to the translator of Heeren, ships belonging to Hindoos went to sea; but it needs to be ascertained. History has been so much mutilated that most students of history have no way to know these facts, because their history professors do not have. But it has been archeologically established that there was trade between the two – Indus and Nile – civilizations in ancient times, as evidenced by objects of Egypt have been excavated in the Indus Valley and Indian in the Nile Valley.

Ship-building Technology in the Indus Valley Civilization

Dr. Poonai (1994: 48-49) cites the following Rig Veda hymn (10-63-10) which confirms that the Vedic Aryans had the technology of ship-building which helped them in their long westward travel for trade with Egypt, Mesopotamia and Bahrain:

146

Inter-civilization Trade: Indus, Euphrates and Nile

"Daiveem naavam svaritraaman aagasamasravantee maa ruhema svastaye" (It means "May we embark upon the good ship of peace and happiness, may it be swift, without defects and without leaks.)

Poonai (1994: 61-68) talks about early emigrations by the Rig Vedic Aryans from Mohenjo-daro and Harappa to various principal sites, such as Iran, Sumer, Mesopotamia, Anatolia, Egypt, Southeast Asia, Phoenicia, the Turanian plains and neighboring lands. Poonai (p.156) has said:

"The different clans established different city states, such as Assyria (Asura Aryan clan), Aggad/Akhad (Aggar), Elam (Eyam/Ayam), Medes (Madai/Medes), Parthia and Persia (Purusham Aryanam), Hittite states (Kshattri), Phoenicia (Nasatya), Kassite territory (Khasi), Mittani (Mitraani), and Babylon (Bhupalan)."

Regarding the dialects of these Aryan clans, Poonai has remarked that into each of the above territories and others like them, the Rig Vedic Aryan clans carried their own versions of *Prakrit*. Both the phonetic values and the symbols underwent modifications peculiar to each state, but the rules governing the use of language survived without major changes. There was no separation of vowels and consonants in any of the alphabets or syllables except in the case of Rome and Greece. In the latter two states (Mittani and Babylon), the rules of grammar also conformed more closely to the rules governing the Rig Vedic Sanskrit.

The hieroglyphic dialect of the Hittites, as observed by Poonai (p.102), is related to the Rig Vedic clan of Lohians / Luvians (in Sindhi and Hindi *lohars*, meaning blacksmiths). It was used by Arzawa, the most powerful of the western states of Anatolia. The cuneiform dialect was used for international communication with governments of other territories. The Hurrian clan of the Rig Vedic Aryans plied the trade routes from southern Mesopotamia across Assyria and Cilicia through the Konya plains to the north-western and the western parts of Anatolia and they gave Sanskritic names to some places and persons, such as *Purushananda* and *Kumani.* Names of other places *Ahhiyawa, Millawanda, Mira, Luka* and

147

Haripala were derived from the Sanskrit words *Aham-yah-wah, Mila-varna, Mira, Loka* and *Haripala* respectively. Some other states bear Sanskrit-related names, such as *Khushala, Tum-Mana, Kassiya, Pala, Kuldeep* and *Narak.*

Poonai (p.190) has talked about certain inscriptions found in the ruins of an ancient fortress 'Karatepe' built in about 680 B.C. by a Rig Vedic Aryan ruler, who bore an obviously Sanskrit name, *Asitavan Das.* This discovery was based on the decipherment of the Hittite hieroglyphic by an American scholar Dr. Gelb (1930). The results of the decipherment were confirmed on the basis of further archaeological records.

Poonai has pointed to another strong evidence of the influence of the Sanskritic dialects in the region. An archaeologist found *'deepam',* a unique item of pottery, a lamp with a wick which burns oil. It is known as 'deep' in Hindi and some other Indian regional dialects. In Sindhi, it is called *'deep'* or *'diyo'.* In Sanskrit the word *'deepam'* means lamp. The name of the Hindu festival "Divali' comes from this. *Divas / deeps/ deepams* are lighted on the occasion of. Divali, the 'festival of lights'. The 'deepam' must have been taken to the Middle Eastern region by Indo-Aryans in remote ancient times.

Sir William Jones, in his Fourth Anniversary discourse, delivered on February 15, 1787, talks about India's commercial connections with Arabia, particularly Yemen:

"... yet, as the *Hindus* and the people of *Yemen* were both commercial nations in a very early age." He told that Hindus traded with the western world "gold, ivory, and perfumes of India, as well as the fragrant wood, called *alluwwa* in *Arabic* and *aguru* in *Sanskrit,* which grows in the greatest perfection in *Anam* or *Cochinchina.* "

Trade Indus had with Euphrates, Nile and other civilizations

Will Durant (1935, p. 395) talks about inter-civilization connections the people of the Indus (Sindhu) Valley made with other civilizations:

"The indications are that Mohenjo-daro was at its height when Cheops built the first great pyramid; that it had commercial, religious and artistic connections with Sumeria and Babylonia."

In footnote Durant explains that according to Coomaraswamy in Britannica Encyclopedia (xii, 2ii-12): "These connections are suggested by similar seals at Mohenjo-daro and in Sumeria (especially at Kish), and by the appearance of the Naga, or hooded serpent, among the early Mesopotamian seals." Durant, in footnote (p.395), also has mentioned:

"In 1932, Dr. Henry Frankfort unearthed, in the ruins of a Babylonian-Elamite village at the modern Tell-Asmar (near Baghdad), pottery, seals and beads which in his judgment (Sir John Marshall concurring), were imported from Mohenjo-daro ca. 2000 B.C."

It is historically established beyond any doubt,

1. that the Indus Valley (Mohenjo-daro and Harappa) had very active and productive commercial intercourse with the north-west Euphrates (Mesopotamia) and Nile (Egypt) civilizations in remote ancient times,
2. that the Indus (Sindhu-Sarasvati) valley people had navigation and shipbuilding technology,
3. that *Suryavanshi* Aryans colonized Egypt, Palestine, and "SURYA" (the Sun), present known as Syria, and
4. that the writing – on the archeologically excavated seals and tablets at Mohenjo-daro and Harappa – indicates that the Indus valley people were literate.

Aryan contribution to the civilizations of Russia and Europe

Childe, in the Chapter 'Role of the Aryans in History' of his book 'The Aryans' (1926, pp. 210-212), has written:

1. "And besides the megalithic tombs were other graves covering the remains of a people – who, whether they were come from South Russia or represented a section of the pre-dolmenic population – were, we believe, Aryan in character." Childe further observes that the interaction of the two types of civilization (Russian and Aryan) was the mainspring of a rapid progress. Western and eastern ideas were blended to a European progressive society.

2. "The gulf between French and Scandinavian culture at the beginning of the 2nd millennium is enormous. The superiority of the former is the measure of the contribution made by the Aryan element to European civilization."

3. "Thus the Aryans do appear everywhere as promoters of true progress and in Europe their expansion marks the moment when the prehistory of our continent (Europe) begins to diverge from that of Africa or the Pacific."

4. "Aryan genius found its true expression in Greece and Rome."

5. The lasting gift bequeathed by the Aryans to the conquered people was neither a higher material culture nor a superior physique, but a more excellent language and the mentality it generated.

In the First Chapter 'Language and Prehistory', Childe emphasizes the significance of spiritual unity, and the concept of Divine Law or Cosmic Order in Aryan culture which was bequeathed to Europeans through their language (I believe Sanskrit) which has ability of abstract thinking. Spirituality, the gem of the Aryan (Vedic or Hindu/Buddhist/Sikh) culture, is too complex for most European thinkers. This was the reason why the scientist Albert Einstein wrote to Nehru that the first part of his book 'Discovery of India' was not easy reading for a Westerner.

Aryan, the Jewel of the White Race

William L. Shirer, in his *'The Rise and Fall of the Third Reich'* (1959, pp. 103-104), talks about Count Joseph Arthur de

Gobineau, who believed that the key to history and civilization was race and the Aryan was the jewel of the White race. He claimed: "The jewel of the white race was the Aryan, this illustrious human family, the noblest among the white race." The Encyclopedia Americana (2003, vol. 2, p.426) writes the same for Gobineau.

The Europeans are craving to be known as Aryans. In fact, they are not. Only Vedic people (present Hindus) are Aryans. How could Gobineau say that the White is the superior race, when he himself says that the 'Aryan' is the jewel of the White race, and that the Aryan is the "noblest among the White race?

Historically, it has been established that Aryans are from Aryavarta (India). I, as an Aryan, will be happy if Germans (or Europeans) call themselves 'Aryans', but I will not like if Gobineau claims that the Aryans are not originally from *Aryavarta*. He seems to believe that the origin of the Aryans is traced back to Asia, not to Europe, the principal abode of the White Europeans. Then, in no way, White European can be original Aryans. It would have been accurate if he had said that the origin of the Aryans is traced back to India, instead of Asia, though India is a part of Asia.

It is hard to understand why European scholars hesitate to give credit for the greatness in the Aryan race to India, legitimately belongs to. How and why does Gobineau think that the origin of the Aryan race be traced to Central Asia, not to India?

It would be a dirty sinful blot on a civilized race to justify persecution of the members of another race. Each and every race has its birth right to believe whatever, it thinks, is right. It is not right to consider any other race to be inferior, and hate it because it is different. I, being an Aryan (Hindu), would not like Aryan association with any race which feels itself superior. It is OK if it calls itself 'a great civilized race.' Civilized people should not feel ashamed of admitting learning from any other race, but not stealing the race of some other ethnic society.

TWELVE

Colonies India Established

"Of the cursory observation on the Hindus, which it would require volumes to expand and illustrate, this is the result: that they had an immemorial affinity with the old Persians, Ethiopians, Egyptians, the Phoenicians, Greeks, Tuscans the Scythians or Goths, and Celts, the Chinese, Japanese, and Peruvians."

Sir William Jones (AR vol.1, p. 426)

All this, what Jones has said about Hindus and ancient India, is not given in most history books. Nehru (1946, p.20) explains why. He complains that history is dominated by Europe, and thus the history of ancient India has been given little attention to leave the pages for the history of modern Europe:

"Most westerners still imagine that ancient history is largely concerned with the Mediterranean countries, and medieval, and modern history is dominated by the quarrelsome little Europe. And still they make plans for the future as if Europe only counted and the rest could be fitted in any where. The history that men and women from India made far from their homeland has still to be written."

153

E. Pococke, in *'India in Greece'* (p.47), talks about colonization of Persia, Colchis, Armenia, and Egypt by India (Hindus):

"The ancient map of Persia, Colchis, and Armenia, is absolutely full of the most distinct and starling evidences of Indian colonisation and what is more astonishing, practically evinces, in the most powerful manner, the truth of several main points in the two great Indian poems, the Ramayana and Mahabharata. The whole map is positively nothing less than a journal of emigration on the most gigantic scale. ... I have glanced at the Indian settlements in Egypt."

Tagore, in *'Towards Universal Man'* (1961, p. 64), has said:

"India has never coveted new territory or scrambled for the spoils of trade. China, Japan and Tibet, who are today so anxious to close their doors and windows against the advances of Europe, cordially welcomed India into their homes as a spiritual guide. India has never sent out her forces for plunder and pillage, but only to carry out messages of peace and goodwill. The glory she won was the fruit of asceticism and that is greater than the majesty of kingship."

Hu Shih, a former Chinese ambassador to USA, has said that India conquered and dominated China culturally for 20 centuries without ever having to send a single soldier across her border.

Gandhi: Modern v/s ancient civilization

Mahatma Mohandas Karamchand Gandhi (1869-1948), comparing modern civilization with ancient civilizations, remarks:

"Modern civilization represents forces of evil and darkness; whereas the ancient civilization, i.e. Indian civilization, represents, in its essence, the Divine force. Many of us believe, and I am one of them, that through our civilization we have a message to deliver to the world."

It seems, Gandhiji considers present Indian civilization as "ancient", and perhaps European civilization as "modern." Gandhiji believes *'Old is gold.'* He explains why Bharat has continued to remain as she was well balanced in her great past:

"We are children of an ancient nation. We have witnessed the burial of civilizations – those of Rome, Greece and Egypt. Our civilization abides even, as the ocean in spite of its ebbs and flows."

Gandhiji has given a helpful prescription to keep the culture enriching itself:

"I don't want my house be walled on all sides and that my windows are blinded. I want all cultures of all countries to come into my house. But I refuse to be wiped away by any culture what-so-ever."

Mahatma Gandhi

Incorporation of good values from other cultures without denting own basic culture helps growth. Closing windows on the outside cultures arrests culture's growth. No culture is perfect and ultimate. Conservatism is inimical for mental hygiene of the society. Open windows to other cultures have enriched Indian culture and it continues to mature to adequately and appropriately meet the demands of the changing times.

Later in this book, the colonies, Hindus had established in their glorious past, are discussed. I know I will not be able to identify all because their history has been distorted, rather mutilated beyond recognition.

Dr. Avul Pakir Jainulabdeen Abdul Kalam (born on Oct. 15, 1931), the father of India's missiles program, has awakened India from its rather long slumber intoxicated by their saintliness. After India conducted its nuclear tests in 1998 under his supervision, Dr. Kalam was quoted as saying:

155

"Unless India stands up to the world, no one will respect us. In this world, fear has no place. ... Only strength respects strength."

THIRTEEN

Ahimsa: Loss of Worldwide Colonies

"At one time India had a place on top of the world; there was no limit to her spiritual daring in the fields of religion, philosophy and science and her forces spread far, annexing new domains. The preceptor's seat India had thus won is now lost; now she must stand as a disciple. The reason is that fear has entered into her soul. Panic made us forbid voyaging on the high seas – whether of water or of knowledge. We belonged to the universe but relegated to the parish".

Nobel Laureate Rabindranath Tagore

Panic came from India's about eight hundred year bondage by Muslims and Great Britain. I believe, strong Hindus got overpowered because of their misconceived Ahimsa, they religiously adored. Dr. A. P. J. Abdul Kalam said: "Fear has no place. Only strength respects strength."

Sword is necessary in this jungle of violent human animals. It has been easy to control ferocious animals – marine as well as earthly – but very difficult to tame the animals in human attire.

Dr. Abdul Kalam (born on Oct. 15, 1931), the father of India's missiles program, former President of India, has awakened India from its rather long slumber intoxicated by their saintliness, blind worshippers of ahimsa. According to Gita, killing killers is nonviolence (*ahimsa*). After India conducted its nuclear tests in 1998 under his supervision, Dr. Kalam rightly asserted:

"Unless India stands up to the world, no one will respect us. In this world, fear has no place. ... Only strength respects strength."

INDIA is REBORN

After the international diplomatic fury against India's "nuclear alleged misbehavior" (as perceived by the hypocritical nuclear powers) abated, India (Bharat) has been increasingly perceived as an emerging world power. It seems to confirm the 'Vedic doctrine of rebirth'. Ancient Bharat is reborn. Her soul did not die.

Ignoring irritants from neighboring adversaries, India has been quietly working diligently in all fields – education, astronautics, internet, space, shipbuilding, defense, nuclear technology, and what not – with her unshakable assured determination to globally establish self as the top world power, as she was in her previous life. Developed nations are seeking her friendship on mutually acceptable terms.

Dr. Abdul Kalam's proclamation – "Only strength respects strength" – has been firmly affirmed in Delhi. He gave to Bharat the missiles. Bharat, in return, appropriately adorned him with the highest civilian award 'Bharat Ratan'. He was nominated as the eleventh President of the Republic of Bharat (2002-07).

Sir William Jones (AR, vol.1, p. 426) talks about the spread of Hindus all over and their affinity with several peoples:

"Of the cursory observation on the Hindus, which it would require volumes to expand and illustrate, this is the result: that they had an immemorial affinity with the old Persians, Ethiopians, Egyptians, the Phoenicians, Greeks, Tuscans the Scythians or Goths, and Celts, the Chinese, Japanese, and Peruvians."

Unfortunately Hindus lost their colonies due to their misconceived *Ahimsa*. Hindus believe *'Ahimsa-Paramo-Dharma'*, meaning *Ahimsa* (nonviolence) is the greatest Dharma. But its universal application in all situations – irrespective of the intension of the enemy and the result – can be suicidal. It became fatally suicidal resulting in loss of not only all colonies, but also own home too. Very sorry to say, I have started hating the sacred and divine *Ahimsa*. I very much hate inappropriate use of *himsa* (violence). I prefer first to give threat of violence which may avert violent attack by enemy. It seems Hindus failed to understand how *Himsa*, in some situations would be necessary to control evil people from hurting innocent people. In some unavoidable situations, *Himsa* (violence) becomes *Ahimsa* in its real sense. No society, from its immemorial inception, has been without violent people, and without external enemies. If there were no evil persons and no belligerent peoples, Rāmāayanā and Mahābhārtā would not have happened in remote ancient times, and in modern times, several civilized nations would not have piled nuclear bombs, though they can be suicidal, as it recently happened in peace-loving Japan. Sorry for being pessimistic. I wish recent Japan's earth quake and tsunami would civilize present hypocritical nuclear powers.

Are we civilized? Has science been civilized?

When looking at present civilizations, it has been hard to understand the meaning of civilization. It is also difficult to worship 'science' as a constructive civilized goddess, when we see its violent deadly products. As a matter of fact, it is neither the fault of the science nor of its products. Fault lies with the man who has lost his divine mission. He has been misusing rather abusing their desirable uses. Mother Earth (*Dharti Mātā*) will be peaceful to live on, only when the man would be at peace with self. Then only he can be at peace with mankind. Shamelessly, weaponry and nuclear energy have become a significant source of the livelihood of some great the so-called civilized nations. For their comfortable survival, they have to make other nations fight or feel threatened, so as to feel dire need for arms and nuclear protection.

Following questions will remain as questions, until man knows self and remains at peace with self:

1. "Does the man want to be peaceful?
2. "Is the man happy to see happy people around?"

3. Why is man against himself?

Mahatma Gandhi (1869-1948), comparing modern civilization with ancient civilizations, remarks:

> "Modern civilization represents forces of evil and darkness; whereas the ancient civilization, i.e. Indian civilization, represents, in its essence, the Divine force. Many of us believe, and I am one of them, that through our civilization we have a message to deliver to the world."

It seems, Gandhiji considers present Indian civilization as "ancient", and perhaps European civilization as "modern." Gandhiji believes *'Old is gold.'* He explains why Bharat has continued to remain as she was well balanced in her great past:

> "We are children of an ancient nation. We have witnessed the burial of civilizations – those of Rome, Greece and Egypt. Our civilization abides even, as the ocean in spite of its ebbs and flows."

To be honest, it is difficult to understand Gandhiji's perspectives on present Indian society. He feels proud of it, but wishes improvement. He has given a helpful prescription to keep the culture enriching itself:

> "I don't want my house be walled on all sides and that my windows are blinded. I want all cultures of all countries to come into my house. But I refuse to be wiped away by any culture what-so-ever."

Incorporation of good values from other cultures without denting own basic culture is a great vitamin to strengthen and enrich own culture. Closing windows on the outside cultures arrests own culture's growth. No culture is perfect and ultimate. Conservatism is inimical for mental hygiene of the society. Open windows to other cultures would let their fragrance in, to enrich our culture. It will continue to mature to adequately and appropriately meet the challenging demands of the changing times.

In most situations, man's ego is critically sandwiched between his superego and id. Man's capability to adequately and appropriately meet the challenges of the time depends on the strength of his ego how it can balance his superego and id. Yudhisthra, because of his superego, put his own brave *Pandava* clan in great trouble. His younger brother Arjuna – a man of balanced strong ego, of course under the guided supervision of Lord Krishna on *Kurukshetra* (Mahābhāratā battle ground) – defeated their evil cousins (*Kauravas*), who were madly driven by their id. On the *Kurukshetra,* Lord Krishna gave Arjuna the Gita *gyan* (knowledge) to enlighten his ego, which was gravely confused and entangled by the conflict whether it would be right to kill his evil cousins, uncles and grand uncles, as required by his divine mission to protect good people. Arjuna was being disintegrated by his kin-*moha* (attachment). Gita suggests that *moha* disables ego. Gita is all the discourse between Krishna and Arjuna while on the battle field *Kurukshetr*. It is amazing that Lord Krishna had the knowledge of psychology and psychoanalysis in remote ancient times over five thousand years back. The modern Freudian psychoanalysis seems to have its origin in or similarity to Krishna's.

Some feel that Gandhiji, because of his superego (mahātmāpan), was not a suitable politician to effectively deal with Bharat's belligerent border enemies. Politics and saintliness (mahātmāpan) can, rather should not coexist. Gandhi was a great Mahātmā. Because of his *mahātmāpan* (saintliness), he may not be able to distinguish self from enemy. He may feel being generous to enemies rather than getting back from them what they have stolen. Super ego is of little utility for a nation when dealing with belligerent enemies, more so on the borders.

Mahātmās (saints) believe in *ahimsa* (nonviolence), as ultimate solution in all situations. It is a wishful thinking. Hindus believe in *Ahimsa paramodharma*. It doesn't mean that violence should never be used. Violence should be used only after all the means and ways have been exhausted. Country needs strength to respectfully survive. Hindu (Aryan) society, from its ancient times, has experienced lot of defeats, mostly, in my opinion, because of its aversion to use sword even when its use becomes necessary.

It is great that Bharat did not financially exploit, nor did culturally abuse their colonies as Britain and some other European powers did. Indians gave them enviable culture and civilization.

FOURTEEN

India in Central Asia

"It is a fascinating chapter in history, though we can study it only in the fine Greek-modeled coins of these rulers and in those sculptures of Graeco-Buddhist art which the ruined Buddhist shrines of the Swat and Peshawar valleys have preserved for us. Then when the great Indo-Scythian empire of the Kushan dynasty had replaced the small Hellenistic chiefships on both sides of Hindukush and had further extended its sway beyond the Indus, it was from the north-western borderland that fervent religious propaganda carried the Buddha's doctrine, together with Graeco-Buddhist art and Indian (Hindu)[80] literary culture, into Central Asia and thence into China. This spread of Buddhism right across Asia may well be considered India's greatest contribution to the civilization of mankind in general."

Aurel Stein[81]

Aurel Stein (1862-1943), a Hungarian archaeologist, who spent much of his life in the service of the British Empire in India,

---

[80]The word 'Indian', in fact implies 'Hindu', and the 'Indian contribution' implies contribution of Hinduism and Buddhism.

[81] Aurel Stein (1862-1943), in his book *'On Alexander's Track to the Indus'* (2001, preface, p. xi), writes about the presence of Buddhists and Indian (Hindu) literary culture in Central Asia.

163

conducted a series of important Central Asian expeditions in the early years of the 20th century. He carried out explorations over the greater part of innermost Asia, and along the whole of those north-western borderlands of India.

Kulke and Rothermund, in '*A History of India'* (1986, p.152), write that the transmission of Indian (Hindu & Buddhist) culture to distant parts of Central Asia, China, Japan, and Southeast Asia without military conquest is certainly one of the greatest achievements of Indian history or even the history of mankind.

Stan/istan countries in Central Asia

Most countries in Central Asia – particularly those with their names ending with 'stan' or 'istan', such as Baluchistan, Afghanistan, Tadzhistan (Tajikistan), Turkmenistan, Turkistan or Turkestan, Kyrgyzstan, Uzbekistan, Kazakhstan, etc.. – could be part of Greater India in her ancient times. '*Sthan/stan*' is a Sanskrit word, meaning 'place'. According to *The Practical Sanskrit-English Dictionary*, by Vaman Shivram Apte (1992, p.1007), '*sthanam*' means "A state, place, spot, site, locality, station, position, etc." Some say that "istan" is a Persian/Iranian word. It is possible. Both Sanskrit and Avestan may have the same or similar word for land. It is known that ancient Sanskrit and ancient Avestan were linguistically very close to each other. History tells that in ancient times Iran was culturally and administratively part of India. For more particulars, please read the Chapter, 'Iran: A Part of Ancient India'.

History needs to ascertain if all these countries with suffix 'stan' or 'istan', like Pakistan, were once part of Bharat (India) or not. Aurel Stein has talked about literary culture into Central Asia.

The question arises: "What were the original names of these countries before they were re-named by their occupiers / invaders? The most recent example of Pakistan will explain it. Prior to the partition of India in 1947, Pakistan, Baluchistan and Vaziristan were part of Bharat (India). In the Chapter 'Afghanistan: A Part of Ancient India' it is shown with irrefutable documented historical evidences that Afghanistan was governed by Hindus and Buddhists before it was occupied by Afghans. All these 'istan' countries (refer to the map on the following page) are in the northwest of India, sharing border with India. When drawing a line around them, beginning at Kazakhstan in the extreme northwest and ending at Pakistan, including Iran, they make a block connecting with India. It suggests that all these, or most Central Asian 'istan' countries, like Pakistan, might be part of the ancient India. The alleged invading Aryans are said to be from Central Asia. In fact, they were Indo-Aryans – Vedic people or Hindus – originally from the extended India of those times. When in trouble, Hindus (Aryans) in those countries, like Hindus in Pakistan, migrated to the mainland India and several of them stayed there and got culturally absorbed.

Istan countries, as part of Greater India

History of the movement of ancient Aryans – 'India→ Central Asia→ India' – has been misinterpreted as 'Central Asia→ India' to validate the ill-founded theory *'Aryan Invasion of India'.*

The north-west of India has always been vulnerable to foreign invasions. The ancient 'Greater India' (Vishaal Bharat) has been dismembered as a result of foreign invasions, excepting Pakistan which was created in 1947 by partitioning British India on the basis of religion. These 'istan' parts of ancient 'Greater India' must have been captured one by one by some tribes, such as Baluch, Afghan, Tadzh/Tajik, Turk, Kyrg, Uzbek, Kazakh, etc. They were renamed after the name of the tribe conquered it, for example, Kazakhstan after Kazakhs, Afghanistan after Afghans, etc.

Stephen Knapp, in *'Proof of Vedic Culture's Global Existence'* (2000, pp. 68-69), shows Vedic connection of most of Central Asian countries:

"In any case, not only are there many words connected with or derived from Sanskrit, there are many places around the world that also reflect their Vedic connection. For example, the places that end with the suffix *sthan,* which is the Sanskrit *stan,* reflect their Vedic connection as found in Baluchistan, Afghanistan, Kurdisthan, Kafiristhan, Turkishan, Ghabulisthan, Kazaksthan, and others, such as Arvasthan which was corrupted to Arabia. Countries like Syria and Assyria show their Sanskrit connection through Sura and Asura communities mentioned in the Vedic epics. Those countries also spoke Sanskrit until they lost their connection with India or Vedic culture. Cities in England show their Sanskrit connection with their corrupted form of *puri* turned to 'bury' as in Shrewsbury, Ainsbury, and Waterbury."

J. P. Mallory, in *'In Search of the Indo-Europeans: Language, Archaeology, and Myth'* (1989, p.53), remarks:

"Moreover, the remains from these steppe Bronze Age sites provide us with some of the finest parallels with common reconstructions for Indo-Iranian culture. The settlement and cemetery of Sintashta, for example, although located far to the north on the Trans-Ural steppe, provides the type of Indo-Iranian archaeological evidence that would more than delight an archaeologist seeking their remains in Iran or India. Next to a small settlement occurs a cemetery of tumulus burials dating to the sixteenth century BC. These contain the remains of large quantities of sacrificed animals, especially horses and dogs which are noted in Indo-Aryan ritual, evidence of chariots, and an assortment of other Indo-Iranian ritual markers."

Indo-Iranian rituals in some 'istan' countries, as indicated by archeological finds, reflect very clearly the presence of Sanskrit-speaking Aryans in Central Asia. The name "Sintashta" of a cemetery seems to have its origin in Sanskrit, and the remains found there reflect Vedic rituals. The dating 'sixteenth century B.C.' of such cemetery evidences that Indo-Aryans were in Central Asia before they might have started migrating back to the mainland India in about 1500 B.C.

Mallory (p. 53) continues to give more evidences to prove that Indo-Aryans were there in these 'sthan / istan' countries, before 16th century B.C.:

"Indeed, it is in the eastern Andronovo variants such as the Bishkent culture of south Tadzhikistan that one encounters again the probable expression of Indo-Iranian ritual in the archeological record. At the cemetery of Tulkhar, male burials were provided with small rectangular hearths, reminiscent of the typical Ahavaniya, the rectangular fire-altar of early Indic priests, while females were provided round hearths, comparable to the Garhapatya, the female-associated hearth fire of the Indo-Aryan house."

History, unfortunately enslaved by rulers, has erased the original names of these countries and the ethnic identities of the ancestors of their present natives. The contents of the book on

Kazakhstan, authored by Dr. Alma Kunanbay, when objectively analyzed, implicitly would suggest that the ancestors and the heritage of Kazakhs seem to have very close religio-cultural association with none, but the Hindus of Hindustan (Bharat or India). Other research-based books on the remaining "istan" countries, I am sure, would help in piecing together my hypothetical thesis that Kazakhstan has historical relationship with ancient Hindu India.

Traces of Kazakhstan: Its heritage in India

The flap of the jacket of *'The Soul of Kazakhstan'* (2001)[82], authored by anthropologist and ethnographer Dr. Alma Kunanbay, reads:

"This formerly nomadic country that sprawls nearly 2000 miles across the middle of Central Asia is rich in culture, tradition and spirituality that dates back thousands of years. Until recently, it was little known outside the region because it lost much of its identity and heritage under the 70-year domination of the Soviet Union, and before that, the Russian Empire. Since independence in 1991, Kazakhstan is reestablishing its own identity and making itself felt in world politics and the global marketplace. Kazakhs, who have been taught under the Soviet system that their nomadic heritage was worthless, are rediscovering their roots and an inherent richness that many of that generation had not known existed. *The Soul of Kazakhstan* is an attempt to help fill that void."

Dr. Kunanbay laments that "it (Kazakhstan) lost much of its identity and heritage under the 70-year domination of the Soviet Union ... who (Kazakhs) have been taught under the Soviet system that their nomadic heritage was worthless." Such brainwashing is done by the victors. Unfortunately, history has not been

---

[82] The essays in "*The Soul of Kazakhstan*" are written by Dr. Kunanbay, photographs by Wayne Eastep, and edited by Gareth L. Steen. It is published by Easten Press, New York.

cooperative to help the subjugated to know who originally they were. It has left a void, some, like Kunanbay, are trying to fill in, as much as possible. I think 'bay', suffix to 'Kunan' can be compared to 'bai' suffixed to a woman's name in the past, as well as in present India to show respect. Youngsters used call my mother 'Reejh' as 'Reejhibai'.

The book does not clearly mention who were the ancestors of the Kazakhs and their original culture and religion. Dr. Kunanbay has described the culture and religion of the Kazakhs, "(Kazakhstan) is rich in culture, tradition and spirituality that dates back thousands of years." This can be interpreted with fair certainty that their religion and culture do not seem to have their origin in Islam, which is only about 1500 years old. Most of its elements, as described by Dr. Kunanbay (pp. 53, 60, 72), seem to be similar to those of the Vedic religion (present Hinduism):

- rich in culture, tradition, and spirituality that dates back thousands of years
- Kazakhstan, as "the spiritual cradle"
- close relationship with nature and their response to nature's influences
- veneration of mountains, caves, rivers, and lakes
- burning incense at sacred places
- solar deities (*Surya Devta),* and "Mother Earth"
- Worship of the deities of fire, sky, earth, water, and fertility

It is surprising to see that the name **'Umay'** of the "protectress of fertility," as noted by Kunanbay, is very close to *'Uma'*, the wife of *Shiva*, the god of fertility (*Shiva Lingam*). Dr. Kunanbay describes the heritage of Kazakhs as thousands years long. No religion, other than Vedic (Hinduism), has that longevity. Spirituality and knowledge (*gyan*) have been significant ingredients of the Kazakhstan's philosophy. All these philosophical ingredients of the Kazakh culture seem to be similar to those of Hinduism.

169

Sufism in Kazakhstan

Kunanbay (p.60) remarks that Sufism is well known in the southern region of Kazakhstan, which is not far away from Afghanistan and pre-1947 India. It has been very much loved by Hindus in India, as evidenced by its significant ingredients, such as mysticism, agnosticism, love, spirituality and Urdu mystic poetic genres, which seem to be similar to Vedic philosophy of India. Thus Sufism in India may be a little different from that in Muslim countries, because in India, there has been mutual influence between Sufism and Vedanta.

Sufism appears to be a blend of Hinduism and Islam. Some believe, Sufism is the result of the influence of Islam on Hinduism and some others believe the opposite. I believe Sufism has lot of Vedanta in it. Swami Vivekananda was a disciple of mystic Ramkrishna (1834-86). Many Muslims do not accept Sufism as Islamic.

Columbia Encyclopedia notes that:

"The development of various aspects of Islamic civilization (e.g. literature and calligraphy), many conservative Muslims disagree with many popular Sufi practices, particularly saint worship, visiting of tombs, and the incorporation of non-Islamic customs. Consequently, in recent centuries, Sufism has been a target for Islamic reformist and modernist movements."

Kabir, born as a Muslim, is loved by almost all Hindus because of his liberal philosophy of life, very close to Sufism. It is not accepted by some Muslims. Hinduism and Sikhism have been enriched by the Sufi philosophy. Sufism is giving so much solace to the life we are living. Its knowledge guides our life to be worth-living.

Rig Vedic Aryans in Anau, Turkmenistan

Dr. Poonai, in *'Origin of Civilization and Language'* (1994, p. 66), writes that excavations at the site of Anau on the plains of

Turkmenistan have revealed that early emigrants from the Indus valley had settled there.

Tocharian Documents in Brahmi Script

Tocharian, spoken by Central Asian people and in the NE Tarim Basin of West China in remote past is now extinct. Some Tocharian documents were found written in Brahmi script. Since Tocharian was written in Brahmi, it can be presumed that its speakers and their land had some relationship with the Indus Valley people who wrote in Brahmi script. The influence of Sanskrit on Tocharian suggests presence of Sanskrit-speaking Indo-Aryans in the land of Tochars in ancient times. Historical research needs to tell whether they were the natives, immigrants, or invaders of the Chinese Turkestan (Tarim Basin). Earlier in this chapter, it has been shown that most of the Central Asia was part of the Extended or Greater India in ancient times.

Dr. Poonai (p. 223) writes that Vedic Aryans, about 4,500 years back, were in the region of the Caspian Sea and the Black Sea, according to some historians, invading Aryans might have come from:

"By about 2,500 B.C., the speakers and potential speakers of these Rig-Vedic Sanskrit-derived languages had reached the northern shores of the Caspian Sea and the Black Sea, the Anatolian coast on the Aegean Sea, the Phoenician coast on the eastern Mediterranean, the northern shores of the Adriatic Sea and the shores of the Gulf of Genoa."

This proves beyond any doubt that the some Sanskrit-speaking Aryans might have returned to India, the abode of their ancestors, in about 1500 B.C. when their kingdoms might have been overpowered by other forces. Those returning Aryans were mistaken as invaders.

171

Indian (Vedic) culture in Central Asia, China, Japan, SE Asia

Kulke and Rothermund, in *'A History of India'* (1986, p.152), talk about the wings of Indian (Hindu) culture flying over most of the countries in Central Asia, China and South-East Asia:

"The transmission of Indian culture to distant parts of Central Asia, China, Japan, and especially Southeast Asia is certainly one of the greatest achievements of Indian history or even the history of mankind. None of the other great civilizations – not even Hellenic – had been able to achieve a similar success without military conquest."

They further write:

"In this brief survey of India's history, there is no room for an adequate discussion of the development of the 'Indianised' states of Southeast Asia which can boast of such magnificent temple cities as Pagan (Burma; constructed from 1044 to 1287 AD), Angkor (Cambodia; constructed from 889 to c. 1300 AD), and the Borobudur (Java, early ninth century AD). Though they were influenced by Indian culture, they were nevertheless part of the history of those respective countries."

FIFTEEN

Afghanistan: A Part of Ancient India

"India is often referred to as the subcontinent. ... In the historical sense of the word, 'India' referred to the territory bounded by the Hindu Kush and the Himalayas, and extended from modern Afghanistan and Pakistan in the west to Bangladesh in the east. South of the basins of the Indus and Ganges, rivers whose sources lie in the mountain barrier to the north, India includes the entire peninsula: the Deccan. This lies between the Gulf of Oman and the Bay of Bengal projecting like a triangle into the Indian Ocean."

Henry Stierlin, in *'Hindu India'* (2000, p.8)

Stierlin has described above the vast geography of ancient India. He continues: "The Greek influence (in 3rd century B.C.) was particularly noticeable, for example, in the treatment of the human figure by the Buddhist sculptors of Gandhara." Gandhara is the present-day city of Kandahar in Afghanistan. The Muslim conquest of Afghanistan could not happen before 8th century. Buddhist statues in Afghanistan in the second or third century B.C. provide definite proof that the region was inhabited at that time by Hindus and Buddhists. 'Hari Rud' river is another evidence of the Hindu presence in ancient Afghanistan. Hari is the name of the Hindu god Krishna.

In fact, ancient India was much larger than a continent. It included Bangladesh, Pakistan, Baluchistan, Afghanistan, Iran, Asia Minor, and several other countries in Central Asia with their

173

names suffixed with 'istan' or 'stan'. History has been silent to tell their original names prior to their occupation by Afghans, Tajiks, Turks, Kyrgs, Uzbeks, Kazakhs, etc. Ancient India, also, ruled over Indo-China and several countries in far South-East Asia, such as Thailand, Cambodia, Vietnam, Java, Sumatra, Bali, and some other islands in Indonesia.

The Columbia Encyclopedia (Fifth edition, p.27) makes a mention of the "rich valley of HERAT on the Hari Rud (Arius) River in the northwest corner of the country (the heart of ancient ARIANA)." The words Arius and Ariana reflect Aryan presence in Afghanistan. Many historians have admitted that there are several evidences reflecting significant presence of Hindus and Buddhists in Afghanistan in its pre-Afghan period. However, the constant invasions from the northwest resulted in loss of several parts of Bharat (India), one-by-one, including Afghanistan, and the most recent Pakistan. Pakistan was not lost because of any invasion, but because of partition of India on the basis of religion in 1947.

Afghanistan, like Pakistan, was a part of India. Iqbal Ali Shah (1938, p. 9) writes:

"Historians believe that the inhabitants of Afghanistan, prior to the Greek invasion, were Hindus. After the decline of the Indo-Scythians, the Hindus were governing and inhabiting the country. They ruled the country till the end of the seventh century when the Arabs conquered Afghanistan and the people of Afghanistan embraced Islam."

Abdul Ali Arghandawi (1984:136) writes:

"Buddhism and Hinduism were practiced in Afghanistan and its remains are still available in northern Afghanistan and other parts of the country. Buddha's 52 meter high statue in Bamian and many stupas dug up in different parts of the country represent Buddhist religion."

Phil Zabriskie, in 'The Outsiders' (National Geographic, February 2008), writes:

174

Afghanistan: A Part of Ancient India

"At the heart of Afghanistan is an empty space, striking absence, where the larger of the colossal Bamian Buddhas once stood. In March 2001 the Talibans fired rockets at the statues for days on end, then planted and detonated explosives inside them. The Buddhas had looked out over Bamian for some 1,500 years. ... The regimes rose and collapsed or were overthrown. The statues stood through it all. But the Talibans saw the Buddhas simply as non-Islamic idols, heresies carved in stone. They did not mind being thought brutish. They did not fear further isolation. Destroying the statues was a pious assertion of their brand of faith over history and culture."

Talibans declined offers from a few museums to remove and relocate them in museums. This reminds me of what I read in a history text about Mahmud Ghaznavi.– known as *'But Shakan'*, meaning destroyer of Idols (*but* = Idol, shakan = destroyer) – who got Hindu idols smashed into pieces when he ruled over Afghanistan in about 10th century A.D.

Alexander Cunningham,[83] in his book *'The Ancient Geography of India'* (1871, p.14), writes that the people of whole Afghanistan spoke Indian language and practiced Hinduism and Buddhism:

"For several centuries, both before and after the Christian era, the provinces of Northern India beyond the Indus in which the Indian language and religion were predominant, included the whole of Afghanistan from Bamian and Kandahar on the west to the Bholan Pass on the south."

On the same page Cunningham describes how later Afghanistan was Islamized:

"In the following century (7th century), as we learn from the Chinese pilgrim, the king of Kapisa was a *Kshatriya* or pure Hindu. During the whole of the tenth century the

---

[83] Kapisa, was one of the 10 separate states or districts of Afghanistan, according to M. Julien's 'Hiouen Thsang,' 1.71.

175

Kabul valley was held by a dynasty of Brahmans, whose power was not finally extinguished until toward the close of the reign of Mahmud Ghaznavi. Down to this time, therefore, it would appear that a great part of the population of eastern Afghanistan, including the whole of Kabul valley must have been of Indian descent, while the religion was pure Buddhism. During the rule of the Ghaznavis, whose late conversion to Muhammadanism had only added bigotry to their native ferocity, the persecution of idol-loving Buddhists was a pleasure as well as a duty. The idolaters were soon driven out, and with them the Indian element, which had subsisted for so many centuries in Eastern Ariana, finally disappeared."

Peshawar, originally known as *Parashawar*

On p. 66, Cunningham writes that the present Peshawar was originally known as *Parashawar*. And that the kingdom of Gandhara was a dependency of Kapisa or Kabul.

Lahore, founded by Lav, son of Rama

Cunningham (pp.166-168) talks about the originality of 'Lahore' and 'Kusawar (or Kasur):

"The great city of Lahore, which has been the capital of the Punjab for nearly nine hundred years, is said to have been founded by *Lava*, or *Lo*, the son of *Rama*, after whom it was named *Lohawar*. ... According to the traditions of the people *Kasur* was founded by *Kusa*, the son of *Rama*, after whom it was named *Kusawar*, which, like the contemporary city of *Lohawar*, has been slightly altered in pronunciation by the transposition of the vowels. The town stands on the high bank of the old bed of the Bias river, 32 miles to the south-south-east of Lahore, and is popularly said to have once possessed *bara kilah*, or 'twelve forts'."

Pushkalavati, Ancient capital of Gandhara

Cunningham, in *"Ancient India as described by Ptolemy"* (pp.41-42), talks about *Pushkalavati,* capital of Gandhara, which was under the administration of Pushkara, the nephew of Rama:

> "The ancient capital of Gandhara was *Pushkalavati,* which is said to have been founded by Pushkara, the son of Bharata, and the nephew of Rama.[84] ... The Greek name of *Peukelaotis,* or *Peucolaitis,* was immediately derived from *Pukkalaoti,* which is the Pali, or spoken form of the Sanskrit Pushkalvati."

Rama was son of *Dashratha,* the king of Kosla, with *Ayodhya,* its capital. *Dashratha* had three wives – Kaushalya, Sumitra, and Kekai. Rama was the only son of the eldest queen Kaushalya, Bharat was the only son of the youngest queen Kekai. Sumitra had two sons, Lakshman and Shatrughan. Rama's son Kush or Cusha was given Africa to govern, as shown later in the chapter 'India in Africa'.

Cunningham (pp.115-117) writes some similar things about Gandhara:

> "The Gandharai – Gandhara is a name of high antiquity, as it occurs in one of the Vedic hymns, where a wife is represented as saying with reference to her husband, "I shall always be for him a Gandhara ewe." It is mentioned frequently in the *Mahabharatā* and other post-Vedic works, and from these we learn that it contained the two royal cities of Takshasïla (Taxila) and Pushkalavati (Peukelaotis) the former situated to the east and the latter to the west of the Indus."

The queen Gandhari was the wife of the Kaurava king Dhrutrashra who was blind. Gandhari was so much devoted to her blind husband, that she blinded herself permanently by a band on

---

[84] Wilson's 'Vishnu Purana', edited by Hall, b.iv.c.4.

her eyes. The Mahābhāratā war was between the two cousin families – the Pandavas, headed by Yudhishtra, and the Kauravas, headed by Dhrutrashtra. On the battle field at Kurukshetra, the Kauravas were led by his eldest son Duryodhana. Gandhara was named after Gandhari, the wife of Dhrutrashtra. There has been controversy over the exact time of the Mahabharatā war, ranging from 1000 B.C. to 5,000 B.C. Consensus seems to be around 3,000 B.C., exact November, 3067 B.C.[85] The date has been based on astronomical calculations.

John W. McCrindle, in *'Ancient India as described by Ptolemy'* (200, pp.116, 117), talks about Gandhara:

"Gandhara (present Kandahar) was one of the most flourishing seats of Buddhism. ... Proklais is the ancient capital of Gandhara situated to the west of the Indus, which was mentioned in the preceding remarks under its Sanskrit name Pushkalavati, which means 'abounding in the lotus'."

On p.362, in notes, it is mentioned that Pushkalavati was named after Pushkala, the son of Bharat, the brother of Rama. It means, Gandhara was under the control of the Vedic Aryans (present Hindus), since the rule of Dashratha, the father of Rama. One of the capitals of Gandhara was *Purushapura* (present Peshawar).

Dr. A. Foucher – in *"Notes surla gèographieanccienne du Gandhāra"* (*Notes on The Ancient Geography of Gandhara*), in the October issue of the *Bulletin de l'École francaise d' Extreme-Orient* (1901) – talks about his scientific mission in India, when he visited in details the Peshawar District, the territory of ancient Gandhara. He talks about Purushapura at Peshawar and Pushkaravati in the immediate neighborhood of Charasadda, where he saw Buddhist sculptures and the inscriptions of Asoka. Foucher (p.2) remarks that Pushtu was spoken in the birth place of Panini. He further states: "But the worst invasions were yet to come and Gandhāra at least remained Indian in manners and language."

[85] Kosla Vepa (ed.), *Astronomical Dating of Events& Select Vignettes from Indian History* (2008, p. 35), as per Kota Venkatachelam *The Plot in Indian Chronology* (1954)

On p.2, it is mentioned:

"In our days when under the rule of the Sikhs and their successors the English, Gandhāra again became part of India, it was all too late to revive the past. ... It is true, there seems to remain a residue of the Hindu population, *banya* families, scattered here and there, in the larger villages and whom for the sake of their trade, the Pathans unable to keep accounts and in consequence incapable of shop-keeping, have been obliged to tolerate."

Foucher (pp.10-13) talks about his tour with Chinese traveler Hiuan-tsang from Purushapura to Pushkaravati, and Hashtanagar. In the neighborhood of the town, they visited a Brahmanical temple, a stupa built by Asoka, and another stupa very high and flanked by its monastery.

Jawaharlal Nehru, in *Discovery of India* (p.107), writes about Gandhara, the present Kandahar:

"The great civil war, which occurred later, described in the Mahabharata, is vaguely supposed to have taken place about the fourteenth century B.C. That war was for the overlordship of India (or possibly of northern India), and it marks the beginning of the conception of India as a whole, of Bharatvarsha. In this conception a large part of modern Afghanistan, then called Gandhara (from which the name of the present city Kandahar), which considered an integral part of the country was included. Indeed the queen of the principal ruler was named Gandhari, the lady from Gandhara."

Nehru (p.202) writes that the well-known town in ancient India "Gandhara (Afghanistan) must have been an important part of Aryan India."

179

Afghanistan and Baluchistan under Emperor Ashoka

The Columbia Encyclopedia (p.164) remarks that the Emperor Asoka (232 B.C.), the grandson of Chandragupta, "brought nearly all India, together with Baluchistan and Afghanistan, under one sway for the first time in history." It also mentions that after his bloody conquest of Kalinga (261 B.C.), Asoka felt remorseful of the sufferings he had inflicted on the people. He resigned from the worldly life for the service of the people and accepted Buddhism and abandoned wars of conquest.

Pre-Afghan name of Afghanistan

Alexander Cunningham, in *'The Ancient Geography of India'* (p.14), remarks that the Indian language and religion were predominant in whole of Afghanistan, and that the great part of the eastern Afghanistan, including the whole of the Kabul valley must have been of Indian descent, while religion was pure Buddhism.

John W. McCrindle,[86] in his work titled *'Ancient India as described by Ptolemy'* (p.82), seems to suggest that Afghanistan was the country of *Paktys* (Pushtus). He writes:

"Klaudios Ptolemaios[87] (in Latin affectionately known as "Ptolemy) was a celebrated astronomer, mathematician and geographer. He was a native of Egypt. He was the first writer on Greek astronomy, based on the works of Hipparchus. His astronomical work titled *Megale syntaxis tes Astronomais* is commonly known by its Arabic title *Almagest or* "great work.""

McCrindle (pp. 81, 82) quotes Max Müller, from *'India: What Can It Teach us?'*, that Afghanistan was known as the land of the Paktys:

---

[86] Dr. John W. McCrindle, in *"Ancient India as described by Ptolemy,"* p. xiii.
[87] Ibid, pp. 81-82.

"In the *Vedas* we have a number of names of the rivers of India as they were known to one single poet, say about 1000 B.C. ... The Indus was known to early traders whether by sea or land. Skylax sailed from the country of the Paktys, i.e. the Pushtus, as the Afghans still call themselves, down to the mouth of the Indus."

But this name came in currency later after advent of Afghans and other tribes. Still its ancient name has not been ascertained. Ludwig, Lassen, and Whitney substitute *Kubha* (Kabul) for the Sarasvati and think the Oxus (present Amu Darya) also must have been one of the seven rivers.

How did 'India' and ''Indus' come around?

McCrindle (p. 82) says that 'India' was derived from Sindhu. Iranians pronounced 's' as 'h'. Thus '*Sindhu*' became '*Hindhu*' (*Hidhu*) and as h's were dropped, at that early time, *Hindhu* became *Indu*. Thus the river (Sindhu) was called *Indu*, thus *Indus* .

I think Bharat is the only country which is shamelessly carrying the name, given by the victors. When speaking in Hindi, it is Bharat, and in English, it becomes India. Even in Hindi, many times it is addressed as India. No other country has two names like this – one in its own language and the other in English. France is France in French, as well as in English. Pakistan is Pakistan in Urdu as well as in English, and so are the names of other countries – Afghanistan, Baluchistan, Thailand, Germany, Switzerland, etc.

History tells that the names of the countries, recently (a few centuries back) have been changed by their victors. The countries of self-respect regain their original names immediately after their independence, as Ceylon became Sri Lanka and so Burma, Myanmar.

Name, especially of a country, has its history. The name 'Ceylon' doesn't evoke her history beyond the time it was bonded. Without history, one will not know his heritage, culture and literature to be proud of. Victors try to hide them. Literature of Sri Lanka goes millennia back to Rāmāyanā. It tells that no wise ruler would be like Rawan. The name 'India' has only a few century-long history, that of shame. The "Indian" is the most shameful name, because it resembles to American Native Indians. Bharat has millennia-long history and literature – Vedas, Upanishads, Shastras, etc. – from its immemorial times. They have been guide for other peoples on the planet, as discussed earlier. Bharat's history, as penned by our victors, brings nothing but shame.

Bharat's metropolis cities – Mumbai, Chennai, Kolkata, Pune, etc. – have regained their original identity to enjoy the respect, their respective proud history had. History, the true story of the people, is important. History – story of positives as well as negatives – has lessons to learn from. No history of a developed or of a developing country has or had only positives, because no country has only positive people. Negative history has also lot of preventive lessons.

It is hard to understand why the post-independence governments of Bharat – Congress as well as BJP – have been enjoying shameful Kumbhakaran slumber over such important issue impacting the honor of the nation. This issue has never come in the Parliament, though the Bharat is given in the Constitution. Very few peoples know Bharat, as the real name of our great nation. Proper name can /should not be translated or changed.

Rig Veda and Afghanistan

R. C. Majumdar, in *'The History and Culture of the Indian People'* (1951, pp. 247-248), writes: "Considering that the *Rig Veda* mentions the Kubha (Kabul), Gomati (Gumal), Kruma (Kurram), and Suvastu (Swat), which lie to the west of the Indus, it is possible that the Rigveda people knew of the existence of the Oxus." On the basis of all this, Majumdar asserts:

"We may thus conclude that the extent of the country, as reflected in the hymns, is Afghanistan, the Punjab, Sind and Rajputana, the North-West Frontier Province, Kashmir, and Eastern India up to Sarayu."

Hertel Brunnhofer, Hertel Husing, and others, however, argue that the scene of the *Rig Veda* is laid, not in the Punjab, but in

Afghanistan and Iran.[88] Brunnhofer relies mainly on the identification of the peoples mentioned in the Veda, with tribes located in Afghanistan, in the inscriptions of Darius, or in later Greek authors. In my opinion, Afghanistan or Punjab or Iran does not make any difference, because Afghanistan and Iran, like Punjab, had been a part of ancient Bharat.

According to the Vedic traditions and other historical, geological and archaeological evidences, it is fact that Afghanistan was a part of ancient India. Kandahar was originally Gandhara, named after Gandhari of Mahābhāratā. According to David Frawley, in 'Gods, Sages and Kings' (1991:83), a region in Afghanistan was known as Gandhara, whose name is mentioned in the *Rig Veda*.

Frawley (1991, pp. 82, 83) – referring to the names of some rivers, such as Sindhu, Kubha (Kabul), Gomati, Krumu, and Mehatmu in a Vedic hymn – rightly seems to have identified their relationship with the Vedic India, in other words the historic relationship between India and Afghanistan. Frawley (1991: 83) remarks:

"Some scholars have used their designations to connect the Vedic people with some home in Afghanistan and Central Asia. Actually there is a more simple and obvious reason for their inclusion. They are the rivers of a region known as Gandhara, the western uplands of India. The name of this region can be found in the Rig Veda itself as associated with sheep (1.126.7). It is an important source for wool, as sheep do well in mountain areas. ... At the time of the Greek visits to India, which followed Alexander (Alexander the Great, 356-323 B.C.), Gandhara was inhabited by traditional Aryan peoples. They were not displaced until the Muslim invasion.

---

[88] Brunnhofer, *Arische Urzeit*, 1910; Hertel, *Indo-Germ;* Husing, *MAGW*, xivi; Winternitz, *HIL*, I, pp. 63-4; and Childe, *Aryans, p.32* (Taken from Majumdar, R.C. et al, p.248).

Afghanistan itself was called 'the land of the Aryans' from ancient times."

SIXTEEN

Iran: A Part of Ancient India

"Iran was one of the first destination sites which came under the influence of the Rig-Vedic Aryan cultural impact. That was so because of its proximity to Aryavarta, the land of the Aryans as India was then called, and because of its location directly in the path of westward emigration from the land. Most emigrating groups were clans of Asura or Assur Rig-Vedic Aryans. One such group colonized an eastern region of the Iranian plateau. They referred to themselves as Ahuras and to God as Ahura Mazda, a name most probably derived from the Sanskrit Asura Mehda, giver of the breath of life."

Dr. P. Poonai[89]

As a matter of fact, Iran was not colonized by India. Iran was from pre-history ancient times, culturally, linguistically and administratively, a part of Aryavarta (India).

In Persian 's' is pronounced as 'h'. Asura became Ahura. Poonai (p.65) explains how the name Persia has been derived from Purusham Aryanam:

---

[89] Dr. P. Poonai in *'Origin of Civilization and Language'* (1994, p.65).

"The Ahuras also called themselves Purushaspa Aryanam, a name most probably derived from the Sanskrit, Purusham Aryanam, the noble people, which later became abbreviated into Parsianam, Parsia, and Parthia."

In ancient times, India enveloped Iran and most of the 'istan' countries in Central Asia as described in the earlier Chapter. Iran, in its ancient times, was culturally and linguistically very similar to India.

Geoffrey Bibby (1969: 278) has said that "... so was Iran governed by India in ancient times."

Will Durant, in *The Story of Civilization: Our Oriental Heritage* (1935, p. 391), describes the scene of the history of ancient India enveloping Ceylon (Sri Lanka), Afghanistan and Persia:

"The scene of the history is a great triangle narrowing down from the everlasting snows of the Himalayas to the eternal heat of Ceylon. In a corner at the left lies Persia, close akin to the Vedic India in people, language and gods. Following the northern frontier eastward we strike Afghanistan, here is Kandahar, the ancient Gandhara, where Greek and Hindu sculpture fused for a while, and then parted never to meet; and north of it is Kabul, from which the Moslems and the Moguls made those bloody raids that gave them India for a thousand years."

Durant (p. 391, foot notes) writes that in 1805, Colebrooke's essay *On the Vedas* revealed to Europe the oldest literature of India, and also "Anquetil-Duperron's translation of a Persian translation of the *Upanishads* acquainted Schelling and Schopenhauer with what the latter called the profoundest philosophy that he had ever read."

E. Pococke, in '*India in Greece*' (p.47), talks about colonization of Persia, Colchis, Armenia, and Egypt by India:

"The ancient map of Persia, Colchis, and Armenia, is absolutely full of the most distinct and starling evidences of Indian colonisation and what is more astonishing, practically evinces, in the most powerful manner, the truth of several main points in the two great Indian poems, the Ramayana and Mahabarata. The whole map is positively nothing less than a journal of emigration on the most gigantic scale. ... I have glanced at the Indian settlements in Egypt."

Name 'Iran' derived from 'Aryan"

Dr. Peter B. Clarke (ed.), in *'The World's Religions'* (1993, p.130), writes that the name 'Iran' is derived from 'Aryan'. He seems to suggest that Iran, in ancient times, was inhabited by Aryans. The old Iranian language Avestan was very close to Sanskrit. C.V. Vaidya, in *'History of Sanskrit Literature'* (vol. I, 1986, p.39), observes that there is significant similarity between Avestic *gathas* and *Rig Vedic mantras*. The word 'gathas' in Sanskrit/Hindi means stories. Some times, it looks as if both are identical. Clarke continues that there is no doubt that the Indo-Aryans and Iranians once formed one people and lived together.

J. P. Mallory (1989, pp. 42-43) states that according to Burrow, Indo-Aryans were once the occupiers of Iran.

T. Burrow, in *'The Sanskrit Language'* (2001, p.4), writes:

"The relations between this ancient Iranian and the language of the Veda are so close that it is not possible satisfactorily to study one without the other. ... It is quite possible to find verses in the oldest portion of the *Avesta,* which simply by phonetic substitutions according to established laws can be turned into intelligible Sanskrit."

Burrow (p.1) observes:

"In the greater part of India today languages are spoken which are derived from a single form of speech which was introduced into India by invaders from the north-west more than three thousand years ago. The invading peoples were known in their language as *arya*, a word which is

187

also commonly used as an adjective meaning 'noble, honourable.'"

Burrow's statement – that the invading people were Aryans, and that the word 'Arya' (in Sanskrit) means 'noble' – clearly suggests beyond any doubt that those alleged invading people were originally Indo-Aryans from India. How then could it be invasion? It was their 'return' to, not 'invasion' of India. The Aryan invasion of India is a myth, a mischievously fabricated theory. Historians, like Burrow and others, who believe in 'Aryan invasion of India', have not been able to identify the country (other than India) which had Aryans as its natives and Sanskrit as its native language.

Burrow, on the same page (p.1), writes that the modern name 'Iran' is ultimately derived from Arya. He further says:

"In conformance with this usage, the term *Aryan* is now used as common name of these peoples and their languages; alternately the term Indo-Iranian is commonly used. To distinguish the Indian branch from the Iranian, the term *Indo-Aryan* has been coined."

This proves that none but Aryavarta (Bharat, India) is the original home of the Aryans and of their language Sanskrit. As a matter of fact, Indo-Aryans must have been residents of also Iran whose language 'Avestan' was one of India's vernaculars like Hindi, Bengali, Marathi, Tamil, Sindhi, Gujarati, etc. Very close linguistic correspondence between Sanskrit and Avestan words – given by Burrow, as shown below – will puzzle many to think if Avestan and Sanskrit were two different languages.

Sanskrit	Avestan/Persian	Meaning in English
Hiranya	Zaranya	Gold
Sena	Haena	Army
Rsti	Arsti	Spear
Asura	Ahura	Lord
Yajna	Yasna	Sacrifice
Hotar	Zaotar	Sacrifying priest
Soma	Haoma	Sacred drink Soma

Aryaman   Airyaman   member of religious sodality

Sanskrit 's' is pronounced as 'h' in Avestan and 'h' as 'z'. Likewise, 'Sindhu' became 'Hindu', soma became homa, and 'Sindhustan' became 'Hindustan.

Will Durant, in *Our Oriental Heritage* (p.406), remarks that Sanskrit was a near relative of the early Persian dialect in which the Avesta was composed.

Benjamin Walker, in *'The Hindu World: An Encyclopedic Survey of Hinduism'* (vol. 2, p 353), writes about inter-mixing of ancient Iranian and Indian (Hindu) gods and deities:

"The Indo-Iranian tribal communities gave place to new territorial kingdoms situated on great rivers and the jungle retreats of the rishis. The old Iranian gods faded in importance and were substituted by deities of new dimensions, Brahma, Siva, Vishnu, Krishna, the Nagas, the Linga."

Benjamin Walker (vol. 1, p.70) talks about the Aryan language whose literary descendants were Avestic in Persia and Vedic in India. It suggests religious, cultural and linguistic closeness between Iranians and Indians (Vedic people) in ancient times. This explains who Aryans were and where they were from:

"They (Aryans) spoke an Aryan language of which the literary descendants were Avestic in Persia and Vedic in India. The immigrant Indian branch has left a vivid glimpse of its faith and customs in the Vedas, which have given their name to the period and their way of life. ... In the country of their ancestors the Iranian Aryans and the Indian Aryans lauded the same gods with the same hymns, and worshipped them with identical rites. Their relationship is today well established, and their 'original home' is now believed to have been at least as far as west as the wide plain between the Oxus and Jaxartes, the cradle of some of the characteristic features of Indo-Iranian culture and religion."

It clearly suggests that the Iranian Aryans and the Indo-Aryans were one and the same people in ancient times when they "lauded the same gods with the same hymns, and worshipped them with identical rites." I don't think they were known as 'Hindus' and 'Persians'. All the people of the subcontinent, including Indians, Iranians, Nepalese, Bhutanese, Sri Lankans, Burmese, etc., must have been called Aryans, as the country was known as Aryavarta, Aryadesh, or Aryabhoomi. The unfounded theory of the 'Aryan invasion' – engineered in London and guided by the world-known British policy "Divide and Rule" – seems to have divided Indians and Iranians who, in ancient times, were one and the same people.

From what Dr. Peter B. Clarke, Mallory, Burrow, and several other scholars have talked about the co-habitation of both – the Indo-Aryans and the Indo-Iranians – it seems they were one people and lived together in ancient times when Iran was a part of Greater India. In my opinion, the term 'Indo-Aryan' is linguistically fallacious, because there were no Aryans other than of those of Indian origin.

Persia: Named after Parsooram, warrior with Axe:

E. Pococke (India in Greece, p.45) has said that Persia was named after Parsooram, the Mahābhāratā warrior with Axe:

> "I have glanced at the Indian settlements in Egypt which again be noticed; and I would now resume my observations from the lofty frontier which is the true boundary of the European and Indian races. The Parsoos, the people of Parsoo-Rama, those warriors of the Axe, have penetrated into and given a name to PERSIA; they are the people of Bharata*."

'Rama', suffixed to the name Parsoo, shows that Iran (Persia) was under the control of India from the days of Rāmāyanā which

---

* Bharata, the name of India.

happened long before 3,067 B.C., the year of the Mahābhāratā war.[90]

According to *'mahabharat@intelindia.com'*, the coastal area of Karnataka and Kerala state in India is known as Parashurama Kshetra:

"Parashurama Bhargava or Parasurama (Axe-wielding Rama), according to Hindu mythology is the Sixth Avatara (incarnation) of Vishnu, belongs to the Treta Yuga, and is the son of Jamadagni & Renuka. Parashu means axe, hence his name literally means Rama-with-the-axe. He received an axe after undertaking a difficult penance to please Shiva, from whom he learned the methods of warfare and other skills. He is a Chiranjeevin, who fought the advancing ocean back thus saving the lands of Konkan and Malabar (Maharashtra-Karnataka-Kerala coastline). The coastal area of Karnataka and Kerala state in India is known as Parashurama Kshetra (Parashurama's area). Some dispute this and say it extends all the way to Mumbai in Maharashtra."

Euphrates as Eu-Bh'rat-es?

Pococke (p.45) writes that the name 'Eu-Ph'rat-es (as Eu-Bh'rat-es) has been given to the principal stream that pours its water into the Persian Gulf.

Dr. Poonai, in *Origin of Civilization and Language* (1994, p. 170), explains the root of the name Persia which resembles to Parshurama:

"The doctrines of the Vedas were therefore widely taught to the noble people of Iran also called Purusham Aryanam a phrase which can be abbreviated to Parsianam or Parthians or Persians."

---

[90] Kosla Vepa (ed.), *Astronomical Dating of Events & Select Vignettes from Indian History* (vol. 1,2008, p.37).

The term 'Parsee' seems to have originated from Parsianam. Poonai (pp. 220,221) remarks:

"The Ahuras were originally a colony of Asura Rig-Vedic Aryans who immigrated from Aryavarta or India into the land of the Purusham Aryanam or Persianam or Persia, as explained earlier. The Asura Rig-Vedic Aryans reached the Iranian plateau readily and in considerable numbers from the earliest times."

Herman Kulke and Dietmar Rothermund[91] do not seem to be clear about the originality of the Aryans:

"A peace treaty of 1350 BC from Boghazkoi in Western Asia, which was then the capital of Hittites, is often quoted as the first document referring to the Aryans. In this treaty, which a king of the Hittites concluded with the ruler of the Mitanni kingdom, the Aryan gods Mitra, Varuna, Indra and the Nasatyas were invoked as witnesses. As these gods thereafter reappeared in the sacred literature of the Vedic Aryans or that this elite was a branch of a larger Indo-Aryan community which had migrated first to India and then to the west. The old Iranian language of the Mitanni, is closely related to the Indo-European language and Iran means 'Land of the Aryans'. Thus some Aryans may have come via Iran to India."

Kulke and Rothermund seem to be confused, as seen by their two contradicting statements: (1) "Iran means 'Land of the Aryans', and (2) "Thus some Aryans may have come via Iran to India." I think they must be talking about their returning to India. Mention of "Aryan gods Mitra, Varuna, Indra and the Nasatyas were invoked as witnesses" clearly shows that both Hittite and Mitanni kings were Indo-Aryans (Vedic people, Hindus).

---

[91] in 'History of India' (1986, p.33).

As a matter of fact, Aryans didn't come to India or Iran from somewhere. They were originally from India who had gone out for trade and colonization. According to Aurel Stein, as said earlier, Indo-Aryans were already in Central Asia. They were returning. The Hittites and Mitanni were originally the natives of India and Iran. C. V. Vaidya, in *'History of Sanskrit Literature'* (1986, p.39), writes that Mitanni were Aryans from the Punjab. They were Vedic Indo-Aryans (Hindus) as evidenced by the names of the Vedic gods invoked in the treaty. These gods were already being worshipped, as evidenced by the Rig Veda in which their names appeared long before 4000 BC. Kulke and Rothermund's statement, "these gods thereafter (after 1300 BC) reappeared in the sacred literature of the Vedic Aryans", seems to be based on the ill-based theory of Aryan invasion of India, according to which the Vedas were composed by the alleged invading Aryans in 1000 BC or even later. But, the Vedas were composed long before that as explained in Chapter Two, 'Vedas: The Most Ancient Scriptures of the world."

As explained earlier, Iran was a part of Greater India. Indo-Aryans, who had gone out of India and had established their kingdoms in Asia Minor region and beyond, were returning to India, when they were routed out by some other forces.

V. Gordon Childe, in *'The Aryans: A Study of Indo-European Origins'* (1926, p.19), writes that Mitannis were warriors *(Kshatries)* from India: "Finally we know that there existed among the Mitanni at this time a class of warriors styled *marianna* which has suggested comparison with the Sanskrit *marya,* young men, heroes."[92]

Childe further talks about the Aryan (perhaps Mitanni and Hittites) dynasts installed in the Mesopotamia region:

"So it is clear enough that the dynasts installed on the Upper Euphrates by 1400 B.C. were Aryans, closely akin to those we meet in the Indus Valley and later in Media and Persia. But their subjects were non-Aryan Asianics, and the rulers had adopted the native language and the

---

[92] Moret, *'From Tribe to Empire'* in 'Cambridge Ancient History'.

Babylonian script for their official correspondence, and apparently acknowledged local gods besides their own."

Similar traits we find among Indian emigrants, particularly Sindhis, the original natives of the Indus Valley (Mohenjo-daro, Sind), who would pick up the vernacular of their adopted country without going to school. I have seen in Jakarta, how fluently my host (a Sindhi gentleman) was communicating with his maidservant in Bahasa, the local language. He had not gone to school to learn that Indonesian language,

Childe (p.19) underlines that the Aryan adventurous movement kept on advancing further and further:

"And the movement which had brought them to the Euphrates did not stop there. During the same period the Tell-el-Amarna tablets mention Aryan princes in Syria and Palestine too – Biridaswa of Yenoam, Suwardata of Keilah, Yasdata of Taanach, Artamanya of Zir-Bashan and others.[93] These two were probably mere dynasts ruling over non-Aryan Semetic subjects."

The personal names of the Aryan princes – like Biridaswa, Suwardata, Yasdata, and Artamanya – look Indic (Sanskritic) rather than Iranian. He explains that 'Birdaswa' has been plausibly compared to the Sanskrit 'Brhad-aswa', meaning owning a great horse – 'brahad = great, and 'aswa' = horse.

Iran means 'Land of Aryans'

Max Müller (1891, pp.292-293) talks about the use of the word "Arya" in Iran and its Zend-Avesta:

"In India, as we saw, the name of Arya, as a national name, fell into oblivion in later times, and was preserved in the term Arya-avarta only, the abode of the Aryans. But it was more faithfully preserved by the Zoroastrians who

---

[93] Cambridge Ancient History, ii, p. 331.

had migrated to the north-west, and whose religion has been preserved to us in the Zend-Avesta, though in fragments only. Now Airya in Zend means venerable, and is at the same time the name of the people."[94]

Ariana or Aryana

The Columbia Encyclopedia (Fifth Edition) writes: that 'Ariana' or 'Aryana' was the general name for the Eastern provinces of the ancient Persian Empire, regions south of the Oxus River (modern Amu Darya). Ariana is included in present East Iran, N and E of Afghanistan, India, and the Indus River.

It may be erroneous to say that 'Arianism', founded in 4th century AD by a Christian priest Arius in Alexandria, had any relationship with Indo-Aryans.

Indo-Aryans and Iranians as one people

The authors of the Vedas and worshippers of Ahuro Mazdao did live together in early ancient times. Iran, as a significant part of India, was the original home of the Aryans. Because of military occupation of Persia (present Iran) by foreign powers, the worshippers of Ahuro Mazdao were separated from the mainstream Sanskrit-speaking Aryans of India. Because of their long separation, the Zend language got heavily influenced by the language of its occupiers. In about ninth century A.D., several Parsees (Zoroastrians) had to leave Persia (present Iran) because of religious persecutions. Some of them, not all, fled to India, the country of Sanskrit-knowing Aryans. They were welcomed because the Vedic (Hindu) India is historically known as a kind-hearted shelter to refugees of various other ethnic peoples including Jews and Buddhists from Tibet.

Parsees, perhaps because of their traditional religio-cultural bond with Hindus, and more so because of historical close relationship their language Zend-Avestan had with Sanskrit, they have felt comfortable and secure in Hindustan. They have very

---

[94] Lassen, *Ind. Alt. b. i. 8. 6.*

well mainstreamed on all counts – culture, language, food and ethnic dress Sari. They have advanced a great deal economically as well as educationally. Parsees have adopted Gujarati, as their language, because they first came to Navsari and Surat, big towns of Gujarat. They have been free to practice their religion and culture. Parsees, in general, are peace loving people. Most of them are well-educated and financially well off. If you want to be happy in your adopted home, heed the advice of the elders: "Behave, think, and feel like a Roman when you are in Rome."

As a matter of fact, as explained earlier in this chapter, in remote ancient times, Iran was a part of Greater India (Vishaal Bharat), and their languages – Sanskrit and Zend-Avestan – were linguistically too close to be seen as two different languages.

Max Müller, in *'The Science of Language'* (1891, p.289), remarks:

"Sanskrit and Zend share certain words and grammatical forms in common which do not exist in any other Aryan languages; and there can be no doubt that the ancestors of the poets of the Vedas and the worshippers of A*huro mazdao* lived together for some time after they had left the original home of the whole Aryan race."

It is clear that Max Müller considered Aryavarta (India) as the "original home of the whole Aryan race." On p. 295, Max Müller emphasizes the same that Aryavarta is the original abode of the Aryans:

"That *Aryan* was used as a title of honour in the Persian Empire is clearly shown by the cuneiform inscriptions of Darius. He calls himself Ariya and Ariya-*kitra*, an Aryan and of Aryan descent; and Ahuramazda, or, as he is called by Darius, Auramazda, is rendered in the Turanian translation of the inscription of Behistun, 'the god of the Aryas.' Many historical names of the Persians contain the same element. The great-grandfather of Darius is called in the inscriptions Ariyaramna, the Greek Ariaramnes (Herod, vii. 90)."

The suffixes *"ramna"* or *"ramnes"* in the names of the grand father of Darius *'Ariyaramana'* or *'Ariaramnes'* need to be noticed which reflect the name of Hindu god Rama. This is also found in present Hindu names, like 'Venkatraman', 'Raghviraman', 'Sitaraman', etc.

Max Müller (1891, p. 296) remarks: "The modern name of Iran for Persia still keeps up the memory of this ancient title." He (p.298) continues to tell about the presence of the element of Arya in the names of both the countries – Armenia[95] and Ireland. He clarifies: "And it s maintained by O'Reilly, though denied by others, that this *er* is used in Irish in the same sense of noble, like the Sanskrit *arya.*"

Max Müller (1891, p.294) writes that some other countries in the region craved for Aryan title: "As the Zoroastrian religion spread westward, Persia, Elymais, and Media all claimed for themselves this Aryan title. Hellanicus, who wrote before Herodotus, knows of Aria as a name of Persia."

Max Müller (1891, p.297) traces the countries in the north-west of India, where the name of Arya has spread:

"We have traced the name of Arya from India to the west, from Arya-avarta to Ariana, Persia, Media, more doubtfully to Armenia and Albania, to the Iron in the Caucasus, and some of nomad tribes in Transoxiana. As we approach Europe the traces of this name grow fainter, yet are not altogether lost."

Max Müller (1891, p.298) talks about the two roads open to the Aryas of Asia took to Northern Greece and along the Danube to Germany. It is now certain beyond any doubt that the Aryans from India (Aryavarta) were there in the Caucasus, Central Asia, and Europe, who, on their return to India in about 1500 B.C., were mistaken as invaders.

C.V. Vaidya, in *'History of Sanskrit Literature'* (1986, vol. 1, pp. 39-40), is attempting to give lingual (Sanskrit and Avestan) evidences to establish that in ancient times, the Indian Aryans and

---

[95] De Sacy, *Memoire*, p. 47; Lassen, *Ind. Alt. i. 8.*

Iranians, not only lived together, but also were one people. He writes that the Avestic *gāthās* and *Rig Vedic mantras* were extremely similar and some times identical. By the way, *'gāthās'* is a Sanskrit word, meaning stories. Therefore, Vaidya feels:

"Argument again in favour of a late date for the Rigvedic hymns is sought to be derived from the extreme similarity of Avestic gāthās and Rigvedic mantras which are sometimes identical. There is no doubt that the Indo-Aryans and the Iranians once formed one people and lived together. They naturally have some mantras in common. But we must remember that Zoroaster did not himself compose these *gāthās*. He only preserved what had come down for centuries and even if we take 550 B.C. as the date of Zoroaster, that cannot be the date of those *gāthās*. Indeed, as the Hindus have preserved the Vedic mantras intact for thousands of years, because they have become sacred, so also must the Avestic gāthās have been preserved intact for thousands of years before they were taken up by Zoroaster for his new religion."

The above is an irrefutable evidence that there was close relationship between India and Iran, and so between Sanskrit and Avestan, and so between Hinduism and Zoroastrianism.

V. Gordon Childe, in his book *'The Aryans: A Study of Indo-European Origins'* (1987, p. 20), writes that according to Eduard Meyer, "Indians and Iranians had lived together as one body and had worshipped these very deities in common before the Indians had occupied the Indus Valley."

In my opinion, Eduard Meyer is wrong in saying that Indians had occupied the Indus Valley. As a matter of fact, they were its natives.

SEVENTEEN

India in the Mediterranean

"Again, there is nothing that we know of in prehistoric Egypt or Mesopotamia or anywhere else in western Asia to compare with the well-built baths and commodious houses of the citizens of Mohenjo-daro. In those countries, much money and thought were lavished on the buildings of magnificent temples of gods and on the palaces and tombs of kings, but the rest of the people seemingly had to content themselves with insignificant dwellings of mud. In the Indus Valley the picture is reversed, and the finest structures are those erected for the convenience of the citizens."

Sir John Marshal[96]

We can know Middle-east better through the Indus Valley civilization. Sir John Marshal, in Nehru's, *Glimpses of World History* (2004, p. 217), has talked about the points of difference and superiority of the Indus Valley people to their contemporaries of Egypt and Mesopotamia. Sir John Marshal (Nehru, p.216) praises the Indus civilization:

"One thing that stands out clear and unmistakable both at Mohenjo-daro and Harappa is that the civilization hitherto

---

[96] Sir John Marshal, in Nehru's, *Glimpses of World History* (2004, p. 217).

revealed at these two places is not an incipient civilization, but one already age-old and stereotyped on Indian soil, with many millennia of human endeavour behind it. Thus India must henceforth be recognized, along with Persia, Mesopotamia, and Egypt as one of the most important areas where the civilization processes were initiated and developed."

The history of the Indus Valley suggests that its people were adventurous traders and merchants, always in search of the countries with which they could establish commercial connections, and also the countries to colonize. Trading allowed them first to step in, establish their businesses, and then know how to establish their kingdoms. It seems the European colonists – British, French, Dutch, Portuguese, Spanish and Germans – had learnt the science and the art of colonization from the history of the ancient Indus Indo-Aryans.

Aryans did all this in Mesopotamia, Egypt, Asia Minor, Bahrain, Far South-East Asia, Africa and Europe. They had passion for trade and commerce, which kept them always moving vibrantly all around on the planet.

Stephen Knapp (2000, p.81) cites V. Gordon Childe, who, in his book *'The Aryans'*, states that there is evidence that the Aryans had been established in centers on the Upper Euphrates in 1400 B.C. which were similar to the cities of the Indus Valley, and later in Media and Persia. This clearly tells that these Aryans were not the natives of Mesopotamia.

Dr. Poonai, in *'Origin of Civilization and Languag'* (p.169), enlists the names of various Rig-Vedic clans in India and their later middle-eastern cognates:

Rigvedic clans in India	Descendants (Mid-East cognate)
Kshttri	Hittite
Mitra-ani	Mittani
Khasi or Kasi	Kassite
Assur Aryan	Assyrian
Bhupalan	Babylonian
Madai	Mede

India in the Mediterranean

Purusham Aryanam	Parthian, Persian, Iranian
Rigvedic clans in India	Descendants (M-East cognate)
Eyam	Elam
Sumer	Sumer

Dr. Poonai remarks that the closeness of the resemblance between the Sanskritic and the cognate names is a strong evidence of the linguistic contribution of the people of the Indo-Gangetic-Himalayan region to the states of Mesopotamia and neighboring lands including Turkmenistan, Iran, Anatolia, the Balkan peninsula, Southern Europe, Phoenicia, Spain, Italy and Gaul. He has also listed a few main Rig Vedic clans, such as Asuras (Asurs), Aggars, Kshatris, Pals, Singhs, Dasas, Mitras, Khasis, Anandas, and Amars.

Rig Vedic Aryans in Mediterranean region

Dr. Poonai (p. 223) writes that Vedic Aryans, about 4,500 years back, were in the region of the Caspian Sea and the Black Sea from where, according to some historians, invading Aryans might have come to India:

"By about 2,500 B.C., the speakers and potential speakers of these Rig-Vedic Sanskrit-derived languages had reached the northern shores of the Caspian Sea and the Black Sea, the Anatolian coast on the Aegean Sea, the Phoenician coast on the eastern Mediterranean, the northern shores of the Adriatic Sea and the shores of the Gulf of Genoa."

This proves beyond any doubt that the some Sanskrit-speaking Aryans might have returned from the Caspian Sea, the Black Sea, and the Aegean Sea region to India, the abode of their ancestors, in about 1500 B.C. when their kingdoms might have been overpowered by other forces. Those returning Aryans were mistaken as invaders.

Stephen Knapp, as the title of his book 'Proof of Vedic Culture's Global Existence' suggests, writes that the Vedic

201

influence pervaded all over the globe. He (p. 81) writes:

"As we investigate the region and countries of the Middle East, we find much evidence that shows the early influence of Vedic culture. Much of this influence still remains today. This justifies the fact that such influence would not be there if this region had not been at one time a part of the global Vedic Aryan culture and had been administered by Vedic rulers."

Knapp (p.81) talks about several Middle East countries worshipping same gods:

"Numerous countries of the Middle East shared many of the same gods in various ways, although they called them by different names. They also had many similarities in the legends and stories which explained the creation of cosmological realities."

E. Pococke (p.178) writes about the Vedic (Hindu) influence in Babylonian and Assyrian empires:

"That a system of Hinduism pervaded the whole Babylonian and Assyrian empires. Scripture furnishes abundant proofs, in the mention of the various types of the Sun-god, Bal-nat'h, whose pillar adorned "every mount," and "every grove;" and to whose other representative, the brazen calf,[97] the fifteenth of each month was especially sacred."

Even now, among Hindus, the mid of the lunar month, because of full moon, is considered sacred. It is known as *Purnamassi.*

---

[97] Nanda

Was Cabba at Mecca a Hindu worship place?

Captain F. Wilford, in Sir William Jones's Asiatic Researches (p. 257), tells the story of two doves "found by Mohammed in the *Cabba* at *Mecca;* which they claim, with some reason, as a place of worship belonging originally to the *Hindus.* " Research is needed to validate Wilford's claim about the White Islands and Cabba.

Aryan Kingdoms in Syria and Palestine;

Knapp (pp. 81-82) talks about the Aryan princes in Syria and Palestine, who, according to him, were rulers, not permanent residents there:

"There are also tablets at Tell-el-Amarna that mention Aryan princes in Syria and Palestine. But these Aryans were not necessarily permanent residents of the area, but dynasts who ruled over the non-Aryan subjects of the region. This would explain why some scholars such as Jacobi, Pargiter, and Konow accept the deities of the Mitanni in the Upper Euphrates in Syria and Palestine as being Indian, introduced to the area through a Sanskrit speaking people who came from the Punjab."

Knapp (p.82) further writes:

"Furthermore, L. A. Waddell claims that the first Aryan kings can be traced back to at least 3380 B.C. They had a capital north of the Euphrates near the Black Sea in Cappadocia in 3378 B.C., and these Hittite kings of Cappadocia bore Aryan names. This means that the Aryans had been very well settled in the area during this time."

The Hittites

According to Knapp (pp.82, 83), both the Mitannis and the Hittites were eastern people with their roots in Aryan race of India.

Documents from Boghaz-Koi, Asia Minor (present Turkey), translated in 1917, show that they spoke an ancient language which was related to or derived from Sanskrit. Knapp (p.83) writes that according to D.D. Kosambi in *The Culture and Civilization of Ancient India* (p.77), the Hittite people were known as the Khatti, possibly derived from the Sanskrit word *Kshatriya* or from the Pali Khattiyo.

Knapp (p.82) further writes:

> "The Hittites were known to have worshipped a god called Inar, most undoubtedly the Vedic Indra, which the Larousse Encyclopedia of Mythology (p.85) mentions as a god who had come from India with the Indo-European Hittites. There is also a book that has been found in Anatolia on horse training that contains technical terms in perfect Sanskrit. Thus the Hittites were certainly part of Vedic culture and a migratory wave out of the Indian region."

According to Dr. Poonai, *'Origin of Civilization and Language'* (1994, p. 228), the Hittites were descendants of the *Kshattri* clan of *Rig-Vedic* Aryans. At one time they had occupied the whole of Anatolia and during that occupancy, as a result of their Sanskritic heritage they gave Sanskritic names to many places and persons in Anatolia, for example, Purushananda, Pala, Haripal, Marasantiya, Kuldeep, Sarvagun, Asitavan Das, Naram Singh, etc.

The Mitanni

Knapp (pp.82-83) writes that the Mitanni from North India appeared as a ruling tribe in Mesopotamia, Syria, and Palestine. The clay tablets found at El Amarna in the 15th century B.C. bore names of the Mitanni kings of Syria, namely Artatama, Artamanya, Saussatar, Sutarna, Subandu, Dusratta, Suwardata, and Yasdata. He further writes:

> "Later on, the treaties between the Hittite king Shubbiluliuma and the Mitanni king Mattiuza are shown

to invoke the Mitanni gods Mitra (Vedic Mitra), Indaru (Indra), Uruwna (Varuna), and Nashattiya (the Nasatyas). Herein we can see that the Mitanni gods had names similar to the Vedic gods. The Mitanni people were also called the Maryanni."

Knapp (p.83) writes:

"Childe, in his book *The Aryans* (p.19), compares this name (Maryanni) to the Sanskrit word *marya,* meaning young men or heroes. This word is used in the *Rig-Veda* (3.54.13 & 5.59.6). Thus, it is likely that the Mitanni could hardly be anything but part of the Vedic culture and from India. However, as they moved from their native land, they shed their culture. The Mitanni people were a group from the Vedic Purus."

Knapp also talks about Hugo Winkler, who in 1907, identified the names of the four Vedic gods – Indra, Varuna, Mitra, and the Nasatya twins – along with ten Babylonian and four Mitannian gods who were invoked as witnesses to a treaty signed in 1360 B.C. between the kings of Mitanni and the Hittite. The question arises: "Why Vedic gods?" Because, both the Mitanni and the Hittite, the principal parties in the treaty, were *Khshtries* originally from India. Babylonian gods were also invoked, because they considered it as a right diplomatic practice to recognize the gods of the country they were in.

Childe, in *The Aryans* (p.30), remarks:

"The Indians' language approximates most closely to that of Mitanni documents and has been preserved from a remote date in the hymns of the Rigveda. This priceless document also furnishes precious historical data."

The Sumerians

According to Knapp (2000, p.83), it is not sure that the Sumerians were a part of the Vedic civilization. But, in many other ways they seem to be like Vedic people. He explains:

> "The Sumerian theology, which is very similar to the Vedic version, can still be found in the detailed texts dating back to 1900 B.C. ... So presently it is not clear which were the Sumerian gods or which were carry-overs from the Vedic Aryans, to whom the Sumerians at least were closely related if not a part of Vedic civilization. ... The images of the gods were worshiped by being given offerings of food and drink, fruit, incense, and new garments on festival days. This is the same system used in worshiping the Vedic deities in India."

Hindus in Mesopotamia, Asia Minor, and Central Asia

Pococke, in his book 'India in Greece' (pp. 45, 46), talks about presence of Hindus in ancient Mesopotamia, West Asia and in Central Asia, south of Caucasus. He (pp. 45-46) writes that an emigration took place from Indian districts of Bopalan (Bhopal) and Bhagulpoor (Bhagalpur) and their neighborhoods to north-west. They established their colonies "along the southern banks of the Euphrates in Mesopotamia (present Iraq), they are called singularly enough 'ANCO-BAR-I-TIS,' that is, 'ANGA-POOR-I-DES,' the country of Anga-poor. 'Anga' is that district which, in classical Hindoo writings, includes Bengal proper and Bhagulpoor."[98]

Pococke (p.179) talks about the *Suryavansi* settlements (colonies) in the Middle East region:

> "The martial bands of the Surya Vansa (Surya = sun, and Vansa = descent) will now be briefly contemplated, in their Syrian settlements; more especially those in which they acted so prominent a part, as the fierce and warlike opponents of the favoured Children of Israel."

---

[98] Wilson, Sansc. Lex. "Anga," "Bhagulpoor" (Boglipoor) is a district in the province of Bahar (Bihar).

India in the Mediterranean

Harry H. Hicks and Robert N. Anderson,[99] in *'Ancient India and Vedic Aryans: New Discoveries, Scientific Procedures and Implications for History'*, write:

> "There were some migrations to the West. Gimbutas felt that around 20th century B.C., the 'movement of Asiatic peoples was responsible for the break-up of the Old Empire of Egypt.' There were movements into Mesopotamia, and further west into Anatolia."

It has been shown in this chapter that Hindus had established their kingdoms (Mitanni, Hittites) in Egypt, Syria, Asia Minor and Mesopotamia. According to the Columbia Encyclopedia (p. 163), in ancient times most Oriental and Occidental civilizations intersected in Asia Minor. It clearly shows that in ancient times, there were peoples of several ethnic backgrounds in Central Asia including Asia Minor, from the East as well as from the West. It is evident that they were traders, not the natives of Central Asia.

Vedic Aryans in Nevali Cori (Anatolia) in 7000 B.C.

B. G. Sidharth[100] was startled to see a sculpture of the head of a Vedic priest, excavated at Nevali Cori in Anatolia (present Turkey) by archeologists headed by Prof. Harald Hauptmann of Heidelberg. Sidharth, himself, had gone to the Nevali Cori site. Sidharth, talking about the head, remarks: "It is identical to the head of a Vedic priest, so common in India even today. The sculpture represents a clean shaven head with the typical plait or *shikha.*" I had fortune meeting with the Prof. Sidharth at the Birla Center eight years back when I started my research on the history of Ancient India, which has been distorted and mutilated.

---

[99] Sharma and Ghose (ed.), *"Revisiting Indus-Sarasvati Age and Ancient India"* (1998, p.353)
[100] B.G. Sidharth, in "A Lost Anatolian Civilization: Is It Vedic", Research Communication, 1992.

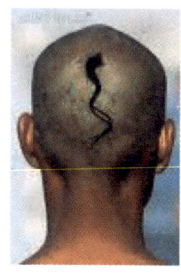

Head with *shikha*

It reminds me of my childhood, when, as a part of the *Janeoo* (Sacred thread) ceremony, my head was clean-shaven, leaving only *Shikha,* snake-like a bunch of hair at the back top of my head. In my Sindhi language, it is called *'Choti'.* It is a custom among Hindus, particularly Brahmins to have *Janeoo.* Only Hindus (Vedic people) do it. Unlike several other Hindu communities, all Sindhi Hindus wear Janeoo. My father used to say that all Hindus, irrespective of their caste, should have Janeoo.

Sidharth talks about the antiquity of the Nevali Cori civilization compared to the Rig Veda's:

"The Nevali Cori civilization could be identified with the Rig Vedic civilization. ... Nevali Cori site goes back to beyond 7000 B.C."

The age of *Nevali Cori* reflects the age of the *Rig Veda* which is much older than the *Nevali Cori.* It should not puzzle us. We know Aryans have been adventurous from too remote ancient times. History tells *Swastika* was every where – in Americas, Europe, Africa, South-east Asia, etc. Who else other than Vedic Aryans (Hindus) would have taken *Swastika* every where? They took the Swastika to Americas about ten thousands years back.

Aryan invasion of Asia Minor

Grahame Clark, in *"World Prehistory: A New Outline"* (1969, p. 214), under the subtitle *'Post-Harappan chalcolithic cultures in the Indus and Ganges Basins'*, writes:

"Precisely when Aryan-speakers first entered the subcontinent is still open to discussion, though it may be relevant that documentary sources, notably the archives of clay tablets at the Hittite capital of Boghazkoy, point to the arrival of Aryan-speakers in Asia Minor during the fifteenth and fourteenth centuries B.C. In so far as we can picture them from the epic-chants, hymns, prayers and spells that make up the Rigveda, the Aryans were copper or bronze-using barbarians, who gained their living from stock-raising and cereal farming, occupied timber and thatch houses and used horse-driven chariots for sport and war."

How could the Aryans, who used horse-driven-chariots for sports in such ancient times, be called barbarian? Even in present times, only few can afford such luxury. During those times, since there were no industries, agriculture was the only way of life. So the people, engaged in stock-raising and cereal farming, should not be considered as barbarians. Clark does not specify from where those Sanskrit-speaking Aryans came to Asia Minor during the fifteenth and fourteenth centuries B.C. In my opinion, Aryans were in Asia Minor, long before fourteenth century B.C., as evidenced by the Hindu priest-like head, excavated at the Nevali Cori (Anatolia), which according to radiocarbon analysis dated beyond 7000 B.C.

Who were those Aryans, Grahame Clark is talking about their entering in Asia Minor? From where did they come? Seeing their ethno-cultural characteristics such as – Sanskrit numbers and Indic names of the colors of the horses in the chariot-war-training manuals, Sanskritic names of some towns and persons, cremation, names of Hindu gods invoked in treaties between Hittite and Mitanni rulers, etc. – it can be said beyond any doubt, that they were Indo-Aryans who must have gone there from no where else, but from Aryavarta (India). Since they were warriors who had established their kingdoms, they must be from royal families. This negates the theory, 'Aryan invasion of India'. It was their return to, not invasion of India.

Some historians say that Aryans invaded Asia Minor in 1800 B.C. According to the Columbia Encyclopedia (p.163), "The Hittites established the first major civilization in 1800 B.C." But, as per archeological evidences, it can be said that Aryans were there in Asia Minor even before 7000 B.C. It seems the historians and the Columbia Encyclopedia did not take in account the archeological evidences, as discussed earlier (pp. 210-211) about the Nevali Cori civilization.

It is possible that later in about 1500 B.C., when Aryans in Asia Minor and in neighboring states were in trouble, most of them stayed there and got culturally and linguistically absorbed, and some decided to return to India, the country of their ancestors. Being warriors from royal families, on their return, they might have traveled in armored horse-driven chariots. They might have confronted violent resistance from the then natives of India who might have mistaken them as invaders.

Grahame Clark (1977, p. 271) writes:

"We know from the radiocarbon analysis that the metropolitan sites came to an end in all probability as early as c. 2000 B.C. and even secondary sites in the Indus basin by c. 1750 B.C. When the Aryan speakers first reached India is still unknown. Internal evidence suggests that the society mirrored, in the earlier parts of the Rigveda, was accustomed to copper and bronze, but ignorant of iron, something that would put the earlier waves of immigration back before c.800 B.C. How far back is still unknown, but the occurrence of the names of gods familiar from the Indian pantheon in the treaty between Hittites and Mitannian rulers dating from c.1380 B.C. suggests that the mythology of the Aryan speakers reflected in the Rigveda had taken shape around the middle of the second millennium B.C."

The invocation of Vedic gods in 1380 B.C. clearly suggests that the alleged invading Aryans were Vedic people, not strangers or foreigners to India. It also suggests that they must have been there long before 1380 B.C. The time of the arrival of the Aryans in India has been speculative, rather unknown. I think it is because the invasion didn't happen, as their one time massive entry. They were not invaders. They must have returned as family or in small groups of families, as it is happening now with overseas Indian migrants {known as NRIs (Non-Resident-Indians)}, returning to India. Since there was difference in the circumstances affecting the departure of the early Aryans from the ancient India, there would be difference in the mode of their return too from that of the present overseas Indians.

According to the Columbia Encyclopedia, Mitanni, an ancient kingdom, was established in the 2nd millennium BC, in NW Mesopotamia. It was founded by Aryans but later was made up predominantly of Hurrians, with Washshukanni as its capital. Mitanni controlled Assyria for a period and was militarily engaged to hold back Egyptian forces intent on conquering Syria. Later friendly relations developed between Mitanni and Egypt. But in 1335 B.C., Mitanni, in their war, fell to the Hittites as well as to Assyrian forces.

In my opinion, some of the Mitanni Aryans – known as Mitrani *Kshatriya* from the NW of India, Sindh and Punjab – when defeated and dislodged from there, must have thought of returning to India, the country of their ancestors. It was their return to, not invasion of India. Historians need to understand the confusion around this, and reconstruct the Aryan-related ancient history of India. These historical Aryans are originally from Aryavarta (India). 'Arya' is a Sanskrit word and it has frequently occurred in the Vedas and other Vedic scriptures, including the Bhagvad Gita. Aryans are being misperceived as foreigners to India who allegedly invaded India in about 1500 B.C. No historian, among such host of misguided confused historians, has been able to prove the originality of the invading Aryans and their homeland. Such ill-based concept – identity and originality of the Aryans – has confused the history of the world, the Aryans have played significant role in.

211

Indo-Aryan elements in Asia Minor and its vicinity

Mallory (1991, pp. 37- 41) says that there were distinctly Indo-Aryan elements in the Mitanni kingdom. This is evident from a Hittite text[101] on the horse-training and chariot, authored by Kikkuli, a Mitanni, in which Indic (Sanskrit) names of numerals – *aika* (Indic *eka* = one), *tera* (tri = three), *panza* (*panca* = five), *satta* (*sapta* = seven), *na* (*nava* = nine) – and the colors of the horses, such as *babru* (Indic *babhru* = brown), *parita* (*palita* = grey), and *pinkara* (*pingala* = reddish). The Mitanni's word *marya* is the same as the Vedic *marya* meaning warrior. Even Sanskrit names of the Mitanni kingdoms, divinities, towns (Tepe Giyan), and personal names evidence Indic (Hindu) influence in the Mitanni kingdom.

The Columbia Encyclopedia (p.167) gives names – Ashurbanipal (I, II, III, IV), Shalmaneser (I, II, III, IV, V), etc of the kings of some kingdoms in Assyria, ancient empire of West Asia, which developed around the city of Assur, or Ashur, on the upper Tigris River and south of later capital Nineveh, the beginning of 3rd millennium B.C., continuing to about 8th century B.C. The Encyclopedia writes that Ashur was Assyria's chief god. The gods of the Babylonians and Hittites were also honored. The names of the kings, mentioned above, seem to have their origin in Sanskrit.

Dr. Poonai (1994, p. 156) has given the names of the kingdoms, the Rig Vedic Aryans had established:

States founded by some Rig Vedic clans

Rig Vedic Aryan Clans	States founded by them
Assur or Ahura Aryan	Assyria
Aggar	Aggad or Akkad
Evam or Ayam	Elam
Medai or Medes	Land of Medes
Purusham Aryanam	Parthia
Purusham Aryanam	Persia

---

[101] Mallory *in the Search of the Indo-Europeans* (pp.47-38).

212

Kshattri	Hittite States
Nasatya	Phoenicia
Khasi	Kassite territory
Mitra-ani	Mittani
Bhupalan	Babylon

The different clans established different city states, such as Assyria (Asura Aryan clan), Aggad/Akhad (Aggar), Elam (Eyam/Ayam), Medes (Madai/ Medes), Parthia and Persia (Purusham Aryanam), Hittite states (Kshattri), Phoenicia (Nasatya), Kassite territory (Khasi), Mittani (Mitra-ani), and Babylon (Bhupalan). In ancient times, because of transportation limitations, states or countries were as small as cities. This affected languages. Each city-state has its own language spilling over the adjacent ones. Those have been considered as dialects which gradually merged and developed into full-fledged languages, growing correspondingly along with their respective developing city governments.

Regarding the dialects of these Aryan clans, Dr. Poonai (p.156) has said:

"Into each of the above territories and others like them, the Rig-Vedic Aryan clans carried their own versions of Prakrit. Both the phonetic values and the symbols underwent modifications peculiar to each state, but the rules governing the use of language survived without major changes. There was no separation of vowels and consonants in any of the alphabets or syllabaries except in the cases of Rome and Greece. In the latter two states (Mittani and Babylon), the rules of grammar also conformed more closely to the rules governing the Rig-Vedic Sanskrit."

The hieroglyphic dialect of the Hittites, as observed by Poonai (p.102), is related to that of the Rig Vedic clan of Lohians/Luvians (blacksmiths).

Some kingdoms in Mesopotamia (2500-1150) were ruled by Vedic Aryans, as suggested by their names, closer to Sanskrit –

Mesannepada and Annepadda (around 2500 B.C.); Umma (around 2360, B.C.); Rimush (2304-2296) and Manishtushu (2295-2281, B.C.), sons of Sargon; Naramsin (2280-2244 B.C.); Ishbierra, king of Isin (1953-1921 B.C.); Urninurta (1859-1832 B.C.); Gungunum (1868-1842B.C.); Sudarna, son of Artadama and grandson of Saushsatar (1500 B.C.), Assuruballit (1366-1331); Shalmaneser- I (1275-1247); etc. Sudarna was a Mitanni king. The names seem Sanskritic.

Yet better research is needed to ascertain their linguistic origin and the ethnic originality of the kings and their history. Sargon extended his contest into Anatolia and his grandson brought Akhad to the zenith of his power and peaceful accomplishments.[102]

William L. Langer (ed.), in *The New Illustrated Encyclopedia of World History* (vol.1, 1975, p.34), talks about the Hurrians (Biblical Horites) who, in small numbers, started entering northern Mesopotamia and the East Tigris country in the late 3rd millennium. Major invasions of these people began about 1700, and by 1500 B.C. they had penetrated into the whole of Mesopotamia, Syria and Eastern Anatolia, and Palestine. The situation for Mitanni kingdom changed and they started losing power.

The earliest Hurrian texts are from Mari (18th century B.C.). Other texts come from the Hittite archive of Boghazkoy (14th-13th centuries) from Ugarit and from Egypt.

Langer was surprised to see that the Hurrian royal families seemed to be Indo-Aryan. He remarks that the ruling class of the Hurrians bore not Hurrian, but Indo-Aryan names. The Aryans overpowered both the Hurrians and Kassites, and established themselves as an aristocracy and probably won their position as chariot-warriors. It becomes strange to see that Aryans were fighting against Hurrians and Kassites who were also Aryans, originally from India. It seems confusing to know who those Aryans were when Mitanni, Hittites, Kassites and even Hurrians were Indo-Aryans. I can understand they, though originally being

---

[102] William L. Langer: *The New Illustrated Encyclopedia of World History*, (1975, vol. I, 32.

from India, were fighting among themselves. It is known that even brothers fight over property.

Langer (1975, p. 34) writes that small Hurrian principalities were united toward 1500 (B.C.) into the Kingdom of Mitanni with its capital at Washukkani on the Khabur. At its widest extent, it controlled Alalakh and Qatna in Syria on the west, and Nuzu and Arapkha, as well as Assyria, on the east. Sudarna I (c1500) was the earliest of the great kings of Mitanni.

No country in the region had Sanskrit or any Indo-Aryan, as its native language. Indo-Aryan rulers naturally had Vedic (Hindu) names and Sanskrit as their family language. Sanskrit influence in the region was evident, as English and Arabic linguistic influence is evident in India. Indo-Aryans were the royal (ruling) class, hence, only the members of the ruling families bore Sanskritic names. Some cities, also, bore Indic names. History tells that only ruling families, being Vedic (Hindus), unlike non-Aryan commoners, cremated their bodies. The chariot-training manuals had Sanskritized numbers, and the names of the colors of the horses (like *bhooro*) were also Sanskritic. The names of the members of the ruling families were slightly corrupted by the local people. The names of Hindus who went to the Caribbean countries as indentured workers only over 160 years back are being spelt a little different, for example, 'Dev' as 'Deo', 'Ashok' as 'Ashook', etc. We can imagine what would have happened to the names of those Aryans, who had gone there over 3500 years back.

Langer (p.32) talks about the legends related to the Akhadian and Mesopotamian kings:

"Later legends, including those of the epic tale *King of Battle,* describe Sargon as extending his conquests into Anatolia and even across the sea to Crete. Rimush (2304-2296 BC) and Manishtushu (2295-2281 BC), the sons of Sargon, consolidated the empire. Naramsin (2280-2244 BC), Sargon's grandson, brought Akhad to the zenith of its power and peaceful accomplishment. He was the first of the Mesopotamian kings to claim divinity, and to style himself "king of the four quarters (of the world)."

Langer also mentions that in the Akhadian era, the arts and trade with distant Indus Valley flourished. Why would not their trade flourish with the Indus Valley, their original land?

Langer (p.32) then tells about the end of the power of the Sargon's dynasty:

"Sharkalishharri (2243-2219 BC), the last of Sargon's line, reigned in a time of troubles, defending his narrowing borders against the blows of surrounding barbarians. After him ephemeral kings held Akhad for some years longer, but the city fell about 2180 B.C. to Guti hordes from the Zagros."

The names of the Sargon's family – Rimush, Manishtushu, Naramsin, Sharkalishharri and other – seem to be Sanskritic. So many Indo-Aryans had gone out of India long back to this region and had established their kingdoms. After long residence in the land of a non-Sanskritic language, their names got corrupted by the influence of the non-Sanskritic native language.

Such situation of Sargon's defeats (pp. 31, 32) and defeats of earlier Mitanni kings (p.34) – Sudarna, Saushastar, Artadama, Tuishrata, etc. – made the Aryans too powerless, and loose to decide their future. Some stayed there and got absorbed and some attempted to return to India, the country of their ancestors. Their return on armored chariots was mistaken as their invasion.

It seems there was some exchange of religious concepts between Sumerian and the natives of the Indus civilization: "The Sumerian gods in early times were closely bound by natural phenomena, the powers of creativity, fertility, and forces confronted in the cosmos."[103]

Dr. Poonai, in *'Origin of Civilization and Language'* (p.190), has talked about certain inscriptions, found in the ruins of an ancient fortress 'Karatepe' built in about 680 B.C. by a Rig-Vedic Aryan ruler – bear obviously a Sanskrit name 'Asitavan Das', based on decipherment of the Hittite hieroglyphic by an American

---

[103] William L. Langer *"The New Illustrated Encyclopedia of World History"* (1975, P.31).

scholar Dr. Gelb in 1930. The results of the decipherment were confirmed on the basis of further archaeological records.

Dr. Poonai (p.104), talking about archaeological and linguistic evidence of Rig Vedic Aryan ancestry in Anatolia, has pointed to another strong evidence of the influence of Sanskrit in the region is provided by an archaeologically found unique item of pottery '*deepam*' (lamp with a wick which burns oil). In Sanskrit the word '*deepam*' (or *deep*) means lamp.

Deepam

Deepam must have been brought in Anatolia by Indo-Aryans for its use in house for light. In those ancient times there was no electricity. *Deepam* (or *deep*) is used in Vedic (Hindu) religious rituals, and festivals, particularly *Divali* or *Deepavali* (diva/deep means lamp) to celebrate the arrival of Lord Rama in Ayodhya, the capital of his kingdom, after defeating the demon Ravana of Sri Lanka, and also to celebrate his return home after completing fourteen years of his self-imposed exile. On *divali*, light by these earthen *deeps* (or divas or *deepams*) is ritually preferred to electric bulbs. During *Divali* time, these earthen *deeps* (or divas/*diyas*) are being imported and sold in Indian shops worldwide where Indian (Hindu, Sikh, Buddhist and Jain) population is significant. I have seen Deepams being sold in Indian stores in America during *Divali* times. The word *"Deep"* has so much significance among Hindus, that they would love to name their daughter "Deepti" to bring light to the family. Deep brings light of Sri Ram's knowledge.

The people, who migrated from India to the Asia Minor region, were mainly of the *Kshatri* (warrior) descent, mostly from the Sindhu-Sarasvati (Indus) Valley which covers Sindh, Punjab, Baluchistan, Rajasthan, and Gujarat. They took with them the horse-driven chariot technology which helped them in establishing their kingdoms overseas. In those ancient times, horse was considered on the top to bring speed on the battle field. There is mention of chariot (in Sanskrit '*Rath*') in *Rig Veda* (10-63-14), the oldest of the Vedas:

"Yam devaso rotha vaajasaatau yam sursata maaruto hitepaartar yavanam ratham Indra sanasim."

Rath was used in the Mahābhāratā war, in which Lord Krishna was the driver and Arjuna was the warrior fighting with a bow for shooting arrows at the enemies. It is also said that in the Mahābhāratā war *agnibans* (fire arrows) were also used and also the arrows which could create clouds to densely cover the sun and then dispel them off.

EIGHTEEN

India in Ancient Europe

"Clans, whose martial fame is still recorded in the faithful chronicles of North-Western India, as the gallant bands who fought upon the plains of Troy; and, in fact, the whole of Greece, from the era of the supposed god-ships of Poseidon and Zeus, down to the close of the Trojan war, as being Indian in language, sentiments, and religion, and in the arts of peace and war. Much I shall, I doubt not, incontestably establish; much must be left to a future period."

Edward Pococke[104]

Pococke, in *'India in Greece'* (pp.253-258), while talking about Hesiod's history of Greece, remarks that the geographical facts, as recorded on the mountains and rivers of Hellas (ancient name of Greece), seem to be "connected with those people who gave names to these rivers and mountains." His later statement, "the representative to Hesiod of words apparently Greek, but in reality Sanscrit, Thibetan, or the Pehlavi dialects," suggests that 'those people' were Hindus and Buddhists from Indian subcontinent who had colonized Greece in ancient times. He seems to complain about "corrupt orthography, and corrupt history based upon that orthography." Later, Pococke talks about Lamaism, solar or

---

[104] Edward Pococke, Esq. in *'India in Greece or Truth in Mythology'*, published by Richard Griffin and Company, London (1856, p. 12).

Buddhistic forms of worship among the primitive population of Hellas.

Pococke (p.254) remarks that the *Surya Vaanshi* and the *Chandra Vanshi* have been the best colonists of Greece:

> "The great aggregate of the colonists of Greece has already been shown to consist of those two great bodies, the Solar and the Lunar races; each following the peculiar tenets of that faith to which the heads of their respective races gave so strong a bias, viz., either the Solar or the Bud'histic forms of worship. The former was more ancient in its establishment, but the latter more durable. The Lamaic nations, springing up apparently upon the frontiers of the kingdoms of Cashmir and Thibet, have by the population, already shown in Thessaly, been proved to have existed in the latter countries in high antiquity, and the record of the life of Zeus, as drawn by Hesiod, is but a garbled statement of plain facts, in perfect harmony with existing state of Lamaism in Tartary."

Pococke (p.130) writes: "... but that the province of Cashmir and its neighbourhood, and its tribes, and its Maha-bharatian history, are transported to the Hella Nova with almost the faithfulness of lithographic transfer from one material to another."

Pococke (pp. 131-2) remarks that Greece has practically become as primitive as India, and that the people of India were primitive even from the most ancient times.

Pococke (p. 131) talks about "Rajatarangini", in his opinion, the most authentic document, as an historical foundation on India-Greece connection:

> "The most authentic document which north-western India possesses – (and north-western India is now made synonymous with Greece, more especially with northern Greece,) – is the Rajatarangini. The Rajatarangini, written at Cashmir, the identical point whence the Cassiopæi, or "people of Casyapa," set out on their emigration into north-western Greece, is a dynastic record of the princes

of that far-famed valley, whose chronicles ascend to the venerable antiquity of B.C. 2448."

Pococke, in the footnote (p.131) tells that Raja Tarangini is not one entire composition. It is a series of compositions written by different authors at different times of different circumstances, as per Prof. Wilson's very copious and learned treatise on the Hindoo History of Cashmir, *Asiatic Researches* (vol xv).

Pococke (p.9), talking about the evidences of Indian colonization of Greece, describes various things looking like Indian – such as beautifully embroidered shawls, numerous ornaments of ivory, tasteful ample produce of the loom, elegant workmanship on the golden jewelry, constant use of the war chariot both by Greeks and Asiatics. On p.255, Pococke talks about the presence of the people of the Himalayas and Buddhist priesthood. On p. 256, he talks about 'The High Lama Town and "a sect of Buddhists so ancient and so extensive as to give a name to a vast tract of country in which they had settled." He mentions that a village bore its name as "Grihya", which, it seems has its origin in Sanskrit word 'Griha' meaning house or habitation.

Pococke (p.12) gives more evidences of Indian (Hindu) presence in Greece:

"Now, the whole of this state of society, civil and military, must strike every one as being eminently Asiatic; much of it specifically Indian. Such it undoubtedly is; and I shall demonstrate that these evidences were but the attendant tokens of an Indian colonization, with its corresponding religion and language. I shall exhibit dynasties disappearing from Western India, to appear again in Greece."

Pococke (pp.18-19), while referring to the identity of structure, of vocables, and inflective power, in the Greek and Sanskrit languages, remarks:

"Every day adds fresh conviction produces fresh demonstration, of this undeniable fact. The Greek language is a derivation from Sanscrit; therefore, Sanscrit-speaking people – i.e., Indians, must have dwelt in Greece, and this dwelling must have preceded the settlement of those tribes which helped to produce the corruption of the old language; or, in other words, the people who spoke that language – i.e., the Indians, must have been the primitive settlers; or, at least, they must have colonized the country so early, and dwelt there so long, as to have effaced all dialectic traces of any other inhabitants; just as the Saxons displaced the feeble remains of the dialect of the ancient Britons, in this island, and imparted a thoroughly Saxons stamp to the genius of the English language."

Pococke explains that the long stay of Indians (Sanskrit-speaking Indo-Aryans) in Greece was cause of the impress, Sanskrit left on the regional dialects of Greece. It is clear that the philological similarities, Sanskrit has with Greek, are not genetic or cognate, as several linguists feel. Greek and Sanskrit can not be lingual genetic sisters because they are geographically too distant, and culturally and historically too different from each other.

Pococke (p.19) speaks high about the lofty effect, the Indo-Aryan colonization left on the language, philosophy, religion, political institutes, etc. of Greece:

"But, if the evidences of Saxon colonisation in this island – (I speak independently of Anglo-Saxon history) – are, strong both from language and political institutions, the evidences are still more decisive in the parallel case of an Indian colonisation of Greece, – not only her Language, but her Philosophy, her Religion, her Rivers, her Mountains, and her Tribes; her subtle turn of intellect, her political institutes, and above all the Mysteries of that noble land – irresistibly prove her colonisation from India."

It would be interesting to analytically examine what Garraty & Gay (1981, p. 97) have said about the migratory journey of Aryans from Greece into India via Iran:

"The Aryans ("noble ones") were part of a large Indo-European migration which left a common cultural heritage from Greece through Iran into India. The religious and social institutions of these invaders are reflected in the oldest stratum of the Veda (sacred "knowledge") – the most revered sector of traditional Hindu religious literature. The tribes were led by an aggressive warrior aristocracy mounted on horse-driven chariots, and armed with copper and bronze weapons of good quality."

These invaders from Greece into India, whose religious and social institutions are reflected in the Vedas, can not be other than Vedic Indo-Aryans (Hindus) who had colonized Greece in about 2448 B.C., as talked about by Pococke in his book 'India in Greece or Truth in Mythology'. The story would have been clear if Garraty & Gay had given the year of their trip to India. They can not be Greeks, nor any other Europeans. How would Vedas reflect their religious and social institutions, if they were not Indo-Aryans? Indo-Aryans (Hindus) were in Greece since long and they were known as charioteers and warriors (Khshatries). They must be in trouble. Therefore, they were returning to India, the country of their ancestors.

Stephen Knapp, in 'Proof of Vedic Culture's Global Existence' (2000, p. 165), sheds some light on 'India in Greece':

"In looking at the Greek culture, we find many connections between it and the Vedic civilization. Many people and scholars tend to view Greece as a source of western civilization. However, it is seldom realized that the original Greek culture was itself Vedic. This is not to say that no one has recognized the similarities. Even as far as 1830 we can find on pages 61-2 from volume II of Narrative of a Journey Overland from England to India by Mrs. Colonel Eldwood, where she sees the Vedic influence in Greece."

Knapp (pp.165-166) tells what Mrs. Elwood has said about the relationship between Hindus and Greeks in remote ancient times:

"The striking analogy between some of the Hindoo fables with those of the Greeks, would induce us to believe that the Greeks and Hindus must, at an early age, have had intercourse, and possibly Pythagorus, with the doctrine of the Metempsychosis, may have imported some of the adventures of the Indian gods and ascribed them to the Greek deities."

Krishna, a god of Greeks?

It is interesting, but too hard to believe what Knapp (p. 166) has said about Krishna, as a god of Greece:

"The fact that Krishna was the God of Greece is proved by the silver coins made by Agathaclose, a Greek ruler of the 2nd century B.C. These coins bear the imprint of Lord Krishna and His brother Balarama and are on display in several museums. Furthermore, a large mosaic of young Krishna playing the flute, standing cross-legged under a tree while grazing cows, hangs in the museum in Corinth. This was obviously salvaged from a local Krishina temple which proves this city was once a center of Vedic culture with temples of Krishna. We can recognize that as the Vedic culture moved from India to Egypt to Greece, etc., much of the philosophy stayed the same, although the names and artistic characteristics of the gods changed with time."

Heraklessle is Harekrishna

Knapp (p.167) further writes about India's cultural connection with Greece. He explains the origin of the Greek "Hera-klessle" in Vedic "Hare-Krishna":

"Greek writers like Pliny referred to Hari Krishna as Heracles. This is traced back to the way the early Greek writers who visited India said that the city they called Klessleboro (Mathura) was the capital of Krishna worship. The Greeks pronounced the name Krishna as *klessle,* and Hare or Hari as *hera.* Thus came the name of Heraklessle, or Heracles and Hercules, who is the muscular man who played prominent roles in the Greek myths."

Lord Krishna loved cows, he considered cow as mother, because like mother, cow gives milk, the first food the infant gets right from his/her birth. Therefore, Hindus don't eat cow (beef) meat. Krishna is known by some names connected with cow such as Gobind and Gopal, meaning protector of cows (Go = cows + pal = protector). In Sanskrit, cow is known as "go".

Jawaharlal Nehru, in *Discovery of India* (1946, p. 92), writes about the influence of Indian philosophy on Greece and Christianity, as contained in the Upanishads:

"Early Indian thought penetrated to Greece, through Iran, and influenced some thinkers and philosophers there. Much later, Plotinus came to the east to study Iranian and Indian philosophy and was especially influenced by the mystic element in the Upanishads. From Plotinus many of these ideas are said to have gone to St. Augustine, and through him influenced the Christianity of the day."

Nehru (p.115), talks about India's contacts with Greece in ancient times: "It is interesting to note that Panini mentions the Greek script. This indicates that there were some kind of contacts between India and Greece long before Alexander came to the East."

Alexander must have known from Greek history about the greatness of India which lured him to capture India. He made attempt, but could not succeed. Circumstances did not cooperate with him.

India Reborn

Plato: Influenced by the Vedic philosophy

Talking about the triumph of the East and the Hellenistic Age, Herbert J. Muller (1958, p.15) has elaborated on how Greeks profited immeasurably from their spiritual trade with the East:

> "At the same time, Plato's own thought was so fertile because it was not a classically ordered system but an exploration of various possibilities, a sensitive response to various influences, including Oriental thought. Its historic influence has stemmed chiefly from his inclination to a transcendental idealism, another worldly kind of spirituality that is more typical of India than of Greece in its heyday."

Plato (429 B.C.) was a Classical Greek philosopher and mathematician. He was a student of Socrates,

According to the 'World Book Encyclopedia' (1993, vol.15, p.504), Plato believed in the immortality of the soul and reincarnation:

> "Plato believed that though the body dies and disintegrates, the soul continues to live forever. After the death of the body, the soul migrates to what Plato called the realm of the pure form. After a time, the soul is reincarnated in another body and returns to the world. But the reincarnated soul retains the dim recollection of the realm of forms and yearns for it. Plato argued that people fall in love because they recognize in the beauty of their beloved the ideal form of beauty they dimly remember and seek."

Both – immortality of the soul and reincarnation – are the ancient basic doctrines of Hinduism and also of its offshoots Jainism, Buddhism and Sikhism. Buddhism was founded by a Hindu prince Siddhartha Gautam (563 to 483 B.C.). He was known as Buddha (enlightened) at the age of 35 when he attained supreme enlightenment.

A popular love song from an Indian movie echoes the belief in reincarnation, *"Aisa lagta hai ki ham agle janam men kahin mile honge."* (It seems we must have met somewhere in our previous life).

M. P. Pandit – in his book, *'Traditions in Mysticism'* (1987, p.121), has highlighted a study by Dr. Vassilis Vittaxis, a former Greek ambassador to India. Dr. Vittaxis, brings to light the similarities and differences between Indian philosophy and the philosophy of Plato. For example, he likens the *nous* (mind) of Plato to the *Atman* of the Upanishads." He further draws parallels between Plato's *Division of Society* and the caste system, 'Plato's Guardians, Warriors, Craftsmen have close resemblance to the Indian Brahmin, Kshatriya, Vaishya.'

Vedic philosophy left impress also on the rest of Europe.

Swetadweepa, or the White Island in Europe

Captain F. Wilford[105]has talked about *Swetadweepa,* or the White Island in the West:

"The sacred Isles in the West of which *Swetadweepa,* or the White Island, is the principal, and the most famous. In fact, it was the holy land of the *Hindus.* There the fundamental and mysterious transaction of the history of their religion, in its rise and progress, took place. The White Island, this holy land in the West, is so intimately connected with their religion and mythology, that they can not be separated and of course, divines in *India* are necessarily acquainted with it, as distant *Muselmans* with *Arabia.* This I conceive to be a most favorable circumstance; in the present case, the learned have little more to do with than to ascertain whether the White Island be England, and the Sacred Isles of the Hindus, the British Isles. After having maturely considered the subject, I think they are."

---

[105] 8th volume, Chapter VII, of *Asiatic Researches*, (ed) Sir William Jones (1787: 246).

I wish Wilford had explained how the White Island, the holy land in the West, was so intimately connected with the religion and mythology of Hindus. He (p.249) has made an interesting observation:

> "But in the course of conversation, my pandit, and other learned natives, often mentioned most interesting legends, bearing an astonishing affinity with those of the western mythologists."

Benjamin Walker, in *'The Hindu World: An Encyclopedic Survey of Hinduism'* (1968, p.468), talks about the *Svetadvipa* (White Island):

> "Svetadvipa (Sveta-dvipa, White Island) in Hindu cosmology* represents the sixth island continent surrounding Jumbu encircled by an ocean of ... Frequently mentioned in Sanskrit literature, it clearly refers to a place, the exact location which is not known. The *Mahabharata* speaks the white people of Svetadvipa on the northern shores of the Ocean as worshippers of Narayana, a thousand-rayed god. ...There has been much speculation about this place, which remains the mysteries of ancient Indian geography. It has been variously identified with Greece, with Greek kingdoms of Parthia, and with Scythia, the country of the Sakas, because an alternative name for Svetadvipa was *Sakadvipa. An ancient Brahmin* caste of India known as *sakadvip* are traced to the maga priests of Persia. Others identify Svetadvipa with Tibet, China, Japan, Palestine, even with Britain, since the name of the island suggests white-skinned inhabitants."

Benjamin Walker also in the end thinks that it would be "Britain, since the name of the island suggests white-skinned inhabitants."

India in Ancient Europe

Harry H. Hicks and Robert N. Anderson,[106] in *'Ancient India and Vedic Aryans: New Discoveries, Scientific Procedures and Implications for History'*, talking about Asiatic migrations, write: "Druids and their priests are believed to have arrived in the British Isles ca. 3000 to 2500 B.C. according to British archeological calculations."

John Bently, in Asiatic Researches (pp.377- 497), talks about the influence of the *Vedas* in Europe and Persia.

Nehru (*Discovery of India*, p.92) write::

"The rediscovery by Europe, during the past century and a half, of Indian philosophy created a powerful impression on European philosophers and thinkers."

Nehru (pp. 92-3) says that Schopenhauer, the pessimist, is often quoted in this connection:

"From every sentence (of the Upanishads) deep, original and sublime thoughts arise, and the whole is pervaded by a high and holy and earnest spirit. ... In the whole world there is no study ... so beneficial and so elevating as that of the Upanishads. ... (They) are products of the highest wisdom. It is destined sooner or later to become the faith of the people."

Aryan contribution to Russia and Europe

Childe, in the Chapter *'Role of the Aryans in History'* of his book *'The Aryans'* (1926, pp. 210-212), has written:

1. " ... graves covering the remains of a people, who, whether they were come from South Russia or represented a section of the pre-dolmenic population, were, we believe, Aryan in character."

---

[106] Sharma and Ghose (ed.), *"Revisiting Indus-Sarasvati Age and Ancient India"* (1998, p.353)

2. "The gulf between French and Scandinavian culture at the beginning of the 2nd millennium is enormous. The superiority of the former is the measure of the contribution made by the Aryan element to European civilization."

3. "Thus the Aryans do appear everywhere as promoters of true progress and in Europe their expansion marks the moment when the prehistory of our continent (Europe) begins to diverge from that Africa or the Pacific."

4. Aryan genius found its true expression in Greece and Rome."

5. The lasting gift bequeathed by the Aryans to the conquered people was neither a higher material culture nor a superior physique, but a more excellent language and the mentality it generated.

Childe, in the First Chapter *'Language and Prehistory'*, emphasizes the significance of spiritual unity, and the concept of Divine Law or Cosmic Order in Aryan culture which was bequeathed to Europeans through their language (I believe Sanskrit) which has ability of abstract thinking. Spirituality, the gem of the Aryan (Vedic or Hindu/Buddhist/Sikh) culture, is too complex for most European thinkers. This was the reason why the scientist Albert Einstein wrote to Nehru that the first part of his book *'Discovery of India'* was not easy reading for a Westerner.

NINETEEN

India in Ancient Americas

"Hindu intercourse with America is still perhaps a startling point to many. But what I have said in this chapter and elsewhere, suggests the inference that bold Hindu mariners had early circumnavigated the earth, visiting foreign lands in every continent. ... Hindu knowledge of the roundness of the earth, her vastness, her seven continents and seven oceans, 49 big islands, ocean currents, submarine volcanoes abounding in the Pacific, etc., leave no doubt of the Hindu knowledge of, and intercourse with, America."

Dr. Mazumdar[107]

"The one and the only reason why we don't know about India's true role in human history is our self-imposed ignorance of Indian mythology, history and traditions."

Gene D. Matlock

Gene Matlock was born in Kansas, in 1928. Since his early childhood, he has been fascinated by India, and her institutions and philosophies. Matlock[108] decided to research Mexican Indians to see if there was Hindu India in them, as claimed in some Indian books. He conducted a rigorous research on the origins of Native Americans and find if some of their rituals, icons, and traditions can be effectively traced back to India. With passage of long time

---

[107] Dr. Mazumdar in *'The Hindu History'* (pp. 216-217), taken from Gene D. Matlock, *'India once ruled the Americas'* (2000, p.106).
[108] Gene D. Matlock, in 'India once ruled the Americas', (2000, pp. 45-...)

and change of several generations in between, it is understandable that memories must have been covered by different layers of memory-dust. But heritage is so important to man that he, when prompted, would be able to x-ray through the dusty layers to have glimpses of his origin, although faint. I think Matlock had such experiences. He also records that some even got angry that they would not like to talk about their origin traced back to India because of caste system their ancestors might have left India. It should be noted that in those ancient times, when their ancestors might have left India, there was no caste system in India. It came recently about a few centuries back.

After a great deal of study, he told an American historian who is considered as an "American authority" on Indian history that he had read the works of two Indian historians, P.N. Oak and Paramesh Choudhury. Matlock writes: "However, this authority, blinded by his own religious and historical preconditioning, confidently replied: "Don't read these books. Those two authors are weirdos. They preach that India once ruled the world." Matlock replied: "Had you lived and traveled for years in such places as Mexico and Central America, observing the wealth of Indian deities, place names, Sanskrit words and traditions there, as I did, you'd become a weirdo also."

History can be true and authentic only when the historian starts his research with his clean untarnished mind to fill it with the facts as they come to him. He should have no religion, no ethnicity, no missionary agenda, which could unconsciously creep in to color the facts with his own biases. He should have respect for ethnic and cultural differences. He should respect the other sacred scriptures as he respects his own.

During the 40s at college in Mexico, Matlock met two gentlemen – (i) a brilliant Hebrew cabalist who had a profound knowledge of Hindu sacred books and (ii) an English ex-Bengal lancer who had retired in Mexico. He says that he and both of them were in total agreement that "Mexico reeked with the smell of God Shiva and other Hindu traditions."

Matlock (p.46) writes:

India in Ancient Americas

"Many Native Americans, some of whose tribal names, physical appearance, religion, legends, and traditions are as Indian as "curry and rice", won't even discuss this matter with me."

Matlock (p.48) writes:

"Although many Chinese adventurers did take up residence in the Americas, it may be that the Chinese were generally interested only in trading – not in colonizing and interacting socially, spiritually, culturally and politically with the Native Americans. However, the evidence is overwhelming that the Native Americans preferred both the good and bad aspects of India's spiritual, cultural, political, and social institutions. Not only that, it's more than probable that the Native Americans were just transplanted brothers of the Indians. There seems no other way to explain this anomaly."

Matlock (p.48) talks about Mr. Chaman Lal. Because of his political problem with the British government, the Crown revoked his passport effectively turning him into a man without a country. Mexico was one of the few countries to give him asylum. He spent rest of his life in Mexico. A few glimpses of some of the Mexican people impressed him with their some connection with Hindus. He, after rigorous research in Mexico, authored the book, *'Hindu America'*.

Matlock (p.48) writes that Mr. Lal, while traveling all over Mexico naturally concluded what is immediately obvious to any one who has studied India's history and mythology: "India once enjoyed some degree of hegemony in Mexico."

He (pp. 48-49) further writes about Mr. Lal's findings that Mr. Lal's book concentrated mainly on India's religious and cultural affinities with ancient Mexican, Central and South American civilizations, using just a minimum of linguistic evidence. However he did acknowledge that several Native Indian languages had Sanskrit roots:

"At present we are studying the native tongues and find that at least as far as Nahuatl, Zapoteca, and Maya languages are concerned, they are of Indo-European (Sanskrit) origin."

I don't deny that Sanskrit may have philological resemblances with Nahuatl, Zapoteca, and Maya languages. But it will be erroneous to conclude that all these language have common origin or that the Nahuatl, Zapoteca, and Maya languages have their origin in Sanskrit. They are historically different and geographically too distant from Sanskrit to make a linguistic family.

Same way, it will be wrong to postulate, as Matlock[109] seems to, that India is the origin of the American Native Indians. It has been historically established that several Hindus had migrated to Americas in prehistory ancient times and left some religious, cultural and linguistic impressions on the Native Americans.

Sanskrit inscriptions found in Peru

According to *Samvad*[110] (December, New Delhi, 1997, p.3), the German scholar Kurt Schildmann claims that his study of ancient inscriptions, discovered in Peru and USA, show that they are similar to ancient Sanskrit, suggesting sea fares from India might have reached Americas long back.

Matlock (p.49) writes that the official historian of the Mexican Government has said in *'General Outline of the History of Mexico'* that Hindus reached America first: "What is called the discovery of America is the meeting of two great currents of races of people, who, after a separation extending over many centuries, were again joined after going right around the earth."

Matlock (p.49) seems to have broad-minded inclusive perspectives on humanity, not divisive as some other scholers have:

---

[109] Ibid, p.47.
[110] Dr. Jagat K. Motwani, "None But India (Bharat): The Cradle of Aryans, Sanskrit, Vedas & Swastika" (2010, p.27).

"Mr. Lal voices my own conviction that regardless of our different colors, and the like, we are essentially one race. All the so-called "races" of mankind are just the result of selectively breeding individuals having like recessive characteristics."

In my opinion, the idea of 'ONE RACE' is too inclusive to distinguish the individuality of a race from others. There are several different races. They should be studied individually. There can be a few common basic attributes of humanity which may be similar or even identical. Such theory of 'ONE RACE' would threaten the anthropology.

I can understand what Matlock is saying that some Native Americans would like to know their ancestors and some would vehemently oppose the research. All Native Americans do not have one heritage, because to start with the Asians, who migrated to Americas via Bering Strait in about 8000 B.C., were from various Asian countries, including China and India. They linguistically as well as culturally assimilated and submerged with the original natives so much that they all became one people, although with some fainted distinguishing religio-ethnic traces. Native American Indians, before massive Asian immigrants, had their own heritage which needs to be identified and understood how much they have preserved its originality. The ancient immigrants into Americas were never known as Chinese or Indian, etc.

Some Native Americans have or had Swastika; but I believe that they were not conscious of its association with the Vedic religion. Some readers may argue that the Vedas were not known in those ancient times. They are wrong. The melting of the Himalayan glaciers – which happened in 8000 B.C. – is mentioned in the Rig Veda. It tells that the Rig Veda, oldest of the four Vedas, was at least ten thousand years old, and so were its language Sanskrit and religious symbol Swastika.

Historians William Brandon in *'Indians'* (1969), Harold E. Driver in *'Indians of North America'* (1869), and Henry Bramford Parkes in *'A History of Mexico'* (1988) have identified several socio-cultural characteristics of American Native Indians, such as – the *Swastika*, cremation, a priestly caste, brownish complexion, incarnated gods, sacrifice rituals, worship of nature gods (fire, rain, earth, trees, sun, etc), worship of the serpent god *(Nagdevta),* pottery, textiles, half-man half-animal god, carving of wood, blowing of the conch (*Shankh*) in temples, carving of elephant on pillars of one Maya temple, oral transmission of religious poetry from generation to generation – seem to be similar to those of the people of the Vedic India. All this supports my theory that some of the migrants – who traveled from Asia to Americas via Siberia, Bering Strait and Alaska during the Ice Age about ten thousand years back – were Vedic Aryans from India.

Hindus in Central America

From right: Sita, Rama, Laxman, & sitting Hanuman

Sir William Jones (Asiatic Researches, vol.1, p. 426) writes about INCAS (royal families) of South America, as the descendants of Sri Rama, the *Surya Vanshi,* meaning members of the Sun Heritage. Pococke [111] (pp. 250-251) writes:

"Rama (the Indian Bacchus) is represented as a descendant from Surya, or the Sun, as husband of Sita, and the son of a princess named Causelya. It is very remarkable that the Peruvians, whose INCAS boasted of the same descent, styled their greatest festival RAMA-Sitva; whence we may suppose that South America was peopled by the same race who imported into the farthest parts of Asia the rites and fabulous history of Rama."

In support of what Sir William Jones has said above, Pococke (pp.178-179) talks about the "Feast of Raymi" (read as Rāma) being celebrated as "the most magnificent national solemnity" in Peru. This suggests that Rāma, the *Suryavansi* Raja (King) of Ayodhya, India, might have ruled over Peru in ancient times.

Elephant in Meso-America and Maya Civilization

Gunnar Thompson[112] writes: "Contact between Asia and Meso-America is more clearly indicated by the presence of motifs representing the long-nosed Hindu deity, Ganesa – the elephant god." The traces of the Hindu god Ganesa in the Mayan religion clearly suggest that the Vedic people (Hindus) were in Meso-America in ancient times. Thompson (p.141) further writes:

"The long-nosed god is a common feature of Mayan religion, even though elephants were never present in ancient Central America. All of the features of Asian elephant gods are present, including earspools, skirts, phallic aprons, prayer postures, bracelets, head projections, human hands and feet, scrolled eyes, and yin/yang motifs. Like its Asian counterpart, the Mayan deity, Chac, was associated with rain."

---

[111] Sir W. Jones, Asiatic Researches (vol. 1, p.426).

[112] Gunnar Thompson in 'Nu Sun', pp.140-144.

Carving of elephant on pillars of one Maya temple supports the above elephant evidence.

Shri Ganesh

Lotus common in Maya & Hindu-Buddhist religions

Thompson (p. 144) observes that Asian contact with Maya is further indicated by a unique usage of the lotus motif which Hindus and Buddhists regarded as the point of emergence for cosmic power to enter the physical world. Lotus was used as a symbol of religious power in both cultures – Hindu as well as Maya. Hindus consider lotus as a pious and sacred flower.

Goddess Lakshmi sitting on lotus[113]

---

[113] Google, significance of lotus in Hinduism

The flower LOTUS (Sanskrit *Padma*) has great symbolical significance in Hinduism.[114] It is rooted in mud, floats above in clean water. It represents beauty and non-attachment, meaning not attached to the dirt. Great message: "Keep above the evils of humanity." Bhagvad Gita (5,10) says:

> "One who performs his duty without attachment, surrendering the results unto the Supreme Lord, is unaffected by sinful action, as the lotus leaf is untouched by water."

The same way, in my opinion, attachment to dear ones can bring pain in case of loss or separation. Better remain concerned and do what you are expected to do for your dear ones, but don't get too emotionally attached and lose yourself.

Other similarities between Bharat & Meso-America

Thompson (p. 143) records other similarities between India and Meso-America, such as similar pottery houses and the wheeled toys. On pages (64-67), Thompson talks about trade between India (Calcutta. Madras) and Indonesia through sea-routes, and ship building technology of Hindus:

> "This was not the earliest maritime venture from the subcontinent. Hindu books dating to the fifth century B.C., the Puranas and Jatakas, describe epic sea voyages reaching as far as Malaysia and Indonesia."

During my family vacation to Maui, Hawaii, in July 2000, I found a black stone resembling *Ling*, surrounded by a rectangular border made of small white pieces of stone. Within the space around the ling-like erect stone, lay a few beautiful flowers and leaves, as seen in the picture given below. The space was kept very clean, reflecting the respect and the sanctity of the place. There were two signs – one in the front of the stone, "KAPU" and the

---

[114] Ibid.

other, a little farther away in the left corner, "KUULA STONE." "Kapu", in the Pacific Islanders' dictionary, means "sacred, forbidden place", and "Kuula" is the name of a fishermen's god. The following morning, I, along with my host friends Khanu and Indira Chandnani, went to the Kihei Public Library to find some answers and explanations regarding the significance of the Kuula Stone because it greatly resembles Shiv Ling, which is on display in many Hindu temples. It represents fertility and production. On the front lawn of the library we found the same erect stone with the signs "Kapu" and "Kuula." The librarian called the place a "shrine". We were told that fishermen go there to present their first catch to the Kuula god and pray for continued abundance (heavy catch) from the ocean. Research is needed to find if there is any relationship between Kuula and Shiva Ling.

Kapu on a Hawaiian island

TWENTY

Far South-East Asia under Vedic Influence

"Indian civilization took root especially in the countries of South-East Asia and the evidence for this can be found all over the place today. There were great centres of Sanskrit learning in Champa, Angkor, Srivijaya, Majapahit, and other places. The names of the rulers of various states and empires that arose are purely Indian and Sanskrit. This doesn't mean they were pure Indian, but it does mean that they were Indianized. State ceremonies were Indian and conducted in Sanskrit. All the officers of the state bear old Sanskrit titles and some of these titles and designations have been continued up till now, not only in Thailand but also in the Moslem states of Malaya."

Nehru, *'Discovery of India'* (1946, p.207)

Nehru (p. 202) writes about the colonizing waves of Indians (Hindus and Buddhists) over the South-East Asia:

"From the first century of the Christian era onwards wave after wave of Indian colonists spread east and south-east reaching Ceylon, Burma, Malaya, Java, Sumatra, Borneo, Siam, Cambodia, and Indo-China. Some of them managed to reach Formosa, the Philippine islands and Celebes. Even as far as Madagascar (whose) the current language is Indonesian with a mixture of Sanskrit words."

Nehru (p.202) remarks that "the names that were given to these settlements were old Indian names," for example 'Kamboja' for present Kambodia.

Nehru: The Influence of Hindu Art abroad

Nehru (1946, p.207) talks about the influence of Indian Art abroad:

"These records of ancient empires and dynasties have an interest for the antiquarian, but they have a large interest in the history of civilization and art. From the point of view of India they are particularly important, for it was India that functioned there and exhibited her vitality and genius in a variety of ways. We see her bubbling over with energy and spreading out far and wide, carrying not only her thought but also her other ideals, her art, her trade, her language and literature, and her methods of government. She was not stagnant or standing aloof, or isolated and cut off by mountain and sea."

It would have been more clear and accurate if the words "Indian' and 'Indianized' were replaced by 'Hindu' and 'Hinduized' respectively. The word 'Indian' is a broader term which includes other present sections of the Indian society – Christians, Muslims, Jews, Zoroastrians, etc. – were not active in the historical process, being talked about. In fact, Hindus and Buddhists had gone to the SE Asian region during much earlier times. They spread Bharat's Sanskrit, Vedic culture, philosophy, ideals, art, and literature there. The words India and Indian came in use later, when Bharat was named as India, Bharatiya as Indian, and Sindhu as Indus by Westerners. The words 'India', 'Indian', and 'Indus' are misnomer when you talk about the history of spread of the Bharatiya culture all over in earlier times.

Nehru: Greater India (Vishāl Bharat)

Nehru adds:

"Her (India's) people crossed those high mountain barriers and perilous seas and built up, as M. Rėnė Grousset says, 'a Greater India politically as little organized as Greater Greece, but morally equally harmonious'. ... But M. Grousset refers to the wider areas where Indian culture spread: 'In the high plateau of eastern Iran, in the oases of Serindia, in the arid wastes of Tibet, Mongolia, and Manchuria, in the ancient civilized lands of China and Japan, in the lands of the primitive Mons and Khmers and other tribes in Indo-China, in the countries of the Malayo-Polynesians, in Indonesia and Malay, India left the indelible impress of her high culture, not only upon religion, but also upon art and literature, in a word, all the higher things of spirit."[115]

Stephen Knapp, in *'Proof of Vedic Culture's Global Existence'* (2000, p. 81), talks about the spread of Vedic influence over vast area in Southeast Asia and then it traveled to Europe too:

"By studying some of these connections and similarities we can see how much how many of these cultures are connected to each other and related to the earliest traditions that came out of the Vedic Aryan civilization. We also recognize how the Vedic influence extended over a vast area and traveled west into Europe and other regions and affected these countries in greater or lesser degrees."

Knapp adds:

"Ancient India no doubt covered a much larger area of land than it does today and spread much farther to the north and west. At least there are historical indications showing that the Aryan influence was felt over long distances. The Vedic gods, for example, were over a wide area."

---

[115] Civilizations of the East' by Rėnė Grousset, vol. II, p. 276.

Concept of *Dev Raja* (God King)

Garraty and Gay (1972, pp.355-357) speak about influence of the Indian culture on Southeast Asia:

"Culturally the strongest external influence on early Southeast Asia was exercised by India. Hinduism and Buddhism spread widely in the area, bringing with them the art of writing, along with new deities, epics, and mythologies. From India came the idea of a despotic God-King who must be supported by his subjects as their necessary link with the supernatural forces that control the world. Brahman priests were employed by ambitious Southeast Asian rulers hoping to expand their dominions and, through consecration as divine kings, to legitimize their conquests. ... The earliest state of which clear evidence survives was Funan, founded in the Mekong Delta not later than the first century A.D. by Kaundinya, the "King of the Mountain." Funan was a maritime state, and `maintained commercial relations with India, Persia, and China. Its greatest king was *Jayavarman (d.514), who lived in a palace with a tiered roof, rode on an elephant, and governed walled cities where inhabitants prized gold, silver, pearls, and engraved ornaments, and who delighted in cockfighting and pigfighting."

Garraty & Gay further talk about its farther spread in the region:

"West of Annam and Champa arose in the ninth century the Khmer empire of Cambodia. It was the Khmers who elevated the principle of the *deva-raja*, or God-King, to the highest peak it attained in Southeast Asia. During the reign of *Suryavarman II (1113-c.1150) the building of the mighty temple complex of Angkor Wat began."

According to Nehru (p.205), the greatest of these states was the *Salendra Empire, or the empire of *Sri Vijaya, which became the dominant power both on sea and land in whole of Malaysia by the eighth century. At the height of its power it included Malaya, Ceylon (Sri Lanka), Sumatra, part of Java, Borneo, Celebes, the Philippines, and a part of Formosa, and probably exercised suzerainty over Cambodia and Champa (Annam), which was a Buddhist Empire. A great ruler, Jayavarman, united the small states in the ninth century and built up the Cambodian Empire with its capital at Angkor. The Cambodian state lasted for nearly four hundred years under the succession of great rulers Jayavarman, Yashovarman, Indravarman and Suryavarman (all the four were Hindus).

*Jayavarman, Suryavarman, Salendra, Sri Vijaya are Hindu names

According to Nehru (p.205):

"The capital became famous in Asia and was known 'Angkor the Magnificent,' a city of a million inhabitants, larger and more splendid than the Rome of the Cæsars. Near the city stood the vast temple of Angkor Vat. The empire of Cambodia flourished till the end of the thirteenth century, and the account of a Chinese envoy who visited it in 1297 describes the wealth and splendour of its capital. But it suddenly collapsed, so suddenly that some buildings were left unfinished."

Nehru (p. 203) remarks:

"Trade and adventure and the urge for expansion drew them to these eastern lands which were comprehensively described in old Sanskrit books as the *Svarnabhumi*, the Land of Gold or as *Svarnadvipa*, the Island of Gold."

Nehru (1946, p.203) praises ancient Bharat as a naval power and for her well-developed and flourishing shipbuilding industry:

"It is clear that shipbuilding was a well-developed and flourishing industry in ancient India. We have some

245

details and particulars of the ships built in those days. Many Indian ports are mentioned. South Indian (Andhra) coins of the second and third centuries A.C. bear the device of a two-masted ship. The Ajanta Frescoes depict the conquest of Ceylon and ships carrying elephants are shown."

It is beyond believing what Nehru (p. 203) talks about an interesting Tamil inscription in 1088 A.C. which refers to a 'Corporation of the Fifteen Hundred':

"This was apparently a union of traders who were described in it as brave men, born to wander over many countries ever since the beginning of the Krita age, penetrating the regions of the six continents by land and water routes, and dealing in various articles such as horses, elephants, precious stones, perfumes, and drugs, either wholesale or in retail."

Kulke and Rothermund, in *'A History of India'* (1986, p.152), write that the transmission of Indian culture to distant parts of Central Asia, China, Japan, and Southeast Asia without military conquest is certainly one of the greatest achievements of Hindu history or even the history of mankind.

Influence of India over the Art & the Culture of the SE Asia
No conquest or invasion, no forced conversion

Philip Rawson, in *'The Art of the South East Asia'* (1990, p. 7-8), writes about Indian colonization of the Far South-East Asia:

"The culture of India has been one of the world's most powerful civilizing forces. Countries of the Far East, including China, Korea, Japan, Tibet and Mongolia owe much of what is best in their own cultures to the inspiration of ideas imported from India. The West, too, has its own debts. But the members of that circle of civilizations beyond Burma scattered around the Gulf of

Siam and Java Sea, virtually owe their very existence to the creative influence of Indian[116] ideas. Among the tribal peoples of Southeast Asia these formative ideas took root, and blossomed. No conquest or invasion, no forced conversion imposed (upon) them. They were adopted because the people saw they were good and that they could use them."

Rawson further writes:

"The small colonies of Indian traders, who settled at points of vantage along the sea routes into the islands and around the coast of Indo-China, merely imported with them their code of living, their conceptions of law and kingship, their rich literature and highly evolved philosophy of life. They intermarried with prominent local families; and dynasties evolved capable of organizing extensive kingdoms within which their populations could live ordered and fruitful lives. ... But archaeology may yet reveal more about the history of Indian colonization in the more remote parts of the Southern Seas."

Rawson's remark "They intermarried with prominent local families; and dynasties" reminds me of its parallel to Akbar's marriage with Jodhabai of a Rajpoot royal family. It was a prudent political and diplomatic strategy to stay strong in the captured country. When in Rome, behave like a Roman. The same was true about the adaptability and flexibility of the character of the Hindu and Buddhist art in their adopted countries in SE Asia, as described by Nehru (p.204):

"Indian art was flexible and adaptable and in each country it flowered afresh and in many new ways, always retaining that basic impress which it derived from India. Sir John Marshal has referred to 'the amazingly vital and

---

[116] Better to be specific. Instead of "Indian", it should be "Vedic" or "Hindu".

flexible character of Indian art' and he points out how both Indian and Greek art had the common capacity to 'adapt themselves to suit the needs of every country, race, and religion with which they came into contact."

"Indian art derives its basic character from certain ideals associated with the religious and philosophic outlook of India. As religion went from India to all these eastern lands, so also went this basic conception of art. Probably the early colonies were definitely Brahminical, and Buddhism spread later. The two existed side by side as friends and mixed forms of popular worship grew up. This Buddhism was chiefly of the Mahāyāna type, easily adaptable, and both Brahminism and Buddhism, under the influence of local habits and traditions, had probably moved away from the purity of their original doctrines. In later years there were mighty conflicts between a Buddhist state and a Brahminical state but these were political and economic wars for control of trade and sea routes."

Adaptability has been the most significant acumen of the Indian traders and businessmen, particularly those who have been engaged in inter-civilization and international trade adventures. Necessity is the mother of invention. It also comes naturally to them, apparently in heritance. 'Vaishya' (business men) is the third on the caste-ladder, after *Brahamin* and *Kshtriya*. It has been the most important and perhaps the largest caste-segment of the Hindu society, which has kept India vibrantly lucrative since her pre-history ancient times, excepting the dark period of her subjugation by Muslims and later by the Britain. During Muslim period public money was squandered and spent on tombs, etc., and the Britain exploited India economically in various ways.

As a matter of fact, only Vaishya alone did not venture overseas to colonize countries far away from home. They did not have *Kshatri* muscle nor the *Brahmin* brain. All the three – *Brahmin, Kshatri* and *Vashya* – jointly were adventurous. Their joint coordinated effort was needed. I believe that all the three –

Brahmin, Kshatri and *Vaishya* – have been embodied in every Hindu in varying degrees to use what is appropriately required in the situation, the person is confronted with. I don't believe that caste (kind of occupation) is hereditary. One's occupation depends on one's aptitude and the circumstance. Man becomes meaningfully successful, only when there is mutually desired coexistence between aptitude and circumstances. The economic health of a society depends on the inter-occupation flexibility and mobility, the society encourages.

Hindu colonization, different from the European and Muslim

I would like to differentiate the Indian (Hindu) colonization from the European and Islamic. Hindus did neither use sword nor did economically lure the colonized people to change their religion. Hindus know that for everybody religion is sentimentally too precious to give up. Christians did not coerce them to get converted but lured them through baits of free education and health services.

Tagore, in *'Towards Universal Man'* (1961, p. 64), has said that India has never coveted new territory and that she has never sent out her forces for plunder but to carry out message of peace and goodwill.

Rawson has rightly talked about the influence of Indian (Vedic) ideas which took root and blossomed in the countries of the South-East Asia, India culturally colonized peoples without conquest.

Hindus in Indochina and Indonesia

According to *the 'World Book Encyclopedia'* (1984, vol.10, pp.168-179), Hindus and Buddhists had established their kingdoms in Indochina and Indonesia. Indochina extends into the South China Sea from the mainland of Southeast Asia. It includes Kampuchea (Cambodia), Laos, and Vietnam. The Encyclopedia writes:

"Indochina has long been a crossroads of peoples and cultures. It has been invaded from what is now Thailand on the west, from China on the north, and from the sea on the east. Most of the people of Indochina originally came from the plains and mountains of Central Asia. Some of the earliest tribes came from the islands now part of Indonesia. From the 900's to the 1700's, China and Thailand fought for control of Indochina. France gained control of the region in the 1800's and held it until 1954. The French called the region *French Indochina.* "

According to the Geneva Agreement of 1954, the nations of Kampuchea, Laos, and North and South Vietnam were formed.

The WBE (p.169) writes that the Khmer people, who entered what is now called Kampuchea about 100 A.D., claimed that the peoples of India, China, and the Indo-Malay were their ancestors. The Khmer ruled most of Indochina from the Gulf of Thailand to China between the 800's and 1400's with Angkor as its capital.

Similarities between India and Indonesia

The history has talked lot about the similarities between India and Indonesia, such as:

1. Similarity of the Indonesian language with Sanskrit, as reflected by the names, such as *Sumatra, Sukarno, Suharto, Jaya, Putri, Kalimantan, Jakarta (Jaya-karta), Yogiakarta, Surakarta, Madura, Sukabumi,* etc.
2. Worship of ancestors and nature.
3. Some of its traditional musical instruments similar to those of India.
4. Puppet dramas playing stories from Hindu epics.
5. Hinduism in Bali.
6. Dances, particularly in Bali, very similar to Hindu classical dances.
7. Batic designs of clothes, etc

All these seem to suggest the presence of Hindus and Buddhists in Indonesia prior to the advent of Muslims there in 1400's.

The WBE (vol.10, p.170b) remarks: "Buddhism and Hinduism were significant religions on the islands, hundreds of years ago. One of its islands is called 'Irian Jaya' (WBE, p.171) which seems to compare with 'Aryan Jaya."

The WBE (vol.10, p.176) talks about Indian (Hindu and Buddhist) influence on Indonesians:

"Indian influence, especially Hinduism and Buddhism began to affect Indonesian life strongly during the A.D. 400's. Small kingdoms had begun to develop especially in Java and Sumatra. Indonesians, like Hindus, believed that a king was either a god in human form, or was descended from a god. Influences of Indian architecture show clearly in early Indonesian temples. In the villages, Indian legends became part of local puppet plays."

Hindu and Buddhist kingdoms in Indonesia became rivals for power for hundreds of years. The Hindu kingdom called Mataram was established in Central Java. (The word 'Mataram' in Sanskrit/Hindi means mother.) It later fell to a Buddhist king Sailendra who later established the kingdom called Srivijaya in southern Sumatra. The kingdoms of Singosari and Madjapahit were ruled by Prince Widjaya. Buddhist kingdom of Srivijaya (600's-1200's A.D.) expanded from Sumatra and became a great sea power. The Hindu kingdom of Madjapahit controlled much of Indonesia in 1300's, before Islam began to spread in 1400's.

According to the WBE (vol. 10 p. 177), the trade in Indonesian waters was at first controlled largely by Srivijaya, the region's sea power. Their power generally came from the production of rice. Madjapahit became the first Indonesian kingdom to base its power on both rice production and commerce. The Indonesian islands were crossroads in expanding international trade, involving merchants of many lands, including Arabs, Indians, Chinese, Persians, etc. They traded several goods including porcelain, textiles, raw silk, spices and scented woods for Indonesian products. Such Asian goods were also traded in Europe. The Italian traveler and merchant Marco Polo visited the islands in 1292 to establish Italy-Indonesia trade relations. Muslim from Arabia and

India came to Indonesia in 1400 A.D. as traders, and later established themselves as the rulers. Melaka gained control of the important trading route through the Strait of Malacca, between Malaya and Sumatra. Melaka became a major trading power. Its ruler converted to Islam spread to various regions of Indonesia.

Note: The names – Mataram, Sailendra, Srivijaya, Sumatra, Singasari, Maljapahit, and Widjaya – have their origin in Sanskrit.

Maldives and the Indus Valley civilization

Maldives (formerly Maldive Islands) are in the Indian Ocean. The Columbia Encyclopedia writes:

"Maldivians are of mixed Indian, Sinhalese and Arab stock. ... The Maldivians were originally from South Asia. In the 12th century, Islam was brought to the islands. ... The Maldives obtained complete independence (from Britain) as a Sultanate in 1965."

Graham Hancock,[117] in *'Underworld: The Mysterious Origins of Civilization'* (pp. 286-287), writes that Thor Heyderdahl[118] makes a case that there is real history behind the Redin[119] myth. Peter Marshal reports a Maldivian tradition about the phenomenal maritime abilities of the Redin with supernatural or even god-like powers flying swiftly across the sea in their boats with sails and oars.[120]

Hancock (p.286) remarks that this is "strangely reminiscent of the imagery of the *Rig Veda* (cited in chapter 7) concerning the

---

[117] Graham Hancock, op. cit

[118] Thor Heyerdahl, *The Maldives Mystery*, London: Unknown Paperbacks, 1988.

[119] Ancient oral traditions of Maldives speak of a mysterious people – the Redin – who, in the opinion of Heyerdahl, were 'a former people with more than ordinary human capacities'.

[120] Amin, Mohamed, Duncan Willets and Peter Marshal, *Journey through the Maldives*, 16, Camerapix Publishers International, Nairobi, 1992.

Asvins – who are several times praised for having conducted a daring rescue in the deeps of the Indian Ocean."

According to Thor Heyerdahl (Hancock, p.287), the Redin probably originated in north-west India, the primary setting of the *Rig Veda*. Heyerdahl,[121] after visiting Gujarat and the great Marine dockyard of the Indus-Sarasvati civilization at Lothal where cowrie shells from Maldives (*Cyprea Moneta*) have been excavated amongst the ruins and are to be seen in the site museum. Thor Heyerdahl comments:

> "I was convinced that at least the Hindu element in the Maldives had come from the north-western corner of India. And probably the Hindus were not even the first to have made the journey straight south from the Gulf of Cambay to the Maldives. Perhaps earlier sailors in the days of Mesopotamian and Indus Valley seafaring had been led by the sun to the Equatorial Channel, and survived in legend as the Redin."[122]

It should be noted that "north-western corner of India" can not be other than Sindh and Punjab in the Indus Valley. Hancock (pp. 280-281) seems to suggest that the sculptures, *stupas* and pyramidal *hawittas,* excavated in the Maldives, are similar to those of the Buddhists of Sri Lanka and the Hindus of South India. Buddhism was extensively present on the Maldives before advent of Islam in 12th century.[123] A Sanskrit text of Vajrayana Buddhism dating back to the ninth or tenth century A.D. is the earliest surviving legible inscription thus far found in the Maldives.[124] It seems definitely Hinduism must have preceded Buddhism in the Maldives. According to the *Encyclopedia Britannica,* Micropaedia (vol. 10, 837), Dhivehi, the Maldivian language, belongs to the Indo-European family and is related to Sanskrit and thus also to

---

[121] Heyerdahl, op. cit., p.159.

[122] Ibid, p.312.

[123] Kon Tiki Museum, 'Archaeological Test-Excavations on the Maldive Islands', Occasional Papers, vol. 2, 66, Oslo, 1992.

[124] *Dhivehi Writing Systems,* 5, National Centre for Linguistic and Historical Research, Maldives, 1999.

Sinhalese, one of the two languages of Sri Lanka (the other being Tamil). Clarence Maloney[125] remarks that a Tamil/Dravidian sublayer exists in Dhivehi, which suggests that Hinduism was present in the Maldives before the Buddhist period. Buddhism is an offshoot of Hinduism.

Phallic Sculptures in the Maldives

Hancock (p.280) talks about Siva Linga in the Maldives:

"Interestingly, large numbers of 'phallic' sculptures have been recovered in archaeological excavations in the Maldives – for example amid the ruins of a vast temple complex in North Nilandhoo Atoll.[126] I was able to study a collection of such objects from different parts of the archipelago, and in my opinion, despite some idiosyncrasies, they are nothing more nor less than Sivalinga."

It is amazing that India had colonized almost all South-East Asian countries, such as Malaya, Ceylon (Sri Lanka), Sumatra, Borneo, Celebes, Philippines, Formosa, Cambodia, Champa (Annam), China, Korea, Japan, Tibet, Mongolia, Indonesia, Siam, Java, Laos, and Vietnam. Some of them were administratively colonized, and some were only culturally influenced.

---

[125] Clarence Maloney, *People of the Maldives Islands,* Madras, 1980, cited in Kon Tiki Museum, op. cit., 70.
[126] Mohamed Amin et al. op. cit. p. 12.

TWENTY-ONE

India in China and Turkistan

"Though Buddhism was not recognized as a third state-religion before the year 65 A.D., under the Emperor Mingti,[127] Buddhist missionaries had reached China from India as early as the third century, 217 B.C."[128] One Buddhist missionary is mentioned in the Chinese annals in the year 217; and, about the year 120 B.C., a Chinese general, after defeating the barbarous tribes north of the desert of Gobi, brought back as a trophy a golden statue, the statue of Buddha. The very name of Buddha, changed in Chinese into Fo-t'o and Fo[129], is pure Sanskrit, and so is every word and every thought of that religion. The language, which the Chinese pilgrims went to India to study, as the key to the sacred literature of Buddhism, was Sanskrit. They called it Fan (an abbreviation of Fan-lanmo)."

Max Müller[130]

---

[127] M. M.'s *Buddhist Pilgrims, Selected Essays,* vol. ii. P. 234.

[128] *Foe Koue Ki,* traduit par Remusat, Paris, 1836, p. 41.

[129] *Methode pour dechiffrer et transcrire les noms sanscrits qui se rencontrent dans les livres chinois, inventee et demontree* par M. Stanislas Julien, Paris, 1861, p. 103.

[130] Max Müller, in *'The Science of Language'* (1891, p.196).

Brook Larmer, National Geographic, (June, 2010, pp.124-145), talks about the Buddhist art, as reflected by the statues and paintings in the galleries in 492 Mogao caves near Dunhuang, a Silk Road oasis in northwest China. The paintings and statues were carved on high cliffs in dunes of China's Gobi desert, in the fourth century A.D.

In Cave 130, a statue of a seated 89 feet tall Buddha has been found. It is one of the Mogao's three largest statues of the Tang dynasty. Mogao's tallest Buddha (Tang dynasty) at 116 feet, peers out of Cave 96-a nine-story pagoda.

About Xuanzang, a Buddhist Monk, who travelled for about sixteen years along the Silk Road in AD 629, Larmer (NG, p. 130) writes:

"What kept Xuanzang going, he wrote in his famous account of the journey, was another precious item carried along the Silk Road: Buddhism itself. Other religions surged along this same route – Manichaeism, Christianity, Zoroastrianism, and later Islam – but none influenced China so deeply as Buddhism, whose migration from India began sometimes in the first three centuries A.D. The Buddhist texts Xuanzang carted back from India and spent the next two decades studying and translating would serve as the foundation of Chinese Buddhism and fuel the religion's expansion."

Judith H. Dobrzynski, in 'Halting Cultural Evolution: Along the Silk Road, China' (NY Times, July 15, 2004, the Arts Section), writes the same. She describes the sculptures of Buddha, among other artifacts carved into the cliffs near Dunhuang, China, between the 4th and 14th centuries. The caves and cliffs were covered with elaborate Buddhist wall paintings portraying visions of heaven and earth in ancient China.

John W. McCrindle, in 'Ancient India as described by Ptolemy' (pp.10-12, footnotes) writes:

"He (Mr. Holt, an eminent Chinese scholar)[131] believes therefore with M. Gosselin that the Kattigara[132] of Ptolemy was probably not far from the present Martaban, and that India for a considerable period up to the 7th century A.D. dominated over Cambodia."

McCrindle (p.9 footnote) writes that China for nearly 1000 years has been known to the nations of Inner Asia under the name of Khitai, Khata, or Cathay, e.g. was for some centuries at that period (B.C. 111 to A.D. 263), only incorporated as part of the Chinese Empire.

Hu Shih, a former Chinese ambassador to USA, has said that India conquered and dominated China culturally for 20 centuries without ever having to send a single soldier across her border.

Hiuen Tsang in search of Indian wisdom and Knowledge[133]

Pandit Nehru, in his letter of Birth Day greetings to his daughter Indira, talks about the Chinese traveler Hiuen Tsang who came to India over thirteen hundred years ago in search of wisdom and knowledge. His thirst for knowledge was so great that he spent many years in India braving many dangers, facing several obstacles and learning and teaching at the Nalanda University, near the city of Pataliputra, now known as Patna. Nehru writes:

"Hiuen Tsang became very learned himself and he was given the title of 'Master of the Law' – the Law of the Buddha – and he journeyed all over India and saw and studied the people that lived in this great country in those far-off days."

---

[131] McCrindle, op. cit., footnote pp. 11,12.

[132] McCrindle, ibid, p.9, footnote., that the location of Kattigara has been fixed very variously. Richthofen identified it with Kian-chi in the Gulf of Tong-king, and Colonel Yule agrees with Richthofen's view. He further says: "For 1st, Tong-king

[133] Nehru's letter (Glimpses of World History, 2004, p. 1) to his daughter Indira Gandhi on her birthday, October 26, 1930. Indira's birthday, according to Gregorian Calendar, takes place on November 19. However, according to the Samvat era, it was observed on October 26.

Nehru (2004, p. 2) further writes about Tsang that he wore a strange attire, round his waist copper-plates and on his head a lighted torch. When asked the reason for his curious get-up, he replied that "his wisdom was so great that he was afraid his belly would burst if he did not wear copper-plates around it; and because he was moved with pity for the ignorant people round about him, who lived in darkness, he carried the light on the head."

I think whatever Hiuen Tsang said about wearing the light on the head was in joke. He was a modest person. He identified himself with the common man around him. He meant that he was wearing light to dispel his own darkness (ignorance) being mirrored in the people around him. He believed no extent of knowledge could quench his thirst for knowledge, because it is limitless and depthless.

All this evidences close cultural relationship between the peoples of China and Bharat. Changing time should not forget and hurt such relationship.

Nehru's History Lessons to Indira from Jail

It is amazing that Nehru[134] gave World History lessons from jail to his daughter Indira regarding the three great persons who have impacted the world:

1. Jeanne d' Arc (Joan of Arc, 1412-1431), a national heroine of France, and a recognized saint of the Roman Catholic Church,
2. Vladimir Lenin (1870-1924), a Russian Marxist, who started the Great Revolution which has changed the face of Russia and Siberia, and
3. Mahatma Gandhi (1869-1948), who with "the magic of his message steals into the hearts of India's millions – men and women, and even little children who have come out of their little shells and become India's future soldiers of freedom.

Great people don't waste even a second of their life.

---

[134] 'Glimpses of World History' (2004, pp. 2, 3).

It is true that Bapuji has enkindled flame of patriotism in hearts of the millions of Indians – young and old, men and women, and also children, the future budding soldiers – creating an unending stream of brave dedicated soldiers to defend her fragile borders.

Sir Marc Aurel Stein

Hungarian archaeologist Sir Marc Aurel Stein (1862-1943) writes: in his book[135] about the presence of Buddhist and Indian (Hindu) literary culture in Central Asia and China:

"It is a fascinating chapter in history ... it was from the north-western borderland that fervent religious propaganda carried the Buddha's doctrine, together with Graeco-Buddhist art and Indian (Hindu) literary culture, into Central Asia and thence into China. This spread of Buddhism right across Asia may well be considered India's greatest contribution to the civilization of mankind in general."

Stephen Knapp, in *'Proof of Vedic Culture's Global Existence'* (2000, pp. 236, 237), has gives several evidences of the Vedic influence in China, as provided by P. N. Oak, given in his book *World Vedic Heritage* (pp. 564-566). I am giving only a few (following 6) of them, as under:

1. The ancient international highway connecting India with China, Russia, and Iran was called *'Uttarapatha'*, which, he says, is a Sanskrit word. I know that in several Indian vernaculars (Hindi, Sindhi, Gujarati, etc.) it means 'Northern Road' – Uttara means northern and path means road.
2. Entire region around surrounding China was steeped in Vedic culture.
3. Until the Mahabharata War (3138 B.C.), like the rest of the world, China too spoke Sanskrit and practiced Vedic

---

[135] *'On Alexander's Track to the Indus'* (2001, preface, p. xi).

culture. After the war, it gradually lapsed into a state of segregation and isolation developing a distinct identity in script, pronunciation, language and art.

4. Both Sir L. Wooley and Arnold Toynbee speak of an earlier ready-made culture coming to China – the Vedic, Hindu culture from India with its Sanskrit language and sacred scripts.

5. The contemporary astronomical expertise of the Chinese, as evidenced by their record of eclipses, the organizing of sacrifices to propitiate the deities of these astral phenomena, the philosophy of the Chinese, and their statecraft, all point to a Vedic origin. That is why from the earliest of times we find Chinese travelers visiting India very often to renew their educational and spiritual links.

6. Auriel Stein found some evidences:

- Evidence of Indian rule in Turkistan and Khotan in the form of coins and inscriptions and the use of an Indian language in its administration up to the 3rd century A.D.
- Officials bore Indian names, for example – Nandsena and Bheem.
- The use of Sanskrit words, such as *Lekhaharak* for the person who gathers and delivers mail (postman or clerk), *Doota* for messenger, and *Chara* for spy.
- He mentions: "In the upper Pamirs and in Tibet too, the Vedic civilization was to be seen everywhere."

Knapp (pp..237-238) mentions what Count Biornstierna has observed on page 85 of his book *The Theogony of the Hindus*: "What may be said with certainty is that the religion of China came from India."

Acupuncture originated in India or in China?

Knapp (p. 238) observes that the alternate form of medicine known as acupuncture, as a matter of fact, has its origin in an ancient Sanskrit text on acupuncture. As an evidence, he says: "In

Korea academics, students are correctly told that acupuncture originated in India."

Shiva Linga & Shiva Temples in ancient China

Knapp (p.238) writes that the remains of a Shiva temple have been found in Fjiyan province at Quanzhou on the south-eastern coast of China which still has an over five meter tall *Shiva Linga* with Tamil inscriptions. Knapp cites a very striking evidence of Chinese' belief in Shiva Linga that "Even as late as 1950, childless Chinese women would go to invoke the blessings of the deity for motherhood."

Knapp (p. 238) writes that Professor Dr. Raghu Vira found a pillar, erected in 1104 in the village of Hsuan-wu, Lo-yang district, with a Sanskrit text written from top to bottom, and from left to right. He also writes that in the rock-cut temple at Tun-huang, and also one in Kung-hsien, one can find "carved images of Ganesh with other deities, such as the sun, moon, Cupid, and the nine planetary divinities."

Knapp (p.238) writes that all this evidence[136] is corroborated by a Chinese dignitary, Yuag Xianji, member of the Chinese People's Political Consultative Conference, who, speaking at the C. P. Ramaswamy Aiyar Foundation, Madras, March 27, 1984, said:

"Recent discoveries of ruins of Hindu temples in Southeast China provided further evidence of Hinduism in China. Both Buddhism and Hinduism were patronized by the rulers. In the 6th century A. D. the royal family was Hindu for two generations. The following Tang dynasty (7th to 9th century A. D.) also patronized both Hinduism and Buddhism because the latter was but a branch of Hinduism."

Yuag Xianji (pp. 238-239) further said:

---

[136] *World Vedic Heritage*, p. 1285

"Religious wars were unknown in ancient China. The Chinese worshiped Shivambhu, the Chinese name for Durga. The resurgence of Hinduism and the decline of Buddhism in India after the 7th century had its echo in China with temples of Mahadeva coming up. The temples had Hindu priests. In the 6th century members of a Chinese ruling family were known by their Hindu pet names as Narayan and Shiva Dasa respectively. Hinduism still exists in China in the guise of Buddhism. Buddhist monasteries have a Hindu touch and many of them could be mistaken for Hindu temples as they are full of idols similar to the Hindu pantheon."

The word 'Shivambhu' compares to 'Shambhu', common name in India. Kulke and Rothermund, in 'A History of India' (1986, p.152), write that the transmission of Indian culture to distant parts of Central Asia, China, Japan, and Southeast Asia without military conquest is certainly one of the greatest achievements of Indian (Hindu) history or even the history of mankind.

TWENTY-TWO

India in Africa

"Lord Rama had two sons, Lava and Kush (or Cush).
Each son was given half of the planet to rule after the
great war between Rama and the demon Ravana. Africa
was an area that was under the rule of Lord Rama's son,
Kush, for which it became known as Kushadvipa. For this
reason the African people were also known as Kushites,
also spelled as Cushites. Thus, Kush is the ancient Vedic
name known for Africa. So the Vedic connection with
Africa goes back no less than the Ramayanic times."

Stephen Knapp (2000, p.107)

Knapp, in *'Proof of Vedic Culture's Global Existence'* (pp. 106-
7), talks about Drusilla Dunjee Houston who wrote a book titled
'The Wonderful Ethiopians of the Ancient Kushite Empire' (three
volumes), in which she indicates that the ancient name for the
landmass of Africa was Kushadvipa. Knapp writes that the name
'Kushadvipa' is mentioned in the *Bhagavat Purana,* also in the
Ramayana, which records the activities and pastimes of Lord
Ramachandra.

E. Pococke, in *'India in Greece'* (1856, p.183), also writes that
the term Cushites is after "Cush", one of the sons of Lord Rama,
and in whose honor the dynasty of "Rameses," or "Rama's Chief,"
took rise. He adds that the members of the same Solar dynasty
(*Suryavanshi*) gave the title to "Ramoth-Gilead," one of the
settlements in Syria.

Pococke (p.183) cites Colonel Tod:

263

"Rameses, chief of the 'Suryas,' or 'Sun-born' (in Hindi 'Surya-Vanshi'), was king of the city designated, from his mother, 'Cushali' (Kaushalya), of which, 'Ayodhia' was the capital. His sons were Lav and Cush, who originated the races we may term 'LAVITES,' and 'CUSHITES,' or 'Cushwas' of India."

Knapp (p.107), giving reference of the Bible in the book of *Numbers* (Chapter 12, verse one), in which it is said, "And Miriam and Aaron spoke against Moses, on account of the Cushite wife he had taken" because she was ethnically different from them. Knapp also observes that most Biblical scholars associate Cush with the area of Ethiopia.

Knapp (p.106) writes:

"In ancient Vedic lore, Africa was known as Kusha Deep or Kushadvipa. Two reasons for this are because large stretches of land were covered by the tall grass known as *kusha* grass in Sanskrit, and after the war between Rama and Ravana, the continent was under the administration of Rama's son Kush or Cusha. African school text books also describe Africans as Cushites, testifying to the above information."

Knapp adds that when Swami Krishnananda hesitantly presented a copy of the Ramayana to Christian monarch Haile Selassic, the monarch responded: "This is nothing new to us. We Africans are Cushites." This motivated Krishnananda to research African text books. He found references of Africans designated as Cushites.

Knapp (p.106) writes:

"The text books provided more evidence of Africa's ancient administration of Cusha. However, the text books wrongly mention Cusha's father as Ham instead of Ram. As previously explained, that is because Rama was spelled in western regions as Rhama. In course of time the "R" was dropped and what was left was 'Ham'."

Knapp (p.107) brings out another fascinating story about the name of ancient Africa:

"Africa in ancient times was also known as Shankadvipa. The word *dvipa* is Sanskrit for island, and *Shanka* in Sanskrit for conch. This was because Africa was like a large island in the shape similar to a conch shell. The English word conch is a derivative of the Sanskrit *shank*. This also shows how the Vedic rulers were so familiar with Africa that they knew its shape as seen from miles above it."

India in Mauritius

Knapp (p.106) writes:

"Other strong Ramayanic links with Africa can be recognized in the island of Mauritius off the eastern coast of southern Africa. The island gets its name from "Marichas," meaning the island of Marichi, who was one of the generals in the army of the demon Ravana, and also a name of the sun. Rama, however, routed all the demons out of the area during the war with Ravana, and made Marichi flee to the stronghold of the demons."

The Random House Webster's College Dictionary defines the word 'Cush'/ 'Kush', as,
1. the son of Ham (Ram, according to Knapp)
2. an area mentioned in Bible, sometimes identified with Upper Egypt, and
3. an ancient kingdom in North Africa, in the region of Nubia.

According to the 'Random House Webster's College Dictionary', Nubia is a region in South Egypt and North Sudan, extending from the Nile to Red Sea.

The word Cushitic (or Kushitic) is defined as "a language family of Africa, a branch of the Afro-Asiatic family, indicating its association with Asia. According to the Columbia Encyclopedia:

1. Cush (or Kush) is an Asiatic nation, perhaps the same as one of similar name in E. Mesopotamia.
2. Ancient kingdom of Nubia, in the present Sudan

Both the Dictionary and the Encyclopedia seem to support Knapp's version referring to Cush's Asian and African connection, and both talk about Cushite kingdoms and languages in E. Mesopotamia, Egypt and Africa (Nubia and Sudan). It would have been better if both had been specific, mentioning Indian instead of Asian, and had explained Cush's historical relationship with Ram (Ham), as Knapp has explained.

Pococke (1856, p.205) has given evidences that "Meroe was indebted for its civilization to India." Sudan as well as Ethiopia had a city named as 'Meroe' in their ancient times. Pococke writes about India's presence in Africa, particularly in Ethiopia and Sudan:

"Philostratus[137] introduces the Brahmin Iarchus, stating to his auditor, that the Ethiopians were originally an *Indian race*, compelled to leave India for the impurity contracted by slaying a certain monarch, to whom they owed allegiance.[138] ... thus Eusebius states that Ethiopians, emigrating from the river Indus, settled in the vicinity of Egypt."

Pococke (p.205) narrates: "An Egyptian is made to remark that he had heard from his father that the Indians were the wisest of men, and that the Ethiopians, a colony of the Indians, preserved the wisdom and usages of their fathers, and acknowledged their ancient origin."

Pococke (pp.211-214), talking about the *'The Promised Land'*, expresses a profound feeling of gratitude to the Great Author of

---

[137] V.A., iii.6.
[138] Ibid., vi. 8.

Truth, thankfully prefaces his remarks with that 'LAUS DEO', which characterized the conclusions of the literary labors of his forefathers. Pococke remarks that the Hebrew lawgiver did not know what the Israelites had to encounter and overcome on the entrance into the land of promise where the fiercest and most warlike of the Solar (*Surya Vanshi*) and Lunar (*Chandra Vanshi*) races had early taken up their abode, and that already the martial bands of these Solar (*Suryavanshi*) Rajpoots were upon their track, and the advance of the fugitives seemed completely barred by the arm of the sea which rolled directly in their front.

Pococke (p. 214) further writes:

"He (perhaps Hebrew lawgiver) has already remarked the extraordinary spectacle of a people of high northerly latitude, in the vicinity of the Himalayan Mountains, and the province of Ladakh, settled in the fertile land of Egypt, and bringing thither its religious rites and various usages of a society that stamp an Indian original. That population is again to be distinctly seen in Palestine, so that both identity of nationality and identity of the era of colonisation, become almost self-evident."

India in Egypt

Gene D. Matlock, in '*India Once Ruled Americas*' (2000, p.2), writes that in an essay entitled '*On Egypt from the Ancient Book of the Hindus*' (Asiatic Researches Vol. III, 1792), British Lt. Colonel Francis Wilford has given abundant evidence proving that ancient Indians (Hindus) colonized and settled in Egypt.

Pococke (p.45), writes: "But to return to the primeval movements of mankind, I have glanced at the Indian settlements in Egypt, which will again be noticed."

Benjamin Walker (ed.), in '*The Hindu World: An Encyclopedic Survey of Hinduism*' (vol. I, p.324), writes: "It is some times contended that Egyptian religious influences left their mark on Hinduism, but little can be said with certainty on the subject."

Hinduism is the oldest religion, much older than the religion of Egypt. Lot has been said earlier about Hindu presence in Africa.

Egypt is in Africa. I am giving here what exactly has been said about this (Egypt and India), and leaving to the readers to decide who has influenced whom or both have influenced each other. Walker continues:

"It has been urged by the exponents of this school of thought (Egyptian religious influence on Hinduism) that the association of the bull with Siva and the reverence for the cow in Hinduism are of Egyptian derivation. They find more than coincidence in the triune deities of the Nile Valley and the triads of the Vedic gods; in the common worship of cows, geese, apes, snakes and birds; in the adoration of the phallus of Osiris and the linga of Siva; in the return of Vishnu as Kalki at the end of time, and the coming of the messianic Osiris. Further analogies were drawn between the theory of the universe as conceived by the Egyptian priests and the Purānic yugas; the doctrine mutually held by both of the judgment and transmigration of souls; the Vedic hymns to the sun god Surya and the Solar hymn of king Akhnaton (II, p. 12). Some Hindu scholars go far as to suggest a Sumero-Egyptian origin for the *Rig-Veda* and trace *Rāmāyana* to Egyptian sources (VII, p. 126)."

In my opinion, neither might have religiously influenced the other. In ancient times, when there was no knowledge of science and when there was little rational thinking, worship of nature, of animals, etc. was possible. And this was also natural that almost all peoples on earth would look like having similar religious affinities with nature and its objects. Desire for continuity of generations would naturally inspire worship of phallus. Therefore, I feel that such similarities between Egypt and India could be coincidental.

But some resemblances between Egypt and India in terms of some proper names, common architectural styles, and motives, decorative motifs on pottery, etc. could be the result of close contacts between the two peoples by way of trade and/or colonization. History tells that in ancient times Hindus established their kingdoms in Egypt, Syria, Mesopotamia, and Asia Minor, as discussed earlier.

To support the theory – that the Vedic religion was not influenced by the Egyptian religion and that it was practiced by some in Egypt in its ancient times – I would like to suggest the evidence of the 'age' factor, that the Vedic religion (Hinduism) is the oldest of all religions. Shiv Ling was found in Mohenjo-daro, proves that the phallus worship was older than that in Egypt. Hinduism is older than 8,000 B.C., as evidenced by the presence of Swastika among Native Americans. First Asians, including some Swastika-worshipping Vedic people from India, arrived in Alaska and Americas in about 8,000 B.C. I don't think that the history of Egypt has talked about the belief of ancient Egyptians in 'transmigration of soul'.

Moreover, history has not talked about any significant migration of Egyptians into India. Dr. Poonai, in *'Origin of Civilization and Language'* (1994, p. 159), talks about the *Rig Vedic* Aryan immigrants into Egypt:

> "Archeological specimens of crania support the conclusion that Rig-Vedic Aryan immigrants arrived in the ancient Egyptian territory from the Indo-Gangetic area about the same time that they reached Sumer and Mesopotamia. …They arrived in the Egyptian area about 6,000-8,000 BC, communicating with each other by means of a skeletal Prakritic dialect".

Was Egypt Kushite (Cushite)?

Robert Draper, in *'Black Pharaohs'* (National Geographic, February, 2008), writes an ignored chapter of history which tells of a time when kings from Deep Africa conquered Ancient Egypt. There-in, he writes about the ancient Kush civilization and Kushites:

> "Explorers who arrived at the central stretch of the Nile River excitedly reported the discovery of elegant temples

and pyramids – the ruins of an ancient civilization called Kush."

Knapp (p.104) writes about Vedic (Hindu) presence in Egypt:

"L. A. Waddell establishes in his book, *Egyptian Civilization,* that Menes, the original founder of Egypt's first dynasty, was the pre-dynastic Aryan Pharaoh that united Egypt. Menes is the Manasyu mentioned in the *Mahabharata* (specifically the Calcutta edition published in 1834, Volume One, Section 94, verses 3695-3697) to which Waddell refers. Manasyu is described as the son of Pravira or Pravireshvara, the son of Puru, and is in the line of the Prabhu of Gopta, or Pharaoh of Egypt."

Knapp further talks about Manasyu:

"Manasyu was known as Manis or Manas (in Sanskrit, 'Manas' means man), in Mesopotamia (the affix *yu* means the *Uniter* in Sanskrit), and some of the seals found in the Indus Valley region refer to Kings Puru and Manis as rulers of the area, including Egypt."

Knapp (p.104) writes about the seals excavated from Mohenjo-daro showing trade connection of its Hindu kings and traders in Egypt region:

"Waddell and other Egyptologists contend that Manasyu or Menes took his military and naval forces and sailed from the Indus region across the Arabian and Red Seas and entered Egypt east of Koptos or Abydos. Koptos was a town, known as an ancient center for trade and still has some of the oldest statues of Egyptian gods."

Manasyu organized Egypt and established Aryan culture, metal industry, irrigation system, and system of writing.

INDEX

Abdul Kalam, Dr. A. P. J., 5, 155, 157-58
Abhimanyu, 47
Accupuncture, 260-61
Aeronautics of ancient India, 43, 158
Aerospace technology, Hindu, 45, 59
Afghanistan, pre-afghan name, 180-81
Agnibaan, 46, 218
Ajanta Frescoes, 246
Alaska, 236, 269
Alexander, the Great, 73, 183, 225
Anderson, Robert, 22, 207, 229
Angkor Vat, temple of, 244-45
Apte, V. S., 55, 164
Arghandawi, Abdul Ali, 174
Arnold, Sir Edwin, 110
Arjuna, 12, 47, 161, 218
Arrian, 19
Aryabhatta, concept of zero, 79, 87, 99

Aryan Race, 7, 13, 30, 35, 58, 124, 151, 196, 203
Aryavarta, 2, 21, 27, 29, 58, 142, 151, 185, 188, 196-97, 211
Jewel of the White Race, 7, 58
Contribution to Russia, Europe, 149-50, 229-30
Aryans in Mesopotamia, 142
Aryans occupied Anatolia, 147
Ashoka, 47, 178-80, 245
Accepted Buddhism, 180
Afghanistan, Baluchistan under, 180
Secret Society, 47-48
Ashook, 215
Ashvamedha, 107
Atmagyan, 97, 99-100
Avesta and Vedas, 20-21
Avestan, 20, 33-35, 79, 123, 164, 187
Avestan and Sanskrit, 20, 33-36, 188-89

Bahrain, 138, 145-46, 200
Balram, Krishna's brother, 244

Bamian, Buddha statue, 174-75
Banerjee, Mamata, 4
Barber, Lionel, 116
Bently, John, 229
Bering Strait, 57, 236
Besant, Dr. Annie, 69, 95, 97, 103-04
Bhajan Belt, 77
Bharat and Knowledge, Diversity: Beauty, not disunity, 7, 85-87, 93
Bharatiya Vidya Bhavan, 95, 113
Bhavabhuti, 30
Bibby, Geofferey, 138-40, 186
Biornstierna, Count, 260
Blavatsky, Helena, 103
Boghazkoi, 143, 192, 204, 209, 214
Bose, Jagdish, 80
Bose-Shah, Malini, 92
Brandon, William, 235
Brunnhofer, Hertel, 182-83
Buddhism in China, 31-32
Burns, Bill, 66
Burrow, T., 123, 187
Burrows, John, 51, 70, 190

Cambodia, 172, 244, 249, 254
Chandragupta, Maurya, 180
Chandrigath, University of, 48
Chankya (Kautilya), 111
Chess, 81
Childe, V. Gordon, 69, 137-38, 141-44, 149-50, 183, 193-94, 198, 200, 205

Childress, David Hatcher, 41-43
Christian, Dr., 105
Christianity, 39, 72, 79, 89, 103, 105-06, 112, 122, 225, 256
Clarke, Peter B., 127, 190
Colebrooke, 66, 186
Colonizing Science & Art, 219
Columbus, 6
Coomaraswamy, 149
Coulson, Michael, 36
Cousin, Victor, 69, 78, 111
Cunningham, Alexander, 175-76, 179-80

Dalit, 116
Darius, 183, 196-97
Dastgir, Ghulam, 37
Decimal system, 80
Deepam, 148, 217
Dev Raja, 86, 244-46
Dhratrashtra, 46, 177-78
Dikshitar, Ramchandra, 43
Dixit, Sheila, 4
Dobrzynski, Judith H., 256
Dodwell, 92
India, absorbent like ocean, 91
Draper, Robert, 269
Driver, Harold E., 235
Dunhuang, 256
Durant, Will, 2, 3, 6, 26-27, 41, 65-66, 78, 81, 106, 110, 112, 116-17, 119-20, 123, 149, 186, 189

272

Durga, 4, 86, 106, 262

Eck, Diana L., 85, 87-88, 90
  diversity unites, not divides,
    87
  diversity of interlocking, 87
  interdependent caste groups,
    87
Egypt, India in, 267-70
Einstein, Albert, 72-73, 77, 150,
  230
Eliot, Sir Charles, 59, 61, 72,
  106
Eldwood, Mrs. Colonel, 224
Emerson, 12, 72, 110

Feuerstein, George, 10-11, 19,
  23
Flying machines, 43, 46-48
Foucher, Dr. A., 178-79
Frankfort, Dr. Henry, 149
Frawley, David, 19, 22, 183
Freudian psychology, 99, 161

Gaimini, 14-15
Galav, T. C., 69, 79, 110, 112
Gandhara, 173, 176-79, 183,
  186
Gandhi, Mahatma, 3, 5, 23, 62,
  64-65, 73, 84-85, 95-126,
  134, 154-55, 160-61, 258
  Salt Satyagrah, 64
  Thoreau, 64
Gandhi, Sonia, 4
Ganesha, 237, 261

Gannon, Sharon, 77
Gargi, Sister (Marie L.Burke),
  102-03, 118
Gargi Vachaknavi, 102
Garraty and Gay, 223, 244
Garuda, 42
Gathas, Avestic, 34, 124, 198
Gautama, Siddhartha, 75, 135
Gelb, Dr., 147, 217
Ghose, Aurobindo, 50, 65-66
  positive in negative, 65
  the nation symbolically, 65
  as a vast prison-house, 65
Ghose, Nabarun, 19, 207, 229
Gita, 6, 12, 37-38, 66, 68-70,
  79, 103-04, 109-110, 157,
  161
Gita, translation in Persian, 38,
  79
Greece, India in 2448 BC, 2, 6,
  17-18, 219-22, 225
Greeks, Krishna god of, 224-
  25
Greeks, Vedic influence on,
  173, 224
Gobineau, Joseph Arthur, 57-
  58, 100-01
Goethe, 12, 27, 78
Granth Sahib, 16, 128
Grousset, Rënë, 243
Gurmukhi, 128

Hagel, 110
Hancock, Graham, 20, 252-54
Hariyappa, H.L., 42

273

Harsha, King, 30
Hastings, Warren, 110
Hazare, Anna, 65
Healy, Mark, 77
Heyderdahl, Thor, 252-53
Hicks, Harry H., 22, 207, 229
Himalayan glaciers, 20, 235
Hindu, 95-96, 181
    Calendar, 19
    Concept of time, 95-126,
        169, 175
    Education, 86
Hindu Temple, 57, 240, 261
Hinduism, 3, 19, 26, 37, 39, 49-
    50, 53-55, 77, 85-86, 89, 91,
    95-126, 169-70, 267-68
    Absorbing power of, 91
    Love for poetry, 38
    monotheism in polytheism,
        49-50
History of ancient India, 153,
    186, 207
Hitler, Adolph, 57-58
Hittites, 143-44, 147-48, 192-
    93, 200, 203-05, 207, 209-14,
    216
Hiuan-tsang, Chinese traveler,
    179, 257-58
Houston, Drusilla Dunjee, 263
Hume, R. E., 11
Hurians, Indo-aryan names,
    211, 214-15
Husing, Hertel, 182
Hu Shih, 154, 257
Hutchins, Francis G., 87

Huxley, Aldous, 51, 70, 79, 112

INCAS, SA descendants of
Sri Rama, 236
Indira, 257-48
Indo-European languages, 26,
    29
Indus civilization, 18, 20, 55-
    56
    Indus & Nile, 18, 140, 146,
        148-49
    Navigators Pococke, 33, 146
    Shipbuilding, 145
    Trade with Yemen, 148
    With Sumeria,149

Jacobi, 22
Jayadratha, 47
Jayaraman, Jayalalitha, 4, 244-
    45
Jones, Sir William, 25, 27, 29,
    72, 128, 148, 152, 158, 203,
    227, 236-37

Kalidasa, 27, 30
Kapu, on Hawaii, 239-40
Kazakhstan, its heritage, 164-
    66, 168-70
Kenoyer, Jonathan Mark, 56
Keyserling, Hermann, 65, 134
Khmer Empire, 244, 250
Khushiram, 128
Kikkuli, chariot training, 212
King, Martin Luther, 63-64
Knapp, Stephen, 16, 21, 78,
    81, 98

Krishna, a Greek god, 86, 173, 224
Krishna, Dr. A.V., 48
Krishnananda, Swami, 264
Krukshetra, 47, 161, 178
Kulke and Rothermund, 164, 172
Kasur, after Kusa, son of Rama, 176-77, 263-64, 266, 269-70

Lahore - Lohawar after, 176
Lakshmi, 4, 86, 106, 238
Language and culture, 38
Larmer, Brook, 256
Lava, son of Rama, 263-64
Life, a great school, 77, 128, 131
Ludwig, Lassen, 18, 195

Mahâbhâratâ, 3, 38, 44, 46-47, 58, 69, 86, 97, 103, 113, 118-19, 128, 143, 154, 159, 177-79, 183, 187, 190-91, 218, 228, 259, 270
Mahâtmâpan, 161
Majumdar, R.C., 182-83
Maldives, 252-54
Mallory, J. P., 33-34, 166-67, 187, 190, 212
Malni, Nirtya Kala Kendra, 92
Maloney, Clarence, 254
Manichaeism, 256
Marconi, 80
Marco Polo, 6, 31, 251
Marshal, Peter, 252

Marshal, Sir John, 149, 199, 247
Matlock, Gene D., 231-35, 267
Mauritius, 91, 93, 265,
Mayavati, 4
McCrindle, John W., 178, 180-81, 256-57
Megasthenes, 6
Mehrgarh, 86
Mesopotamia, 18, 23, 55, 137-39, 142, 147, 149, 193, 199-201, 204, 206-07, 211, 213-15, 266, 269
Hindu kingdoms in, 206-07
Meyer, Eduard, 198
Mitanni, 141, 143-44, 147, 192-93, 200, 203-05, 207, 209, 211-12, 214-15
Mogao caves, 256
Mohenjodaro, 3, 17-18, 55, 57, 117
Mojttabai, Fatehullah, 37, 79
Moksha, 102, 108, 126
Monboddo, Lord, 27-28
Monotheism, 85, 104-07, 113
Motwani, Jagat, 37, 84, 234
Mubarak, Hosni, 113
Muller, Herbert J., 68, 74, 226
Müller, Max, 3, 9, 11-17, 21-27, 32, 35, 61-62, 72-73, 76, 78, 105, 123-24, 142, 180, 194, 196-97, 255
Hindu influ.on Greek philosophers, 73
Hindus excel in, 12-13
Indebted to Vedanta, 71

transcendental Meditation, 31, 108

Sanskrit, the oldest language, 30

Vedas, Unique & priceless, 9

What Vedas teach Europeans, 12

with all wealth, power, beauty, 9

Munshi, Dr. Kanayalal, 5, 113

Mutiny, 1857, 88

Nalanda University, 257

Name change of a country, 181-82

Nanak, 16, 122

Nanakprakash, 128

Narayanan, K. R., 81

Navigation, from Sanskrit word Navgatih, 44, 210

Nazi Germans, 57

Nehru, Jawaharlal, 5, 10-12, 14-15, 17-18, 23, 34, 58-59, 62-63, 66, 71-73, 83-84, 91, 93, 97, 104, 150, 153, 179, 199, 225, 229-30, 241-42, 245-46, 257-58

Absorbing & assimilative power of Hinduism, 91

Bharatvarsha, 117, 179

Christianity, 225

Gandhara, a part of Aryan India, 179

Greater India, 242

history dominated by Europeans, 58, 153

influ. of Upanishads on self, 10

Rig Veda, earliest book of the humanity, 15

SE Asia Shipbuilding, 245

St. Augustine,Upanishads, 225

strong but invisible threads, 89

Svarnabhumi, 245

Nevali Cori in Anatolia, 207-210

Nritaya Kala Kendra, 92

Nirvana, 102-03, 108, 125

Nivedita, Sister (Margaret Noble), 83-84, 97

Oak, P. N., 232, 259

Obama, Barack, 64, 67, 85, 141

In Mumbai, 85

Olcott, Col. Henry S., 44

Om, 77

'OM' - mystic syllable of Hinduism, 77

Oppenheimer, Robert, first chair, 110

Atomic Energy Commission, 110

O'Reilly, 197

Othello, 128

Pain incites adventure, 135

Pandit, M.P., 75, 227
Panini grammar, 36, 178
Parkes, Henry Bramford, 235
Parsooram, Mahâbhârâtâ, 190-91
known as Parashawar, 176
Peshawar, 163, 176, 178
warrior with Axe, 190-91
Phallic Sculptures, 254
Philip, Morris, 22
Pinotti, Roberto, 41, 44-46
Pinjula-Mirror (visual shield), 45
Plato, 68, 72, 74-76, 226-27
belief in reincarnation, 74-75
belief in immortality of soul, 74-75
Upanishads, 75, 227
Vedic influence on, 226
Plotinus, 72, 75
Pococke, E., 33, 51, 85, 137, 146, 154, 186
Poetry, Hindus love, 38
Polytheism, 85, 104-07, 113
Poonai, Dr. P., 34-35, 140, 146-48, 170-71, 185, 191-92, 200-01, 204, 212-13, 216-17, 264
Portfolios assigned to women, 4
Psychoanalysis, 98-99, 108
Ptolemy, 177-78, 180, 257
Pushkalavati, founded by, 177-79

Pushkara, son of Bharata, 179
Pushtu, 178, 180-81

Qaddafi, Col. Muammar, 113

Radhakrishna, B.B., 20
Radhakrishnan, Sir S., 83, 97, 106, 154
Ramakrishna Paramahamsa, 170
Râmâyanâ, 3, 38, 44, 49, 81, 86, 97, 113, 118-19, 128, 159, 181, 187, 190, 263-64, 268
Rameses, or "Rama's Chief, 263-64
Ramnes, 197
RAMA-Sitva, 237
Ram Rajya, 81-82, 119
Rao, S. R., 145
Ravana, 181, 217, 263-65
Rawson, Philip, 62, 246-47, 249
Rebirth, optimism in death, 107, 124, 158
Rehman, Habibur, 37
Reyna, Dr. Ruth, 48
Rig Veda, 14-20, 22-23, 34, 42, 51, 62, 141, 144, 146-47, 182-83, 193, 205, 208-09, 235, 252-53, 268
Afghanistan, 182-84
Robinson, Andrew, 145
Rolland, Romain, 11, 62-63, 72

Roti restaurants, 92
Rückert, 78
Russell, G.W., 12
Russia, Aryan contribution to, 144-45

Sagar, Ramanand, 119
Sagon, Dr. Carl, 50-51, 214
Samvad, 29, 234
Sanjaya, 46
Sanskrit, 6-7, 13, 19-23, 25-39, 51, 53-54, 66-70, 167, 222
Abstract thinking, 150
Adored by Muslims too, 37-38
Inscriptions in Peru
Sarasvati, 29, 234-37
Not common source of European Languages, 32-33, 39, 112
oldest (Max Müller), 27
respect for in Germany, 31
Sanskrit and Avestan, 20, 33, 36, 123, 197
Sanskrit, Avestan sentences, 20, 34-35, 164, 188-89
Three oriental dramas, 30
Saraswati, 4, 86, 106, 149, 181
Satee, not in Vedic period, 119-21
Schelling, 66, 186
Schildmann, Kurt, 29, 235
School of Wisdom, 134
Schopenhauer, Arthur, 10-11, 66-67, 71

Upanishads, comfort in his life & death, 10, 186, 229
Selassic, Haile (Africa), 264
Shah, Iqbal Ali, 174
Shaheena, S., 25, 37-38
Shakespeare, 128
Shakuntala, 3, 27, 85
Sharma, Bhu Dev, 19, 22, 207, 229
Shastri, Satya Vrat, 25, 37
Shih, Hu, ambassador to US, 154, 257
Shipbuilding industry, 146-49, 158, 239, 245
Shirer, William L., 57, 150
Shiva Linga, 169
Shiva Temples, 169
Shudra, 88, 116
Sidharth. B.G., 207-08
Silk Road, 256
Sindhi: A caste-less society, 117, 147
Singh, Dr. Manmohan, 67, 141
Skylax, a Mitanni King, 181
Smith College, 5
Smith, Vincent, 91
Soddy, Frederick, 44
Stan Countries, 164-68, 174
Starr, Chester, 138
Stein, Sir Mark Aurel, 163-64, 193, 259-60
Hungarian archeologist in Central Asia, 163
Stierlin, Henry, 173
Strachey, John, 87

St. Rain, Tedd, 32
Stupa, Bamian Buddha, 179, 253
Sudāma, 214-16
Sufism in Kazakhstan, 170
Sukhamani, 128
Sushrata, father of surgery, 80
Svarnabhumi, 245
Svarnadvipa, 245
Swaraj, Sushma, 4
Swastika, 7, 53-59, 208, 235, 269
   Swastika in Americas, 57
   Swastika in Indus Valley, 55-57
   Swastika of Nazi Germany, 57

Tagore, Rabindranath, 1, 3, 5, 10, 83, 97-98, 127-35, 154, 157, 249
Talibans, Baminian Buddha, 175
Takshasila (Taxila) University, 177
Taxila University, 177
Tedd, 32
Theosophy, 103
Thompson, Gunnar, 55, 237-38
Thoreau, Henry David, 12, 63-64, 72, 79, 109
Thoreau '!Gandhi'! King, 63
Thorndike, Lynn, 51, 70
Thurman, Robert A.F., 77

Time, concept of age of humanity, 50-51
Tod, Colonel (Pococke (p.183), 263
Tòmas, Andrew, 41
Toynbee, Arnold, 260
Trager, James, 56
Tsang, Hiuen, 258
Twain, Mark, 62, 90

UFOs, 47, 49
Upanishads, 6, 10-12, 14, 23, 38, 66-67, 71
   Arthur Schopenhauer on, 10, 71
   Persian translation of, 186
   products of highest wisdom, 71

Vaidya, C.V., 187, 193, 197-98
Varnashram, not caste system, 114
Vasco de Gama, 6
Vedas, 4, 6, 7, 9-21, 23, 29-30, 33, 36, 38, 54-55, 57-58, 61-69, 97, 103, 109, 118, 181-83, 187, 191, 193, 211, 223, 229, 235
   antiquity and source of history, 16-19
   source of history, 16
   Vedas and Avesta, 21, 34-35, 123
   were Vedas revealed?, 14-15
   Vedic emphasis on knowledge, 97

Vepa, Kosla, 46, 143, 178, 191
Vimana text *'Vimanika Shastra'*, 43, 45-46, 70
Vira, Raghu, 261
Vishva Bharati, 134
Vittaxis, Dr. Vassilis, 75, 227
Vivekananda, Swami, 5, 11, 63, 66, 95, 97, 99-102, 170
Voltaire, Francois, 61

Waddell, L.A., 203, 270
Wagner, Richard, 58
Walker, Benjamin, 123, 189, 228, 267-68
Wheeler, Sir Mortimer, 145
Wilford, Captain F., 203, 227-28, 267
Wilkins, Charles, 29
translated Gita into English, 110
Winkler, Hugo, 205
Whitney, 181
Winternitz, 18, 66, 107, 183
Women in ancient times, 7, 102, 117-19
Wood, Michael, 89-90
Wooley, Sir L. (Vedic culture in China), 260

Xianji, Yuag (Chinese worshipped Shivambhu), 261
Xuanzang (Buddhist monk in China), 256

Yuditshtra, 161, 178

Yugabda (3101), 19

Zabriskie, Phil, (Bud. Stuppa in Afgaistan), 174
Zaitsev, Dr. Vyacheslav, 44
Zero, concept of, 47
Zoroaster, 35, 38, 198

References and Bibliography

Abhayankar, K.D & B.G. Sidhartha (eds).*Treasures of Ancient Indian Astronomy.* New Delhi: Ajanta Publications, 1993.

Bahn, Paul G.(ed). *100 Great Archaeological Discoveries.* New York: Barnes & Noble Books, 1995.

Baldi, Philip. *An Introduction to the Indo-European Languages.* Carbondale, IL, 1983.

Bentley. John. *On the Principal Years and Dates of the Ancient Hindus* (written in 1780's). In Sir William Jones (ed). Asiatic Researches (vol.5, Ch. XXI, pp..315-343). New Delhi: Cosmo Publications, 1979.

_____ .*On the Antiquity of Surya Sidhanta and The Formation of the Astronomical Cycles.* in Sir William Jones (ed.) Asiatic Researches (Vol. 6, Ch. XIII. pp.540-593).New Delhi: Cosmo Publications,1979.

_____ On the Hindu Systems of Astronomy, and Their Connection with History in Ancient and Modern times (written 1780's). In Sir William Jones (ed). *Asiatic Researches (*Vol.8, Ch. VI, pp.195-244). New Delhi: Cosmo Publications, 1979.

Bhattacharya, D.K. *Prehistoric Archaeology.* Delhi: Hindustan Publishing Corporation,1972.

Bibby, Geoffrey. *Looking for Dilmun.* New York: Alfred A. Knopf, 1969.

Brandon, William. *Indians.* Boston: Houghton Mifflin Company, 1989.

Burrow, T. *The Sanskrit Language.* Delhi: Motilal Banarsidas Publishers,2001.

Childe, V. Gordon. *The Aryans: A Study of Indo-European* Origins. New York: Knopf, 1926.

_____. *New Light on the Most Ancient East.* New York : Frederick A. Praeger, 1953.

_____. *What Happened in History,* Pelican Books, 1943

Childress, David Hatcher. *Technology of the Gods: The Incredible Sciences of the Ancients.* Kempton, US: Adventures Unlimited Press 2000.

Chopra, Deepak. *Unconditional Life: Discovering the Power to fulfill your Dreams.* New York: Bantam Books, 1992.

Clark, Grahame. *World Prehistory in New Perspective.* Cambridge: Cambridge University Press,1993.

Clark, Grahame & Stuart Piggott. *Prehistoric Societies.* New York: Alfred A. Knopf, 1968.

Clarke, Peter B. *The World is Religions, Understanding the Living Faiths.* Pleasantville: Marshall Editions Limited,1993.

Coedes, G. *The Indianized States of Southern Asia.* Honolulu: An East-West Center Book, The University Press of Hawaii, 1968.

Crawfurd, John. *On the Existence of the Hindu Religion in the Island of Bali* in Sir William Jones (ed.) Asiatic Researches (Vol.13, Ch. II. pp.128-170). New Delhi: Cosmo Publications, 1979.

Cunningham, Alexander *Ancient Geography of India.* Delhi: Low Price Publications, 1871.

Dikshitar, Ramchandra. *'Warfare in AncientIndia'*, Madras: Oxford University Press, 1944..

Dimock, Jr., Edward & et al. *The Literature of India: An Introduction.* Chicago & London: The University of Chicago Press, 1974.

Driver, Harold E. *Indians of North America.* Chicago: The University of Chicago Press, 1969.

Durant, Will. *Our Oriental Heritage.* New York: MJF Books,1935.

_____. *The Age of Reason Begins.* New York, 1961.

Elst, Koenraad. *Indigenous Indians: Agastya to Ambedkar.* New Delhi: Voice of India, 1993.

_____. *Dr. Ambedkar: A rue Aryan*. New Delhi: Voice of India, 1993a.

Embree, Ainslie T.(ed.). *Sources of Indian Tradition* (Vol. 1 from the beginning to 1800). New York: Columbia University Press, 1988.

Feuerstein, Georg, Subash Kak & David Frawley. *In Search Of The Cradle Of Civilization*. Wheaton, IL, USA: Quest Books, The Theosophical Publishing House, 1995.

Foster E. M. *A Passage to India*. Orlando: Harcourt, Inc.,1984.

Foucher, H., translated by H. Hargreaves. *Notes on the Ancient Geography of Gandhara*. Varanasi (India): Bharatiya Publishing House.

Frawley, David. *From the River of Heaven: Hindu and Vedic Knowledge for the Modern Age*. Salt Lake City: Passage Press,1990.

_____. *Gods, Sages and Kings*. Salt Lake City: Passage Press, 1991.

Galav. *Philosophy of Hinduism: An Introduction*.

Garraty, John A. and Peter Gay. *The Columbia History of the World*. New York: Harper & Row, 1981.

Griffith, Ralph T.H. *The Hymns Of The Rgveda*. Delhi: Motilal Banarsidass Publishers Private Limited, 1995.

Gunther, John. *Inside Asia*. New York: Harper & Brothers, 1939.

Hancock, Graham. *Underworld: The Mysterious of Civilization*. New York: Crown Publishers, 2002.

Herm, Gerhard. *The Celts*. New York: St. Martin's Press, Inc., 1976.

Hitler, Adolf. *Mein Kampf (1924)*. Boston: Houghton Mifflin Company, 1971.

Knapp, Stephen. *Proof of Vedic Culture's Global Existence*. Detroit: The World Relief Network, 2000.

_____. *The Power of Dharma*. New York: iUniverse, Inc. 2006

Kunanbay, Alma. *The Soul of Kazakhstan*. New York: Eastern Press, 2001.

283

Langer, William L (ed.). *The New Illustrated Encyclopedia of World History* (Vol. 1 & 2). New York: Harry N. Abrams, Inc., 1968.

Majmudar, R.C.(ed). *History and Culture of the Indian People*. (1st vol). Bombay: Bharatiya Vidya Bhavan, 1951.

_____. *Ancient India*. Delhi: Motilal Banarsidass Publishers, 1952.

Mallory, J.P. *In Search of the Indo-Europeans: Language, Archaeology and Myth*. New York: Thames and Hudson,1989.

Marshal, Sir John. *Prehistoric Civilization of the Indus*. Illustrated London News, Jan.,1928.

_____ *Mohenjo-Daro and the Indus Civilization.*(3 vol.) London, 1931.

Martin, Thomas R. *Ancient Greece: From Prehistory to Hellenistic Times*. New Haven (USA) & London: Yale University Press,1996.

Matlock, Gene D. *India Once Ruled The Americas*. New York: Writer's Showcase, 2000.

_____ . *The Last Atlantis Book: The Atlantis-Mexico-India Connection*. Tempe, Arizona: A Dandelion Books Publications, 2001.

_____ . *From Khyber Pass to Gran Quivira (Kheevira), NM and Baboquivari, AZ*. New York: Authors Choice Press, 2002.

Mattai, Bansraj. *Hinduism*. Denver, Colorado: Outskirts Press, Inc., 2009.

McCrindle, John W. *Ancient India. As Described in Classical Literature*. New Delhi: Oriental Books Reprint Corporation, 1979.

_____ . *Ancient India: As Described by Ptolemy*. New Delhi: Munshiram Manoharlal Publishers Pvt.,Ltd.,2000.

------Motwani, Jagat K. *None But India (Bharat): The Cradlle of Aryans, Sanskrit, Vedas, & Swastika*. Bloomington: iUniverse, Inc., 2010.

_____ . *Ancient History of Bharat and Hindu Identity. in* Sharma, Bhu Dev & N. Ghosh (ed.). Revisiting Indus-Sarasvati Age and Ancient India. Atlanta (USA): World Association for Vedic Studies, USA.1998.

_____ . *Indo-European Languages: Too Diverse for One Family.* In Sharma, Bhu Dev (ed.). New Perspectives on Vedic and Ancient Indian

Civilization. Meerut (India): World Association of Vedic Studies, 2000.

_____. *Indo-European Languages: A Myth*. In Sharma, Bhudev (ed). Contemporary Views on Indian Civilization. Meerut (India): World Association of Vedic Studies, 2003.

Müller, F. Max. *Science of Language (Vol. I)*.New York: Charles Scribner's Sons, 1891._____. *The Six Systems of Indian Philosophy*. Calcutta: Susil Gupte (India) Ltd., 1952.

_____. *India: What Can It Teach Us?* London: New York, Longmans, Funk & Wagnalls Company,1999.

_____. *None But India (Bharat): The Cradle of Aryans, Sanskrit, Vedas & Swastika*. Bloomington: iUniverse. Inc. 2010.

Muller, Herbert J. *The Loom of History*. New York: Harper & Brothers, 1958.

Nehru, Jawaharlal. *The Discovery of India*. Calcutta: The Signet Press, 1946.

Oppenheim, A. Leo. *Ancient Mesopotamia: Portrait of Dead Civilization*.

Chicago, London: The University of Chicago Press, 1967, 1977.

Oppenheimer, Stephen. *Eden In the East: The Drowned Continent of Southeast Asia*. London: Weidenfeld & Nicolson, 1998.

Pococke, E. *India in Greece; or Truth in Mythology*. London: Richard Griffin and Company, 1856.

Poonai, Premsukh. *Origin of Civilization and Language*. Dayton Beach (Florida): Pearce Publishers,Inc. 1994.

Pragiter, F.E. *Ancient Indian Historical Tradition*. New Delhi: Motilal Banarsidas, 1962,1997.

Rawson, Philip. *The Art of Southeast Asia: Cambodia, Vietnam, Thailand,*

Laos, Burma, Java, & Bali. New York: Thames and Hudson Inc., 1990.

Roberts, J.M. *History of the World*. London: Penguin Books Ltd., 1987.

Robinson, Francis (ed.).*The Cambridge Encyclopedia of India, Pakistan, Bangladesh, Sri Lanka, Nepal, Bhutan, and the Maldivas.* New York: Cambridge University Press, 1989.

Rubel, David. *Concise Chronology of World History, 3000 BC -1993.* Nashville: Thomas Nelson Publishers, 1993.

Ruhlen, Merritt. *Guide to the World's Languages.* Stanford, California: Stanford University Press, 1987.

Sacred Symbols: The Celts. New York: Thames and Hudson, 1995.

Shah, Bharat. *Sanskrit: An Appreciation without Apprehension.* New York: Setubandh Publications, 2004.

Sidharth, B.G. *Calendaric Astronomy, Astronomical Dating & Archaeology: A New View of Antiquity and its Science.* Hyderabad: B.M. Birla Science, 1993a..

_____. *The Antiquity of The Rig Veda.* Hyderabad: B.M. Birla Science Centre, 1991.

_____. *A Lost Anatolian Civilization: Is It Vedic?* Hyderabad: B.M. Birla Centre, 1992.

_____. *Date and Place for the Mahabharta.* Hyderabad: B. M. Birla Science Centre, 1993.

Sinor, Denis (ed). *The Cambridge History of Early Inner Asia.* Newcastle (U.K.): Cambridge University Press,1990.

Shirer, William L. *The Rise and Fall of the Third Reich.* New York: Simon and Schuster, 1959.

Stevenson, Victor (ed.). *Words: The Evolution of Western Languages.* New York: Van Nostrand Reinhold Company, 1983.

Stierlin, Henri. *Hindu India: From Khajuraho to the Temple of Madurai.* Koln, New York, London: Paris, Tokyo: Taschen, 2000.

Talgeri, S.K. *The Rigveda: A Historical Analysis.* New Delhi: Voice of India, 1998.

Thompson, Gunnar. *NU SUN. Asian American Voyages, 500 BC.* Fresno (USA): Pioneer Publishing Co., 1989.

Tilak, B. G. *The Orion or Researches into Antiquities of the Vedas.* Poona: Tilak Brothers, 1986.

Walker, Benjam in. *Hindu World: An Encyclopedic Survey of Hinduism* (2 vols). New York: Frederick A. Prueger Publishers,1968.

Wheeler, R. E. M. *Five Thousand Years of Pakistan.* London: Royal India & Pakistan Society, 1950.

Wheeler, Mortimer. *The Indus Civilization.* Cambridge: Cambridge University Press, 1960.

Wilford, Francis. Chronology of the Hindus. In Sir william Jones. *Asiatic Researches* (Vol.5, Ch. XVIII, pp.241-295). New Delhi: Cosmo Publications, 1979.

_____. *An Essay on the Sacred Isles in the West.* Sir William Jones (ed.) Asiatic Researches (Vol.8,Ch.VII,pp.245-375). New Delhi: Cosmo Publications, 1979a.

_____. *A Dissertation on Semiramis, the Origin of Mecca* (written in 1780's). In Sir William Jones (ed.) Asiatic Researches(Vol. 4, Ch. XXVI, pp.361-383). New Delhi: Cosmo Publications,1979b.

_____. *On Egypt and Other countries adjacent to Cali River or Nile of Ethiopia.* In Sir William Jones (ed). Asiatic Researches (Vol.3,Ch.XIII, pp.295-468). New Delhi: Cosmo Publications, 1979c.

_____. *On the Ancient Geography of India* (written in 1780's). In Sir William Jones.*Asiatic Researches* (Vol.14, Ch.VII,pp.373-470).New Delhi: Cosmo Publications, 1980.

Winternitz, M. *History of Indian Literature* (Eng. trans. by S. Ketkar), Vol. I, Calcutta, 1927.

Wolpert, Stanley. *A New History of India.* New York: Oxford University Press, 1993.

Wood, Michael. *In Search of Myths & Heroes: Exploring Four Epic Legends of the World.* Los Angeles: BBC Worldwide Limited, 2005.

Yule, George. *The Study of Language.* New York: Cambridge University Press, 1985.

Encyclopedias

The Encyclopedia Americana

Britannica Encyclopedia

Columbia Encyclopedia

Larousse Encyclopedia

National Geographic

The New Illustrated Encyclopedia

Reader's Digest

The World Book Encyclopedia